A PRIMER ON SOCIAL MOVEMENTS

David A. Snow
UNIVERSITY OF CALIFORNIA, IRVINE
and
Sarah A. Soule
STANFORD UNIVERSITY

CONTEMPORARY SOCIETIES
Jeffrey C. Alexander
SERIES EDITOR

 W. W. NORTON & COMPANY ∞ NEW YORK LONDON

W. W. Norton & Company has been independent since its founding in 1923, when William Warder Norton and Mary D. Herter Norton first published lectures delivered at the People's Institute, the adult education division of New York City's Cooper Union. The firm soon expanded its program beyond the Institute, publishing books by celebrated academics from America and abroad. By mid-century, the two major pillars of Norton's publishing program—trade books and college texts—were firmly established. In the 1950s, the Norton family transferred control of the company to its employees, and today—with a staff of four hundred and a comparable number of trade, college, and professional titles published each year—W. W. Norton & Company stands as the largest and oldest publishing house owned wholly by its employees.

The text of this book is composed in Garamond
with the display set in ITC Fenice.
Book design by Beth Tondreau.
Composition by Matrix Publishing Services.
Manufacturing by Quebecor World, Fairfield.
Production manager: Benjamin Reynolds.

ISBN 978-0-393-97845-2

W. W. Norton & Company, Inc., 500 Fifth Avenue, New York, N.Y. 10110-0017
www.wwnorton.com

W. W. Norton & Company Ltd., Castle House,
75/76 Wells Street, London W1T 3QT
2 3 4 5 6 7 8 9 0

A PRIMER ON SOCIAL MOVEMENTS

Contemporary Societies Series

Jeffrey C. Alexander, Series Editor

CONTENTS

PREFACE

Our primary motivation for writing this book is based on our belief that an understanding of the course and character of human history during much of the past two millennia, and certainly during the past several centuries, is partly contingent on an understanding of the workings and influence of social movements. In looking at the social and cultural landscape in the United States alone over the past two hundred years, it is reasonable to wonder how history might have unfolded in the absence of the abolitionist movement, which sought to abolish slavery; the suffrage movement, which sought to enfranchise women; the labor movement, which sought to reduce the exploitation of workers of all ages; the civil rights movement, which sought to guarantee for all citizens the range of rights that some had been denied for far too long; and the more recent women's and gay rights movements. The importance of these and other movements is not peculiar to the United States but extends worldwide. It merits noting, in this regard, that *Time* magazine's final issue of the twentieth century included among its three major candidates for the person of the century the inspirational leader of one of the more consequential movements of the past century, Mohandas K. Gandhi. Why Gandhi? Because

> He stamped his ideas on history, igniting three of the century's great revolutions—against colonialism, racism, and violence.

His concept of nonviolent resistance liberated one nation
and sped the end of colonial empires around the world. His
marches and fasts fired the imagination of oppressed people
everywhere. (*Time*, December 31, 1999: 123)

Moreover, as the article in *Time* noted, "his strategy of nonviolence ... spawned generations of spiritual heirs around the
world," including Martin Luther King Jr., César Chávez, Lech
Walesa, Benigno Aquino Jr., and Nelson Mandela—all prominent leaders of major, consequential social movements in their
respective homelands of the United States, Poland, the Philippines, and South Africa.

Other names and movements can easily be added to the above
lists, but the movements and names mentioned sufficiently
highlight the fact that some of the major events and figures
of the past century, as well as before, are bound up with social
movements. Thus, the study of social movements not only is an
interesting pursuit in its own right but can also lead to a better
and deeper understanding of the social world. It is our hope that
this book will provide a working understanding of the character
and operation of social movements and, in the process, facilitate
understanding of the world in which they emerge and operate.

Toward that end, we have sought to provide a relatively user-
friendly analytical account of social movements for use in undergraduate courses on social movements and protest, primarily at
an upper-division level, and in introductory graduate seminars
on social movements. By "relatively user-friendly analytical account," we refer to two levels of composition. First, we have
organized the book in a fashion that highlights in an evolu-
tionary and temporal way the course and character of the op-

eration and functioning of movements, from the generation of mobilizing grievances to the various contextual conditions that facilitate and constrain their emergence and operation, to the participation process and the interactive dynamics that affect their course, to their consequences. By pursuing this organizational strategy, we try not only to cover what we consider to be the major discussions and a good deal of the most important literature in the field but also to provide students with major conceptual tools necessary to understand the emergence, operation and dynamics, and consequences of movements. Second, we have sought to write a book that is accessible and interesting to students but not dumbed-down, as are too many introductions to substantive topics of inquiry and research. To enhance the accessibility of the conceptual and analytical thrust of the book, we have tried to anchor our discussions to an array of illustrative case materials on all types of movements in various places. To be sure, research and illustrative case material from the United States is overrepresented, but such material from other countries is prominently featured in the book as well. We have tried to bring to life the many concepts and theoretical discourses invoked by grounding them in concrete examples from the activities of social movements and their participants.

We do not presume that this book, as a primer or introduction to the study of social movements, covers all of the relevant research and writing on the topic. However, we believe that the book is of sufficient conceptual, theoretical, and illustrative breadth and depth to provide a springboard for examination of alternative conceptual schemes and modes of analysis that we have missed or glossed over. It was partly with this understanding that we envisioned this book not as a single, definitive text, but as a primer that could and should be supplemented with empirical, substantive studies of social movements and protest, whether in the form of research articles or monographs. We regard this primer not as a stand-alone book for most courses on movements, whether at the undergraduate or graduate level, but as a conceptual, analytic introduction that can be complemented and supplemented with other textual material.

As with any book, there are numerous others to whom we, as co-authors, are indebted. In addition to our editor, Karl Bakeman, who gently but persistently nudged us along, and the anonymous reviewers of the book manuscript, we are especially indebted to our many colleagues with whom we have taught or co-authored over the years and whose research and commentary on social movements and related collective phenomena have continuously expanded and refined our understanding of their emergence, dynamics, and consequences. Foremost among the colleagues to whom we owe special thanks are: Ed Amenta, Rob Benford, Lis Clemens, Catherine Corrigall-Brown, Dan Cress, Christian Davenport, Jenn Earl, Brayden King, John Lofland, Doug McAdam, John McCarthy, David Meyer, Cal Morrill, Susan Olzak, Francesca Polletta, Belinda Robnett, Marc Schneiberg, Alan Schussman, Sid Tarrow, Verta Taylor, Ralph Turner, Nella Van Dyke, Su Yang, Mayer Zald, and Lou Zurcher (who passed on much too early a number of years ago).

A PRIMER ON SOCIAL MOVEMENTS

Chapter One
CONCEPTUALIZING SOCIAL MOVEMENTS

IT WAS A THURSDAY morning in early May 1989 in Beijing, China. Jia Guangxi, a student at Peking University, rose early, grabbed a megaphone, and set out for the headquarters of the student organizing committee. As other university students poured out of their dormitories, Jia shouted through his megaphone quotations from the constitution: "Citizens of the People's Republic of China enjoy freedom of speech, of the press, of assembly, of association, of procession and of demonstration!" School officials countered, almost simultaneously, exhorting students, over blaring loudspeakers: "Go back to your classes! Don't give in to pressure from your fellow students! Beware of the consequences to yourself and your family!" As if to punctuate these threats, row upon row of uniformed policemen stood menacingly just outside the university gates. But neither the administrative threats nor the physical presence of the police appeared to be much of a deterrent, as 50,000 students, joined by an estimated 250,000 ordinary citizens, flooded the streets to march from the university belt in northwestern Beijing to Tiananmen Square in the city's center.

The sixteen-hour demonstration, which one graduate student claimed "mark[ed] the raising of democratic consciousness of the people," was the latest and the largest in a series of protest events that began when students gathered on April 16 to mourn the death of Hu Yaobang, the former secretary of the Communist General Party, whose tolerance of student demonstrations two years earlier had transformed him, in the eyes of the students, from a party leader to a hero and now a martyr.

This student-led, pro-democracy movement flourished for another month, until the communist regime, which had shown surprising restraint for weeks, unleashed its military in a furor that transformed the Tiananmen Square encampment of students into what *Time* described as the "bloodiest killing ground in Communist China's history."[1]

While the expression of democratic yearnings was repressed in China, it was moving forward at full throttle in the Soviet Union, in Poland, in Czechoslovakia, in East Germany— indeed, in all of Eastern Europe. In fact, the pace and magnitude of pro-democracy mass mobilization in this part of the world was so phenomenal that Soviet-based communist domination could be spoken of in the past tense in less than six months after the Tiananmen Square massacre. Symbolizing this change, perhaps more than anything else, was the fall of the Berlin Wall on November 9. The Wall had stood for nearly a third of the twentieth century as the preeminent physical and symbolic barrier between communism and the free world, between East and West, and now it was being mounted and dismantled by jubilant West and East Berliners. "It was," according to one journalist's description of the event, "one of those rare times when the tectonic plates of history shift beneath men's feet, and nothing after is quite the same."[2]

Clearly, the movements associated with pro-democracy mobilizations in various parts of the world during 1989 were noteworthy social forces, prompting state repression, on the one hand, and contributing to state breakdown, on the other. Powerful stuff, such social movements!

But not all social movements play a significant role in relation to such significant events. Nor are the claims and challenges of all social movements directed at a particular national government or the state. Certainly the thirty-nine adherents of the Heaven's Gate movement, who committed mass suicide in their communal house in San Diego in March 1997 because they believed their deaths would guarantee them heavenly passage aboard a UFO trailing the Hale-Bopp comet streaking across the sky in late March, were not particularly concerned about activities of "the state."[3] Nor was "the state" the focal target of some twenty students and occupants of an on-campus trailer park at the University of California, Irvine, who protested for weeks in the spring of 2004 the planned razing of an affordable-housing site by the university.[4]

Just as there is variation in the scope of significance and target of social movements, so too is there variation in their newsworthiness. Some collective action events and movements become major newspaper stories across the globe. Such was the case with the Paris riots that occurred in the fall of 2005. The dissemination of news of the electrocution of two North African Parisian teenagers and the injury of another who reportedly jumped an electrical substation wall to take refuge from the police quickly prompted some number of youth from the same residential area to take to the streets to burn cars and engage in various acts of vandalism. This set in motion what *Time* described as "a rolling wave of nightly clashes between young Arabs and French riot police that leapfrogged across the suburbs of Paris," eventually reaching "as far east as Dijon and south to Marseilles."[5] The violence quickly became a topic of international news coverage. One study examining how the riots were framed in twelve different newspapers in six countries found, for example, 418 articles on the riots over the three-week period, October 27 to November 18, in which the riots occurred.[6] Worldwide news coverage was much greater, extending well beyond the twelve newspapers examined.

Such extensive coverage of the Paris riots notwithstanding, much, and perhaps most, social movement activity fails to attract widespread national or international media attention. Who, for example, knew about the series of neighborhood, not-in-my-backyard (NIMBY) mobilizations protesting the proposed relocation of the Salvation Army shelter in Austin, Texas, in 1983 except for local residents who read the daily newspaper or tuned in to the local television news? And who, except for local citizens, was aware of the 1992 Christmas Eve march of homeless people carrying banners proclaiming "Still No Room at the Inn" through the streets of Tucson, Arizona, and their subsequent two-week encampment on the lawn in front of the county building?

Even so, hardly a day goes by when some kind of social movement activity or related protest event, whether of local or international relevance, does not receive at least passing media attention, particularly in major large-city newspapers. While reading the November 24, 2004, edition of the *Los Angeles Times*, for example, we found a front-page article immediately captivating. It discussed the escalation of the Ukrainian electoral crisis and alluded to the gathering of "150,000 supporters of the pro-Western opposition leader ... to protest the results of Sunday's balloting."[7] Deeper into the first section, we read that a group of angered citizens gathered outside a school in Mexico City's outskirts to protest "recent child kidnappings" and ended up attacking three anti-drug undercover agents, killing two of them who were misperceived by the protestors to be the kidnappers.[8]

For events more proximate to the site where a newspaper is published, the coverage is likely to receive even greater attention.[9] The March 26, 2006, edition of the *Los Angeles Times*, for example, carried the headline "500,000 Cram Streets to Protest Immigration Bills." The article, which began in the upper right-hand quarter of the front page and continued on an inside page, covered the previous day's march and rally of an estimated 500,000 Angelenos protesting proposed federal legislation to penalize those who hire and aid undocumented immigrants and to build a security wall along the border between Mexico and the United States.[10] A few days later, on March 28, 2006, the same paper carried not only the headline "Immigration Fight Heats Up" but also three different front-page articles related to social movements, including one titled "Massive Student Walkout Spreads Across Southland."[11]

Such news stories and the protest events they chronicle suggest that social movement activity and related protest events are conspicuous and striking features of the social landscape. And that, indeed, is the case, at least in the modern social world, especially considering that much social movement activity occurs beneath the radar of the various media. Moreover, most major social issues involve social movements on one side or the other. Because of such considerations, some scholars argue that we live in a so-called movement society.[12] If so, then understanding our own society, as well as the larger social world in which it is embedded, requires some knowledge and understanding of social movements and the activities with which they are associated. The objective of this book is to provide such an introductory understanding.

Pursuit of this objective requires that we first establish a conceptualization of social movements that is sufficiently broad to include the array of illustrative cases noted above while sufficiently bounded to allow us to distinguish movements from other social phenomena that bear a family resemblance to social movements, such as crowds and the activities of interest groups. Thus, in this chapter, we begin by providing a working conceptualization of social movements. We then discuss the integrative perspective that will guide our formulation of the answers that we develop in response to the five focal questions we elaborate and around which this book is organized.

CONCEPTUALIZATION

We conceptualize social movements in terms of five key elements: first and foremost, they are challengers to or defenders of existing structures or systems of authority; second, they are collective rather than individual enterprises; third, they act, in varying degrees, outside existing institutional or organizational arrangements; fourth, they operate with some degree of organization; and fifth, they typically do so with some degree of continuity. Combining these five elements yields the following definition: social movements are collectivities acting with some degree of organization and continuity, partly outside institutional or organizational channels, for the purpose of challenging extant systems of authority, or resisting change in such systems, in the organization, society, culture, or world system in which they are embedded.[13] Each of the five elements this definition requires some elaboration.

Social Movements as Challengers to or Defenders of Structures or
Systems of Authority

If social movements challenge or defend extant systems of authority, the meaning of 'structures or systems of authority' requires clarification. Even though the concept itself may seem a bit abstract, the surrounding social world is filled with numerous concrete examples. Within the political sector of society, "the state," or national government, is the most obvious and visible example. But other governmental units—such as the "state houses" located in the capital cities of each of the fifty states comprising the United States, county seats, and city hall or the mayor's office—also constitute political structures of authority. Nongovernmental, for-profit corporations, such as Dow Chemical, Nike, and Texaco, are also structures of authority.[14] So are nongovernmental, not-for-profit organizations that range broadly from educational institutions, like Stanford University, Ohio State University, and Miami-Dade Community College; to foundations, like the Ford Foundation and the Mellon Foundation; to professional associations, like the American Psychiatric Association and the American Sociological Association; to religious denominations, like the Methodist, Lutheran, and Southern Baptist denominations. Nongovernmental organizations, like the World Trade Organization and the World Bank, also constitute structures of authority. Various cultural or subcultural beliefs and understandings, mythic figures, and revered documents, such as the Bible, the Koran, and Marx's *Das Kapital*, also can function in an authoritative manner. Sometimes they do so negatively, as when the putatively decadent culture of the 1960s or the culture of secularism is targeted by political and religious movements on the right as sources of sexual license among teenagers and of marital instability; or positively, as when uncertain individuals are told to ask themselves, Is this what Jesus would do? Such examples are neither frivolous nor exceptional, as social movements often challenge and seek to challenge and change existing cultural understandings that function in an authoritative manner.

So what do all of these structures or systems of authority, whether structurally or culturally based, have in common? Two things. First, they are the recognized seats of decisions, regulations, procedures, and guidelines influencing some domain or aspect of the lives of some category of individuals, variously referred to as constituents or adherents in relation to political parties and social movements, as members in the case of voluntary organizations and religious organizations, as employees in relation to places of work, and as stockholders in the case of corporations. To say that a particular structure or system of authority is a recognized seat of decisions regarding some set of relevant interests is to note that adherents or members typically act in accordance with the rules and procedures associated with that structure of authority, and in doing so they are, whether intended or not, granting it a veneer of legitimacy. This does not mean that members or adherents or stakeholders agree with the rules, procedures, or decisions. Nor does it mean that they may not complain or gripe about the procedures and rules, but "institutional bitching," which is widespread in most institutional and organizational contexts, is not the same as contesting collectively and seeking to change the operating rules, procedures, and/or decisions, even though it may be the springboard for the evolution of such challenges. One component, therefore, that structures or systems of authority have in common is that they are the acknowledged seat of rules and decisions relevant to some set of interests for some category of individuals.

A second but less well articulated feature of systems of authority is that they typically are based on underlying sets of interconnected values, beliefs, and interpretive frameworks that rationalize the distribution and exercise of the authority and provide vocabularies of motive that can be used not only to justify adherence to the regulations or procedures but also to challenge their perceived violation.[15] Although this moral and interpretive aspect of structures of authority is shortchanged in much sociological work on the topic, it is especially relevant in relation to social movements because oftentimes it is the disjunction between what authorities command or do and the underlying principles or beliefs they presumably subscribe to or are entrusted to uphold that constitutes the grievance base for challenge. This can be seen clearly in the pockets of movement protest that surfaced in 2002 among Catholic laity in response to the sexual abuse scandal that rocked the church. The following description of a meeting of one such protest group, which called itself the Voice of the Faithful, illustrates this disjunction and the character of this fledgling movement:

> They used to meet Sunday nights at St. John the Evangelist Church in Wellesley, Mass., but the crowd got too big, so now they have broken into cells, gathering nightly by the dozen in parochial school cafeterias or places like this spare church cellar, plotting and testifying under flickering institutional

lights. First up is a man in a gray suit. "If the church were an institutional business," he says, "the hiring manager would be out of a job, and the CEO would be on the next boat out." Next comes a psychiatrist, who calls the Roman Catholic Church a dysfunctional family. Then a theology student, then a young father, then the mother of an abused boy and, finally, Marie Darcy. Darcy has 10 children back home in Merrimack, N.H., but left them tonight to conspire with the Catholic lay group Voice of the Faithful because, well, because it touches on her status as part of the body of Christ. "We are all heirs to Christ, but it doesn't feel that way," says Darcy. "The decisions come down from above, and that's it. The people in the pews quake, wondering what's going to happen."

Into the night the group discusses how to change that, imagining the radical reinvention of the relationship between the flock and leaders that the Voice claims is the American Catholic Church's only road to salvation. Like many Catholics, they are suffering a crisis of confidence as a result of the sexual scandals of the past months, but unlike some others, they see in it opportunity. "If there was ever a time for reform," argues Gisela Morales-Barreto, who attended her first meeting in April, "this is it."[16]

Titled "Rebels in the Pews," the story goes on to note that this contentious lay activity was occurring in one parish after another throughout the United States, largely because of the failure of the clergy to lead their lives in terms of the values and principles they are entrusted to uphold.

This disjunction between the behavior of authorities and the bedrock of principles and values on which their authority is partly based is only one aspect of the story behind the rebellion in the pews, as we will see in subsequent chapters. It illustrates, however, what we mean by structures or systems of authority: coordinated patterns of behavior and orientation, typically among a fairly large number of people, such that the activities, orientations, identities and/or interpretations of one set of actors is subordinated in some fashion to the directives, mandates, and perspectives of another set of actors (superordinates) or privileged cultural texts, narratives, or codes. The nature and degree of individual commitment to the relevant directives or regulations can be quite variable, of course. In some instances, commitment is purely instrumental, based on calculative, interest-maximizing considerations, as when employees do what they are directed to do for extrinsic compensation (for example, wages, salary), or out of fear of incurring sanctions or recriminations (for example, getting fired). In other instances, commitment to follow a mandated line of action is cathectic or affective, based on strong emotional attachment to or identification with an individual, a group, a people, a nation, or a cause, as when citizens are exhorted to heed the call of patriotic duty. In still other instances, commitment to authority is based on moral considerations, as in the case of deferring to the commands of the clergy because they are believed to be part of a sacred hierarchy of authority. Whatever the rationale for acceding to the directions or expectations of authority, whatever its character, it is when the basis of commitment is weakened, dissolved, or violated that the prospect of challenge becomes likely.

The relevance of systems of authority to social movements, then, is that they typically are the target of the challenges mounted by social movements, as illustrated by the previously mentioned student pro-democracy movement that culminated in the Tiananmen Square incident in Beijing, the Christmas Eve march of the homeless in Tucson, and the above-described rebellion in the pews.

Social Movements as Collective Actors

Not only do social movements act in the name of some authority, challenging or defending it, but the action is collective in that it involves some number of individuals, groups, or organizations engaged in joint or coordinated action. Rather than independent or individual action, collective action encompasses any goal-directed activity jointly pursued by two or more actors. Most often we think of social movements as being constituted by some number of individuals working together to press their claims, but they can also be constituted by some number of social movement organizations or advocacy groups who join together to publicly avow their grievances, as has occurred numerous times internationally over the past decade.[17] In Seattle, in late November and early December 1999, for example, well over two hundred organizations and groups joined together as a transnational coalition to protest the World Trade Organization and its activities.[18]

Although social movements always constitute collective challenges, it is important to keep in mind that the challenge can be direct or indirect. *Direct challenges* include straightforward, undisguised, overt appeals and demands, such that the targeted authorities are aware of both the claims and their carriers; *indirect challenges* include movements that seek to change larger systems by changing individuals, movements that are covert and/or ambiguous—covert in terms of the action and its carrier, and ambiguous in terms of the action and the claims. Indirect challenges also include movements that seek to divest themselves of the relevant authority by escaping it.

The fact that challenges can vary in terms of whether they are individual or collective, and whether they are direct or indirect, suggests four general types of challenge when these two dimensions are cross-classified. Type 1, as shown in Table 1.1, includes direct, individual-level appeals and demands that seek to improve some aspect of an individual's life situation relevant to the authority in question, as when a student challenges a professor about a grade, or an employee challenges her boss about her meager raise. Type 2 includes actions that are individualized in the sense of involving little if any coordination, as in the case of various indirect, seemingly disconnected forms of everyday resistance, such as pilfering and foot-dragging at work.[19] Type 3 encompasses direct, collective challenges of the kind typically associated with social movements, ranging from movement-organized marches and rallies to sit-ins and office or building

Table 1.1

TYPES OF CHALLENGE

Level of Action	Direct Challenge	Indirect Challenge
Individual Action	Type 1: Appeals to authority for personal adjustments (e.g., salary raise)	Type 2: Everyday forms of resistance and withdrawal
Collective Action and Social Movements	Type 3: Various forms of targeted protest	Type 4: Exiting from or divesting of authority

takeovers to attempts to revoke state authority, as in the case of the prototypical revolution. Type 4 is exemplified by indirect collective challenges, as when changing individuals is seen as the key to some level of systemic change, as when the connection among the actions, actors, and demands is often ambiguous (for example, some terrorist movements), or as when the collectivity leaves (for example, separatist movements), thereby divesting the authority of its right to control them.

As students of social movements, we are most interested in the collective challenges encompassed by types 3 and 4, although both types 1 and 2 may often contain the seeds for much movement activity. As suggested, the kinds of movements encompassed by Type 3 comprise most of the material that students study. Students of social movements too rarely consider the case exemplified by Type 4,[20] in large part because social movement scholars have generally been more interested in direct challenges to authority, as illustrated by the examples at the beginning of this chapter. Yet, examples abound of indirect collective challenges, such as those waged by various religious movements that have sought to change the world by first changing throngs of individuals or by terrorist groups that seek to undermine confidence in the state by terrorizing unsuspecting citizens.[21] Other examples include efforts to withdraw from or exit the system, ranging from various communal movements (as when spin-offs of the hippie counterculture sought refuge in the countryside of northern California),[22] to separatist and secessionist movements,[23] to some religious cultic and sectarian movements,[24] to mass suicide as the ultimate form of escape or exit, as in the case of the previously mentioned Heaven's Gate cult.[25] We contend that these various forms of exit can be every bit as challenging and unsettling to the relevant authority as are direct collective challenges. For members of a society, a community, a political group, or a religious order to sever their ties with and leave the organization, institution, or community with which they are associated not only challenges the existing structure of authority or regime but also may threaten the exited order by planting the seeds of challenge or exit for other groups. Thus, we count such indirect collective challenges as types of social movement activity.

Social Movements as Extra-Institutional Challengers

Social movements are only one of numerous forms of joint, collective action. Other types include much crowd behavior, as when sports and rock fans roar and applaud in unison; some riot behavior, as when looting rioters focus on certain stores or products rather than others; and some interest group behavior, as when the National Rifle Association mobilizes large numbers of its adherents to write or phone their respective congressional representatives. Since there are numerous examples of joint or collective action that can challenge authorities, it is necessary to clarify what distinguishes social movements from other forms of collective action.

The major axis of differentiation traditionally has been whether the challenges a group mounts are conducted, in part or totally, outside normatively sanctioned institutional or organizational channels—that is, the extent to which some proportion of their activity is extra-institutional. To get a handle on this distinction, it is useful to contrast so-called interest groups and social movements. Interest groups, such as Planned Parenthood and the Christian Coalition, and some social movements, such as the pro-choice and pro-life movements, bear striking family resemblances insofar as they have common interests and objectives with respect to some aspect of social life. Yet there are also important differences. Probably the most important is that they stand in a different relationship to the mainstream political environment or relevant authority. Interest groups are embedded within the political system, as most are regarded as legitimate actors within it. Social movements, in contrast, are positioned outside the authority structure in question either because of the absence of recognized standing or access to it, or because they choose to bypass conventionalized channels of appeal and redress due to distrust of or alienation from the process.

Because of differences in standing, access, and/or orientation, interest groups pursue their collective objectives mainly through institutionalized means, such as lobbying and soliciting contributions, whereas social movements pursue their collective ends mainly via the use of extra-institutional means or tactics, such as conducting protest marches and rallies in public and quasi-public places, building takeovers and sit-ins, and boycotts and encampments. Social movements may sometimes operate squarely within the institutional arena, but their action repertoire is generally skewed in the direction of extra-institutional rather than institutionally or organizationally sanctioned activity. Similarly, interest groups may sometimes adopt the extra-institutional tactics of social movements, but the means through which they advance their interests will generally be channeled institutionally. Sometimes, moreover, existing interest groups and social movements may work together to press common claims and to try to advance shared interests, as Planned Parenthood and the pro-choice movement have done. Interests groups and social movements, therefore, might best be conceived of as different types of "advocacy organizations."[26] They may overlap in a Venn diagram fashion on occasion, but they are significantly different in terms of how they are positioned in relation to relevant authorities and the kinds of modal tactics used to mount their challenges.

Social Movements as Organized Activity

We have emphasized that the challenges mounted by social movements are collective in that they involve joint action in pursuit of a common objective. Joint action of any kind implies some degree of coordination and, thus, organization. Scholars of social movements have long understood the relevance of organization to understanding the course and character of movement activity, but they have also debated about the forms, functions, and consequences of social movement organization. Clearly there are different forms of organization (for example, single organizations versus multiple, networked organizations) and degrees of organization (for example, tightly coupled versus loosely coupled), as well as differences in the consequences of different forms and degrees of organization. But to note such differences is not grounds for dismissing the significance of organization to social movements.

Sidney Tarrow cuts to the heart of these issues when he distinguishes between social movements as formal organizations, the organization of movement activities such as protest events, and social movements as connective structures or networks.[27] Conceptually, the issue concerns neither the form nor consequences of organizations, but the fact that the existence of social movement activity implies some degree of organization. To illustrate, consider the civil rights movement of the 1960s and some of its leaders, such as Martin Luther King Jr. and Stokely Carmichael;

as well as various organizational representatives, such as the National Association for the Advancement of Colored People, the Congress of Racial Equality, the Southern Christian Leadership Conference, and the Student Non-Violent Coordinating Committee. Indeed, it is difficult to comprehend the civil rights movement in the absence of the leaders and organizations associated with it. The same can be said about many other social movements. Take, for example, the student-led pro-democracy movement in Beijing: not only were the actions of demonstrators coordinated, but there were various organizing groups.

Thus, in many movements we see the interests and objectives of a particular constituency being represented and promoted by one or more individuals associated with one or more organizations (referred to in the literature as SMOs [social movement organizations]). While the organizations associated with these movements may vary in a variety of ways, the important point remains that much of the activity, including the relations between participating organizations, is organized. It is because of such observations that a semblance of organization needs to be included as a component of the conceptualization of social movements, but without specifying the character and degree of organization for any specific movement.

Movements as Existing with Some Temporal Continuity

The final element of our conceptualization of social movements concerns the extent to which social movements operate with some degree of temporal continuity. They are relatively episodic social phenomena in the sense that neither their meetings nor protest activities are regularly scheduled events on the community or national calendar. To be sure, social movement events and activities sometimes get placed on the community calendar, but such is typically the result of application and/or negotiation processes with officials rather than routine calendarization of a movement's activities.[28]

To emphasize that movements are temporally episodic is not to suggest that they are generally fly-by-night fads that are literally here today and gone tomorrow. Clearly there is considerable variability in the so-called life course of movements, and some of them do indeed last for a very short time, as with most neighborhood not-in-my-backyard movements. Others endure for decades, as did the Heaven's Gate movement, which was observed in the United States in the 1970s,[29] and the Nichiren Shoshu/Soka Gakkai Buddhist movement, which was introduced to the United States in the early 1960s.[30] Still others persist across generations, alternating between periods of heightened activism and dormancy, as with the women's movement.[31] Furthermore, many, and perhaps most, movements are clustered temporally within "cycles of protest" that wax and wane historically.[32] There is, then, significant temporal variability in the life spans of many social movements.

Continuity, like organization, is a matter of degree, of course. But it is difficult to imagine any social movement making much progress in pursuing its objectives without a fairly persistent pattern of organization and activity. Accordingly, some degree of temporal continuity in the organization and activity of social movements is an essential feature of our conceptualization.

PERSPECTIVES AND QUESTIONS

Having clarified our conceptualization of social movements, we now turn to consideration of our perspective on movements and

the kinds of questions that one must answer to provide a working understanding of the character and operation of social movements. Social movements, like most social phenomena, do not
reveal themselves in a pristine fashion to the observer or analyst.
What is seen or made of some phenomena depends in part on
the vantage point of the observer and in part on the theoretical perspectives through which each phenomenon is viewed and
analyzed. Perspectives frame what is seen because they influence
which questions are asked and, thus, focus light on only some
aspects of the phenomenon.

The study of social movements, just as the study of virtually
all human social phenomena, has been guided by a variety of
substantive standpoints and perspectives. Political sociologists,
for example, are most likely to view social movements through
the lens of political opportunity theory, which focuses attention
on aspects of the political structure that constrain or enhance
the opportunity for social movement activity.[33] Students of organization are more likely to analyze social movements from the
vantage point of resource mobilization theory, which concen-
trates attention on a movement's acquisition and deployment of
resources, such as labor, money, and information.[34] And scholars interested in the sociology of culture and symbolic interactionism are most likely to explore the role of ideology, framing,
identity, and emotion in the operation of social movements.[35]

These are not the only perspectives bearing on social movements today, but they are sufficient to suggest that the analysis
of social movements is fraught with interpretive dangers when
approached from the vantage point of a single perspective. The
probable result is akin to the storied description of an elephant
rendered by six blind men on the basis of the part they touched:

misrepresentation and oversimplification. Such interpretive dangers suggest that there is considerable wisdom to approaching the study of social movements in an integrative fashion that incorporates a number of different perspectives rather than privileging one.

Accordingly, in this primer on social movements, we draw on theorizing and research animated by various perspectives that shed light on different aspects and dimensions of social movements as we elaborate answers to the following focal questions that, we contend, must be addressed to provide an understanding of the character and operation of social movements:

- The first of these questions concerns the generation of the kinds of *grievances* that contribute to the emergence and operation of social movements. We refer to these grievances as mobilizing grievances, and we consider the kinds of factors associated with their development. Specifically, what are the conditions and/or processes that account for the generation of mobilizing grievances?

- The second question explores the contextual circumstances that are requisite for the emergence and operation of social movements. Why is the occurrence of social movements often nested temporally and spatially rather than randomly distributed across time and place? What specifically are the sets of *contextual conditions* that facilitate or constrain the emergence and flourishing of social movements?

- The third orienting question concerns the issue of *participation*. What is the character of movement participation? What are the different ways of participating? What are the determinants that influence who participates in social movement activities, and why? Why do only certain individuals come to participate in movement activity while other similarly situated individuals sit on the sidelines?

- The fourth focal question concerns the *dynamics* of social movements. What happens once a movement has surfaced and is, so to speak, up and running? More concretely, how do social movements go about the business of strategically pressing their claims and dealing with the various relevant actors within their field of operation?

- The fifth and final question we investigate concerns what most scholars and social movement activists consider the bottom-line question: What difference do movements make, and for whom and in what ways? Do social movements play an important role in challenging authorities and generating and halting social change? Are there other functions that they perform? What, in short, are the *consequences* or *outcomes* of social movements?

It is these questions, then, that anchor the five subsequent chapters. It is our hope that our elaborations on these questions provide a good understanding of the character of social movements and the array of factors that affect their emergence, operation, and consequences. We also hope that our work here will stimulate further investigation of a particular movement of interest, of one of the focal questions asked about social movements, or of social movements in general.

Chapter Two
MOBILIZING GRIEVANCES

WHEN INDIVIDUALS COLLECTIVELY challenge authorities via social movements, they typically do so over matters about which they are deeply troubled, have considerable concern, and feel passionately. These troublesome matters or conditions, and the feelings associated with them—such as dissatisfaction, fear, indignation, resentment, and moral shock—can be thought of as grievances. They provide the primary motivational impetus for organizing social movement campaigns and for engaging in social movement activities. Consequently, none of the various sets of conditions necessary for the emergence and operation of social movements is more important than the generation of deeply felt shared grievances, which we define below as mobilizing grievances. After all, it is difficult to imagine most individuals engaging in social movement activity without feeling deeply aggrieved about some condition that is regarded as contrary to the interests, rights, moral principles, or well-being of themselves or others. Think for a moment of the adherents of the pro-choice and pro-life movements, and of those advocating for and against same-sex marriages in the United States. Not only are the adherents of one movement deeply aggrieved by the prospect of the other movement achieving its goals, but their passions about their movement are often palpable and thus worn, metaphorically, on their sleeves. Certainly other motivational factors—such as curiosity, the desire for approval, and peer pressure—may come into play when considering why people align themselves with a particular movement, but these usually are secondary and largely irrelevant in the absence of deeply felt grievances.

The objective of this chapter is to illuminate our understanding of the generation of the kinds of grievances that contribute to the emergence and operation of social movements. We refer to these grievances as *mobilizing grievances*, and we conceptualize them as grievances that are shared among some number of actors, be they individuals or organizations, and that are felt to be sufficiently serious to warrant not only collective complaint but also some kind of corrective, collective action. We focus on factors that generate mobilizing grievances and ask specifically what conditions and/or processes account for their emergence.

We address this question by proceeding along two paths. First, we identify a number of arguments and theses regarding grievances. Second, drawing on the salvageable remnants of this discussion, we elaborate an integrative understanding of the development of mobilizing grievances.

GRIEVANCE GENERATION THEORIES AND OVERSIGHTS

Given the important connection between grievances and social movements, one would think that scholarly understanding of this connection should be well developed theoretically and empirically. Such is not the case, however, as the role of grievances in relation to a movement's emergence and mobilization has been, until quite recently, either glossed over or treated in too simplistic and one-dimensional a fashion. The reasons for this limited understanding can be traced to several unsatisfactory theoretical arguments and/or oversights: the argument that grievances are ubiquitous and therefore relatively inconsequential compared with other conditions that allow for their collective expression; the argument that grievances materialize fully formed out of specifiable objective, material conditions; the argument that grievances can be understood primarily in terms of heightened psychological states or thresholds; and the neglect of grievance interpretation or the process through which mobilizing grievances are partly socially constructed.

Grievances as Ubiquitous and Irrelevant

We begin with a common thesis in the literature on grievances that contradicts much of what we have just said about the importance of mobilizing grievances. The thesis is that grievances are ever-present features of social life and therefore relatively inconsequential for the emergence and operation of social movements. This argument, which surfaced in the wake of the contentious social movement activity of the 1960s and in response to the shortcomings of a number of the other theories we will consider shortly, views grievances as constants and therefore impotent as explanatory variables. Grievances, much like weeds, are thought to flourish naturally and abundantly, irrespective of environmental context or social conditions. Thus, the authors of a well-known article on a series of farm worker movements between 1946 and 1972 write that they "do not deny the existence of" farm worker discontent (or, grievance) but regard it as "relatively constant" and therefore "question" its usefulness "in accounting for either the emergence of insurgent organization or the level of participation by the social base."[1] Similarly, the progenitors of the resource mobilization approach, which we will accent in the next chapter, once took a strong position with respect to the omnipresence of grievances, contending "there is always enough discontent [grievance] in any society to supply the grassroots support for a movement."[2]

If grievances are a ubiquitous feature of social life, which is implied as well by earlier scholars who highlight the conflictual nature of social life,[3] then there is little analytic value in pondering the origins of mobilizing grievances and their relationship to social movements. Far better, instead, to focus almost exclusively on the kinds of structural factors conducive to social movement activity, such as resource flows and political opportunities, which have been the focus of much social movement theorizing and research since the mid-1970s.

There would be no problem with such foci if mobilizing grievances were in fact ubiquitous. But they are not! Individual-level grievances may be ubiquitous, but mobilizing grievances are not. Recall that mobilizing grievances are shared and experienced, or felt, as sufficiently aggravating to warrant not only collective complaint but also joint, ameliorative action. Individual grievances, in contrast, are experienced individually rather than collectively. They typically encompass the kinds of discontents and aggravations experienced on a regular basis by most people, such as dissatisfaction with a raise, office procedures, or one's boss, or having to wait too long for a scheduled physician's appointment or in lines at the bank, the grocery store, the gas station, or on the freeway. These kinds of aggravations, which escalated and became overwhelming for Michael Douglas in the movie *Falling Down,* are ubiquitous, at least in the modern world. But for most folks they are typically regarded as unpleasant aspects of everyday life about which little can be done, or for which the payoffs of doing something are generally thought to be minuscule. Additionally, they rarely congeal into collectively shared grievances that spur collective intervention. Thus, the tendency to jettison grievances as an explanatory variable seems ill conceived in light of the distinction between routine, everyday grievances and mobilizing grievances. To contend, moreover, that the grievances associated with social movement activity are ubiquitous is to presume an automatic link between material social conditions and grievances, which is difficult to sustain empirically and theoretically, as we will see in the following sections. Finally, this questionable assumption and the failure to distinguish between individual and mobilizing grievances gloss over the extent to which the formation of the latter is a function of the interaction of various social conditions and social psychological and interpretive processes.

Grievances as a Function of Structural or Material Conditions
The most enduring argument regarding the origins of mobilizing grievances is that they germinate and flourish in relation to one of two distinct kinds of social structural or material conditions: social arrangements that situate aggregations of individuals in an antagonistic position vis-á-vis one another; and social trends and changes that alter existing social arrangements and patterns of social life. The first set of conditions congeal into what can be thought of as the "group conflict and/or inequality" perspective; the second set of conditions cluster into so-called strain theory.

MOBILIZING GRIEVANCES AS AN OUTGROWTH OF GROUP CONFLICT AND/ OR INEQUALITY. The orienting assumption of this perspective is that mobilizing grievances, and thus social movements, are generated by the unequal distribution of rewards (money, status, and power) and opportunities or life chances in a society. They are, in other words, rooted in conflicts over claims to status, power, and other scarce resources among groups (social classes and racial, ethnic, and religious groups) differentially situated within a social system. The principal progenitor of this perspective historically was the political philosopher and economist Karl Marx, who is best known as capitalism's most trenchant critic and as the father of communism. Writing in the middle third of the nineteenth century, Marx, with his compatriot and co-author Friedrich Engels, depicted capitalist society as a mode of production consisting of two conflicting forces organized as social classes based on their relation to the objects and means of production (for example, material resources, tools, factories, and technology). One class, the bourgeoisie, or capitalists, was seen as controlling the objects and means of production; whereas the other class, the proletariat, owning nothing but its labor power, was subject to economic exploitation and political domination. Given this structurally antagonist relationship between the two classes, Marx portrayed the proletariat as the force of progress that had, as its historical mission, the negation of the existing capitalist system of exploitation and domination and the creation of a new order called socialism. Marx articulated this prophecy in his most famous political tract, *Manifesto of the Communist Party*. As Engels wrote in the preface of the 1883 German edition of the *Manifesto*:

> The basic thought running through the Manifesto ...
> [is that] all history has been a history of class struggles, of

struggles between exploited and exploiting classes, between dominated and dominating classes at various stages of development; that this struggle, however, has now reached a stage where the exploited and the oppressed classes (the proletariat) can no longer emancipate itself from the class which exploits and oppresses it (the bourgeoisie), without at the same time forever freeing the whole of society from exploitation, oppression, and class struggles. ...[4]

The working class, then, was to be the carrier of the idealized movement of all movements: the proletarian revolution. Exactly when this cataclysmic event might occur, however, was not so clear. Marx did not provide a single definitive answer. But running throughout a number of his writings are discussions of several events or trends that can be construed as necessary conditions for the emergence of this vanguard movement. One such set of events includes crises that are internal to capitalism itself, such as an epidemic of overproduction or unemployment. Another is the increasing exploitation and immiseration of the working class. And a third condition is the development of class consciousness on behalf of the working class, a consciousness that signals the transformation of the working class from a "class-in-itself" into a "class-for-itself." The former refers to the objective situation of a class without an implication of members' understanding of their situation in relation to the economic system as a whole and to each other. A class-for-itself, however, arises when members of a class-in-itself become conscious that their fates are joined, that they are the objects of exploitation and oppression, that they share a common enemy, and that any significant change in their objective situation requires dramatic alteration of the social system.[5] Here again, Marx did not clearly specify how or under what conditions this transformative process would occur. Consequently, one is left to ponder and debate whether it would occur naturally or spontaneously when the previous conditions reached a certain unspecified but intolerable threshold, or whether it would have to be organizationally molded and facilitated as Vladimir Ilyich "Nikolai" Lenin, one of the major leaders of the Russian Revolution and architects of the former Soviet Union, pondered and concluded affirmatively in *What Is to Be Done?*[6]

The flow of history in the more than one hundred years since Marx and Engels penned the *Manifesto* clearly calls into question the presumption of a direct, automatic linkage between class antagonisms and the formation of mobilizing grievances of sufficient magnitude to foster working-class revolt. There have been labor movements and strikes and other outcroppings of working-class unrest.[7] But the prophesied proletarian revolution never materialized in advanced capitalist societies for a variety of reasons. Not only did Marx fail to anticipate the evolution and growth of the middle, managerial class, but the immiseration of the working class failed to reach the level of wretchedness that Marx and others envisioned. Additionally, the development of strident working-class consciousness has been neutralized by multiple, cross-cutting associations and identities rooted in ethnicity, race, religion, and gender; by the existence of national, mythic narratives that highlight, as in the United States, shared belief in the prospect of upward mobility; and by the nonclass character of many competing sides of many public issues, such as crime control and the debate over abortion.

Because of such countervailing influences and the nonmaterialization of the hypothesized proletarian revolution, the German sociologist Ralf Dahrendorf suggested a modification of Marx's core thesis by switching the locus of conflict from class antagonisms to organizationally and institutionally embedded conflicts.[8] Such a reformulation suggests a somewhat broader proposition than Marx's class-based thesis regarding the origin of mobilizing grievances associated with collective challenges to authority: they are rooted in underlying conflicts of interest among categories of social actors differentially arrayed hierarchically in a social system. This suggests, in accord with the previous argument, that the basis for conflicts, and thus mobilizing grievances, is ubiquitous. A quick scan of the distribution of resources, privilege, and opportunity in almost any society or organizational context seems to indicate that the above proposition is, in fact, a truism of social life. Yet conflicts do not always materialize, not even when the structural conditions seem ripe for conflict. Moreover, the existence of conflict does not automatically predict the emergence of mobilizing grievances. Consequently, it is clear that the existence of social conflict, whether rooted in class, organizational, or group antagonisms, is not a sufficient condition for the emergence of social movements.

To note that a given condition is not sufficient for the occurrence of a particular phenomenon is not to conclude that that condition is irrelevant or unrelated to the phenomenon in question. It may well be that the presumed connection occurs only in some category of cases or in conjunction with other conditions, some of which may modify the relationship. The later is exactly what Bert Klandermans and his colleagues found in a study of grievance formation in South Africa between 1994 and 1998.[9] The apartheid policies of the pre-1994 government yielded a deeply segregated and divided society, but social movement protest among black South Africans was not as widespread or temporally persistent as one might expect given the profound differences in race-based inequalities. This, obviously, was not due to the absence of grievances among black South Africans. The highly repressive measures of the South African government no doubt functioned to suppress the mobilizing potential of those grievances, as political opportunity theorists would argue. However, the Klandermans study—based on structured, face-to-face interviews with a representative, stratified sample of between 2,220 and 2,286 South Africans aged eighteen and over, conducted annually over the five-year period from 1994 through 1998—revealed not only that the material base of the grievances changed over time from predominately race-based to class-based, but also that the effects of the objective, material conditions were modified by subjective assessments, such as comparative evaluation of one's situation with that of others and the level of trust in the government. In other words, the character and depth of grievance among South Africans was not an automatic artifact of their racial category or socioeconomic situation. On the contrary, it was affected as well by various social psychological factors. We will return to such social psychological factors after considering a second kind of structural argument regarding the well springs of mobilizing grievances.

MOBILIZING GRIEVANCES AS AN OUTGROWTH OF SOCIAL "STRAINS."
An equally persistent idea in the study of social movements, dating back to at least the classical writings of Émile Durkheim,

is that their underlying mobilizing grievances are the by-products of social changes and trends traditionally conceptualized as "strains."[10] Here there are three different arguments: the "disintegration" or "breakdown" thesis, the absolute deprivation thesis, and the "quotidian disruption" thesis.

Disintegration Thesis. This thesis holds that disruptive social changes loosen the threads of social constraint, thus weakening the social fabric and rendering citizens vulnerable to the appeals of social movements.[11] The specific formula advanced to account for disintegrating change varies somewhat from writer to writer, but the core argument is much the same: the traditional sources of social cohesion and integration are weakened or destroyed by war, adverse economic trends, disaster, and the like, thereby causing a rupture or strain in the sociopolitical order that gives rise to grievances that spur social movement activity. Here the mobilizing grievances are seen as springing from the dissolution of social arrangements and patterns of association rather than from conflicts of interests among contending social categories or from social inequalities.

Although this thesis was popular throughout the first two-thirds of the twentieth century, it fell out of favor during the latter third of the century. Disenchantment with it was based in part on a series of studies that contradicted the perspective's central premises. Charles Tilly and his associates, who famously labeled the disintegration thesis "breakdown theory,"[12] provided the most widely cited challenge. In their historical study of protest and rebellion across Europe from 1830 to 1930, they found little compelling evidence linking such collective action to social disintegration. There were, to be sure, significant changes in the social fabric associated with the spread of industrialization, but the collective action of the time sprang mainly out of new forms of organization, thus prompting the Tillys to prophesize that "no matter where we look, we should rarely find uprooted, marginal, disorganized people heavily involved in collective violence."[13] Much subsequent research examining the associational and network characteristics of participants in a variety of social movements has generally confirmed this hypothesis,[14] thus suggesting that mobilizing grievances do not spring automatically from social atomization or breakdown.

Some scholars have also argued that the effect of indicators of disintegration or breakdown applies more to "nonroutine" social movement activity or collective action (for example, violence against property, persons, or both) than to "routine" activity (for example, negotiated and sanctioned marches and rallies).[15] Here again, the findings are not always consistent, but theoretically it makes sense that collective violence against people and property is partly contingent on the relaxation or neutralization of customary restraints, be they moral, legal, or coercive. What, however, accounts for changes in restraint or control remains unclear. One possibility is a decline in government repression, which we will discuss in the following chapter. Another possibility is that the situation is redefined or reframed as intolerable, which we will consider shortly. A third possibility is that some disruptions or strains are more likely than others to congeal into mobilizing grievances.

Absolute Deprivation or Immiseration Thesis. The orienting proposition of this thesis is that dire social, immiserating life conditions—such as the lack of affordable housing, widespread unemployment, inaccessible health care, extreme poverty, epidemic health problems, and disabling discrimination—are the source of mobilizing grievances among those who suffer them. This is a seemingly sensible thesis at first blush, yet research on the relationship between various measures of absolute or objective deprivation and engagement in social protests or movement activities has produced quite mixed findings. Consider, for example, the relationship between unemployment and participation (which can be used as a proxy for felt grievances) both in riots (which often constitute a form of collective protest) and in social movement activity. Initial studies of the urban riots in U.S. cities during the 1960s, using both individual-level and city-level data, generally found that unemployment rates were not positively and significantly related to these riots, but the most recent reexaminations of the city-level data report that cities with higher rates of black unemployment had higher riot rates.[16] Examining protest events that were clearly sponsored and orchestrated by social movement organizations, a study of homeless protest activity across seventeen U.S. cities in the 1980s similarly found that higher unemployment rates were associated with more frequent homeless protest events.[17]

Taken together, these different sets of findings indicate that there is no determinant relationship between measures of absolute deprivation or immiseration and the emergence of mobilizing grievances that incite social movement activity. However, this does not mean that measures of such deprivations may not contribute to the generation of shared grievances. It only says that the relationship is indeterminate, thus prompting questions about the kinds of conditions in which immiserating trends and mobilizing grievances are likely to be linked. One line of inquiry has been to focus on the concurrence of other conditions. For example, in the above-described studies that found support for the association of unemployment with riot and movement activity, other factors were found to interact with unemployment so that the stress or strain produced resulted from the confluence of a number of measures or conditions. In the case of the riot study, for instance, the effect of unemployment was found to be most salient under conditions of interminority competition.[18]

Quotidian Disruption Thesis.　We noted above in discussing the disruption/breakdown thesis that some disruptions may be more likely than others to congeal into mobilizing grievances. It is this proposition that is at the core of the quotidian disruption thesis elaborated by David Snow and his colleagues.[19] In contrast to the disintegration thesis, it is not associational ties and bonds of solidarity that are postulated as disrupted or broken, but rather patterns of everyday functioning and routinized expectations associated with those patterns. The basic argument is that the actual or threatened disruption of the taken-for-granted routines and attitudes of everyday life, referred to as "the quotidian," is especially generative of mobilizing grievances because it renders problematic and uncertain previously habituated ways of conducting one's daily life. The quality or character of everyday life that is routinized may not be easy, and may even be far from being ideal, but the fact that it is routinized means that its practitioners have become accustomed to it and, therefore, are likely to be particularly aggrieved when it is disrupted in the sense that it is no longer sustainable or reproducible. This also makes sense because, according to some theories and research, individuals are especially averse to the loss of what they already have and understand and, therefore, will be highly motivated to recoup what they have lost or to guard against the prospect of such loss.[20] By implication, this suggests that the actual or threatened disruption of the quotidian should be particularly nurturing of mobilizing grievances.

While this makes for a reasonable thesis theoretically, the question arises whether some types of events are more likely than others to lead to disruption of the quotidian. Examination of the emergence of protest and movement activity in a variety of contexts identifies four categories of such disruptive events. One such category includes accidents and disasters that disrupt a community's routines, threaten its existence, and are attributable to human negligence or error rather than to natural forces. An example that generated a sudden escalation of intense grievances and considerable social movement activity was the 1979 partial meltdown of a nuclear reactor in the Three Mile Island area of eastern Pennsylvania.[21] A second category of quotidian disrupting events includes intrusions into or violations of culturally defined areas of privacy and control, such as community space, by strangers or outsiders. Proposed and actual halfway houses, group homes, soup kitchens and shelters for the homeless, and toxic waste dumps constitute well-known examples of such intrusions that almost invariably generate intense mobilizing grievances associated with community and neighborhood movements that cluster under the NIMBY (not-in-my-backyard) acronym.[22]

The third set of events conducive to quotidian disruption entails dramatic alterations in subsistence routines because of changes in the ratio of resources to claimants or demand. In some instances, an unanticipated decline in resources, such as wages or their purchasing power, without any substantial change in demand may nurture the soil for mobilizing grievances, as appears to have been the case with many movements among peasants and farmers. In a study of events preceding peasant rebellions in colonial Vietnam and Lower Burma in 1930 and 1931, for example, it was found that the peasants were not troubled so much by economic exploitation so long as there were enough resources to meet subsistence needs.[23] It thus was concluded that exploitation or deprivation per se are not as unsettling to the peasants as are actual or threatened disruptions to their subsistence routines. This same metric was also found to be at work in Argentina in 2002–2003 when "women's unpaid domestic and caring labor became more difficult and that economic decline hurt poor, working-class, and middle-class women." It was in this context of "unbearable" declining resources that many Argentine women took to the streets in protest as their "consciousness about their place in society changed, and efforts to dismantle gender inequalities gained momentum."[24]

In other instances, an increase in claimants or demand in the face of constant or stagnant resources may stimulate mobilizing grievances, as appears to have been the case in some popular uprisings and revolutions and with some homeless mobilizations. Regarding the latter, one study of homeless social movement activity, associated with fifteen homeless social movement organizations in eight U.S. cities, found that in ten of the cases initial movement activity was prompted in part or fully by the disruption of either individual or organizational routines because of resource deficiencies.[25] In the case of the disruption of individual routines, the typical scenario involved one or more homeless individuals realizing that their taken-for-granted subsistence routines, such as standing in line in soup kitchens or shelters, no longer guaranteed the expected outcome because the growing number of homeless claimants exceeded available meals and/or shelter beds. As a service provider explained when discussing a homeless individual who helped found the National Union of the Homeless: "To get into the shelter, you had to wait in line, and if they fill up, you're just out of luck. Now these lines were not well supervised, so the bigger guys would fight their way in. [He was] a big guy, and it really ripped him up to have to fight other men so that he could sleep indoors on a floor."

A fourth set of events disruptive of the quotidian involves dramatic changes in structures of social organization and control. This appears especially in two contexts: when tightly regimented systems of control, formal or informal, are ousted or displaced and routinized patterns of hierarchy and patronage are disrupted; or when there are dramatic changes in policing practices such that routines that were overlooked before are redefined as fair game for police harassment and arrest and are thus disrupted. In both situations, business as usual is disrupted. Research on prison rebellions has shown, for example, that the major precipitating incident is often a change in wardens and the resultant reconstitution of interconnected systems of formal and informal control that alters prisoners' taken-for-granted routines.[26] Similarly, research on homeless social movement activity has shown that such mobilizations are sometimes sparked by changes in city ordinances and associated policing practices regarding the use of public space by the homeless.[27]

Certainly the prisoners and homeless in question, just as folks who live under the thumb of highly authoritarian political regimes, are likely to harbor various grievances about their life situations, but they have devised a means of making do and thus surviving in a way that often becomes taken for granted and thus mutes the mobilizing potential of those grievances. When this occurs, so the argument goes, it is the disruption of those taken-for-granted routines that is especially likely to be generative of mobilizing grievances. In specifying a connection between specific instances of quotidian disruption and mobilizing grievances, this thesis offers a more determinative connection between underlying social conditions and grievances than the disintegration thesis. Yet it is also clear that mobilizing grievances also often effervesce in the absence of quotidian disruption.

Grievances as a Function of Social Psychological Factors
Social psychological explanations of grievance formation direct attention to certain psychological conditions or states that presumably heighten existing grievances or signal the emergence of new ones. Although structural or material conditions are neither ignored nor dismissed, they are usually treated as nondifferentiated or generalized precipitants of fundamental social psychological states that are regarded as sine qua non conditions for the occurrence of a sufficient level of grievance. In other words, if a certain social psychological state is not reached, then the felt grievances are unlikely to be of sufficient magnitude to spur social movement activity no matter what the underlying structural or material conditions. This logic constitutes what can be thought of as a hydraulic pressure or steam engine model of grievance formation: the hypothesized state, such as frustration, builds up until it reaches a threshold or magnitude that requires release or expression. The classic example of this

sort of theorizing is the frustration-aggression thesis initially developed in 1939.[28] Although the concept of grievance is not a central element of this theory, we propose that heightened frustration over some situation or event can be construed as a proxy for grievance. Additionally, the theory makes clear that when a certain level of frustration is reached, it will seek release even if it means that it is redirected to a safe or more readily available target: that is, a scapegoat. Thus, in exploring the sources of an epidemic of lynching of African Americans in the post–Civil War South, the proponents of the thesis argued that decline of cotton prices (material conditions) increased the level of frustration among poor whites, who took out their heightened frustration on available and relatively safe African Americans.

Since this frustration-aggression thesis was initially elaborated, other more refined hypotheses have been propounded. These include, for example, the relative deprivation thesis, which hypothesizes that mounting frustrations, and thus mobilizing grievances, grow in the widening gap between expectations or aspirations and achievements or attainments, between what folks want or think they should have and what they actually have;[29] and the status dissonance or inconsistency thesis, which argues that a disjunction between two salient statuses, such as education and job prestige or wages, can generate intense frustrations that, by implication, congeal into mobilizing grievances.[30]

Empirical examinations of these social psychological theories are mixed, just as they are for arguments regarding structural and material conditions—and for some of the same reasons. The relationship between the more general condition of frustration, or the more specific states of relative deprivation or status inconsistency, and mobilizing grievances is indeterminate. Sometimes mounting frustrations are associated with apathy, indifference, and inaction; other times, they may prompt citizens to organize collectively and take to the streets to demand that their grievances be resolved; and still other times, they may be associated with the kinds of indirect, individual-level forms of challenge that have been discussed as everyday forms of resistance, such as "foot dragging, dissimulation, false compliance, pilfering, feigned ignorance, slander, arson, sabotage, and so forth."[31] Thus, frustrations or other social psychological tensions alone do not account for such varied responses, but they may be contributing factors.

Frustration, relative deprivation, or status dissonance theories—just as group conflict, disintegration, and absolute deprivation theories—do not take us very far by themselves in explaining the derivation of grievances because they gloss over a number of important social psychological processes and distinctions. First, there is the extent to which assessments of relative deprivation are embedded in multifaceted comparison processes; second, there is the fact that assessments of distributional justice cannot be fully understood apart from parallel assessments of procedural justice; third, there is the tendency to focus on the prospect of gain, or winning new advantages, but to neglect actual or threatened loss; and fourth, there is the neglect of grievance interpretation.

THE NEGLECT OF COMPARISON PROCESSES.　The idea of relative deprivation is predicated on one or more subjective comparisons; otherwise, the notion of "relative" would have no meaning. However, much research attempting to assess the relationship between relative deprivation and social movement activity or protest has either inferred its existence from aggregate statistics of various objective conditions, such as unemployment rates, or treated it in a one-dimensional fashion by focusing on differences in the situation or status of individuals or a group at different points in time. Such assessment strategies are misguided in two ways: First, they skirt the subjective character of relative deprivation. Just because the objective situation of a group is worse at Time 2 than at Time 1 does not mean that the difference will be read as such by the group in question. The difference might go unnoticed or it might be noticed but not interpreted as a grievance, much less one that merits protest. This takes us to the second way in which these assessment strategies are misguided: the failure to give sufficient attention to the multiplicity of ways in which comparisons can occur. For example, comparisons can be intrapersonal or interpersonal and intragroup or intergroup; they can be oriented to different points in time, such as the past or future; and they can be upward or downward. Intracomparisons typically involve individuals or groups assessing their relative attainments or status at two different points in time. Intercomparisons entail comparisons with other people or groups, which can occur at single or multiple points in time. Such comparisons, moreover, are likely to be complicated by the selection of the comparison group and whether the comparison is upward or downward. The effects of such comparisons can be seen in the previously mentioned study of grievance formation in South Africa from 1994 through 1998. While both intra- and interpersonal comparisons were found to contribute importantly to the formation of grievances beyond race and class, interpersonal comparisons were far more important, largely because they provide a better sense of how one's group stands in comparison to other groups in terms of the distribution of valued resources. Temporal comparisons were also important, with those people who thought their current situations were worse than in the past—and/or expected their situations to be worse in the future—feeling particularly aggrieved. As the authors concluded: "Regardless of the objective conditions, comparisons suggesting that one is worse off than others or worse off than in the past, or the expectation that one's situation will be worse in the future, are powerful generators of grievances."[32]

In this study, as with most research examining relative deprivation in relation to social movements, the comparisons examined are typically upward: that is, with people or groups that are higher in some status or economic hierarchy. This is hardly surprising, of course, since relative deprivation does not exist in the absence of such upward comparisons. But this focus glosses over the established observation that people will often make downward comparisons to protect or enhance their self-regard. When this is the case, there also is a disjunction between objective conditions and subjective assessments, which explains in part why assessment of relative deprivation can be a tricky undertaking without considering the various ways in which comparisons can occur.

THE NEGLECT OF ASSESSMENTS OF PROCEDURAL JUSTICE. Such comparisons can also be complicated by whether the outcomes are regarded as fair or unfair, just or unjust. But assessment of the fairness or justice of distributional outcomes, such as differences in wages or grades, can also be complicated by assessment of the procedures through which the distribution in question was derived. Students may not always like the distribution of grades in their classes, but they are unlikely to feel aggrieved if the procedures or metric on which the grades are based are accepted as fair or just. Such observations alert us to the distinction, made by equity theorists in social psychology, between distributive justice and procedural justice.[33] Distributive justice concerns the fairness of the distribution of valued resources or rewards, such as income and grades; procedural justice refers to the fairness of the procedures on which the distributions are based.

This distinction helps us understand that individuals can feel relatively deprived and unhappy about their respective incomes or lifestyles in relation to others with whom they compare themselves and yet not feel deeply aggrieved because they regard the underlying procedures on which those differences are based as being reasonably fair or just. It is in large part because of this kind of calculus that the majority of people in Western societies consider the economic inequality they experience or see as fair or just.[34] And, by implication, it is why folks who are on the wrong end of some distributional scheme in terms of objective criteria do not always consider themselves deprived or mistreated. Another way of putting it is that the mobilizing potential of distributional differences is muted by procedural considerations. This, moreover, is what the previously discussed South African study found. Using trust in government and perceived influence on government as proxies for procedural justice, it was found that variation in these measures moderated the effect of living standard on grievance formation. In other words, objective conditions were less likely to be associated with grievance formation when respondents trusted government or felt that they had some measure of influence.[35]

THE NEGLECT OF ACTUAL OR THREATENED LOSS. Social movements often promise to ameliorate existing social conditions and to improve the life situation of their adherents in one or more ways. Although emphasizing the promise of a better day ahead is more commonly associated with so-called progressive movements, religious-based movements also often direct attention to a utopian future state, as with St. Augustine's "City of God" or the current Christian evangelical movement's enchantment with the presumed advent of "the Rapture." In general, it would appear that the appeals of social movements are often couched in the language of some kind of improved situation or "gain." However, as previously suggested, the kinds of material conditions most directly generative of mobilizing grievances are those that disrupt taken-for-granted, habituated daily routines, or at least threaten to do so. This results in part, as propounded by prospect theory within cognitive psychology, because individuals are especially averse to loss and, therefore, are more likely to take action, however risky, to preserve what they already have than they will to gain something new. If so, then we should expect forecasted or anticipated threats to one's current situation to be important sources of grievance.

Again, the study of grievance formation in South Africa provides confirmatory findings. Among survey respondents sharing the same objective conditions (race and class), those who feared that their life situation would be worse in the near future felt more aggrieved than those who believed their situation would improve.[36] Although hardly a startling finding, it underscores two important points: the effect of objective, material conditions on grievance formation is likely to be moderated by social psychological factors; and the presumed prospect of decline or loss is likely to be an especially potent generator of grievance.

THE NEGLECT OF GRIEVANCE INTERPRETATION. The final troublesome oversight has been the tendency to neglect the extent to which the kinds of social dissatisfactions, personal affronts, and everyday aggravations constitutive of grievances are partly social constructions and thus subject to differential interpretation. This tendency is long-standing and pervasive in that it dates back to the mentioned ideas of Marx and Durkheim regarding the material origins of mobilizing grievances, and it is present in each of the preceding tendencies. If mobilizing grievances are ubiquitous, if they arise naturally and spontaneously in the course of antagonistic group relations or in the face of disintegrative social change or immiserating social conditions, or if they are spawned routinely by intense frustration or relative deprivation, then it is reasonable to expect affected aggregations of individuals to be deeply aggrieved and eager to press their claims through joint mobilization. "If the mere existence of privations" were "enough to cause an insurrection," then, to paraphrase Leon Trotsky, one of the leaders of the Russian revolution, "the masses would be always in revolt."[37] But they are not, as history is replete with examples of aggregations of individuals who are exploited economically, who are deprived relative to their neighbors, and who are objects of stigmatization and differential treatment, but who have not mobilized to collectively challenge the responsible agents, or even some scapegoat, for their situation. Thus, collective protest or social movement activities do not follow automatically on the heels of antagonistic group relations, disintegrating or dire social conditions, or intense frustration, deprivation, or disappointment.

One of the reasons such material conditions or psychological states do not automatically generate mobilizing grievances is that they are subject to differential interpretation. That is to say, the meanings or implications of such material conditions and psychological states for some kind of action are contestable and thus open to discussion and debate. This is evident when we consider what constitutes an injustice. Some scholars have argued that injustice is the primary grievance underlying most social movement activity,[38] but the matter of the kinds of events and conditions constitutive of injustices is rarely self-evident or incontestable. Rather, the designation of some condition as an injustice is typically a matter of interpretation, as suggested by our discussion of the distinction between distributive and procedural justice. Additionally, the resultant negotiated and imputed meanings are not fixed but subject to change as the social context changes. Shifting patterns of interaction and identification are especially likely to alter the meanings we attach to persons, groups, nations, events, experiences, things or material objects, and even to one's biography and self-concept.

The interpretive malleability of one's biography and sense of self, for example, was repeatedly illustrated during the course of Snow's field research on recruitment and conversion to the Nichiren Shoshu Buddhist movement (now called Soka Gakkai International) in the United States during the first half of the 1970s. Whether in the context of a movement meeting or a personal conversation, members would routinely recount not only the various problems they had prior to encountering Nichiren Shoshu and the power of chanting Nam-Myoho-Renge-Kyo but also the observation that they were not fully aware of these problems until they began to chant.[39] As one member, a single male in his twenties, explained:

> Now as I look back I feel that I was a total loser. At that time, however, I thought I was pretty cool. But after chanting for a while, I found out my life before was just a dead thing. The more I chanted, the more clearly I came to see myself and the more I realized just how many problems I had.

Similarly, a single women in her twenties indicated that it was not until she "attended these meetings and began chanting" that she "really began to see that [her] personal life was a mess."

Although such examples of "biographical reconstruction" are commonplace in religious contexts and movements, they are hardly peculiar to just the religious realm, as illustrated by Kathy Blee's study of women in four racist hate movements (Christian Identity, Ku Klux Klan, neo-Nazi, and white power skinheads) in the United States.[40] She found, for example, that her informants "reassessed their interests as women" and "remade themselves in a racist mold" once they joined the movements and became more deeply involved. As she observed in the case of two informants:

> Originally, neither Jill nor Janice was very focused on racism. Both held ill-defined ideas, if any, about their self-interest as whites. Once involved with racist group members, however, each began to consider herself and the world in more racialized terms. Jill changed from a stance of political apathy to

what she described as "racial awareness," Janice from skirting the edges of white supremacy to speaking on its behalf. In the process, both Jill and Janice came to see their interests as diametrically opposed to those of non-Aryans.[41]

In each instance, we see that the grievances invoked to rationalize participation were partly a function of the interpretive process of biographical reconstruction. To note this is not to discount the existence of an empirical substrate to the concerns alluded to by each individual. But each person's account makes clear that whatever issues existed prior to interaction with the respective movements they joined, those issues were not seen as particularly troublesome or pressing until they viewed them from the vantage point of the relevant movement, thus underscoring the importance of grievance interpretation.

Just as biographies may be subject to differential interpretation over time and across different groups or movements, so are collective entities; experiences; events or happenings; and matters that are seemingly even more fundamental, such as whether an event or condition constitutes an injustice that demands intervention and elimination. In light of such observations, it is necessary to step back and examine more closely the contribution of interpretative processes to the generation of mobilizing grievances.

FRAMING PROCESSES AND GRIEVANCE FORMATION

In the past twenty years, a perspective has surfaced within the study of social movements that treats interpretive processes seriously. Referred to as the "framing perspective," it views social movements not merely as carriers of existing ideas and meanings but as important signifying or interpretive agents actively engaged in producing and maintaining meaning for their constituents, antagonists, and bystanders. The concept of framing is borrowed from Erving Goffman's *Frame Analysis* and is rooted in the symbolic interactionist and constructionist principle that meanings do not naturally or automatically attach themselves to the objects, events, or experiences we encounter. They arise, instead, through interpretive processes mediated by culture. Applied to social movements, the idea of framing renders problematic the meanings associated with relevant events, activities, places, and actors, suggesting that those meanings are typically contestable and negotiable and thus open to debate and differential interpretation. From this vantage point, mobilizing grievances are seen neither as naturally occurring sentiments nor as arising automatically from specifiable material conditions, but as the result of interactively based interpretation or signifying work. The verb *framing* conceptualizes this signifying work, which is one of the activities that social movement adherents (leaders, activists, and rank-and-file participants) and other actors (adversaries, institutional elites, media, countermovements) perform on a regular basis.

One way in which framing manifests itself in relation to mobilizing grievances is in terms of diagnostic framing, which is one of the three core framing tasks (for prognostic and motivational framing, see Chapter 4) confronting movement entrepreneurs, leaders, and activists. Diagnostic framing involves two signifying activities: the first is the problematization of an event, social condition, or aspect of life; the second is the attribution of blame or responsibility for the problematized conditions or state of affairs.

Problematization involves an assessment of a given social condition or event as troublesome, unacceptable, unjust, or intolerable and thus in need of repair or change. It may be triggered by a change in conditions or events, or it may entail the reinterpretation of the same conditions or events, thus generating a new or different understanding. In either case, the problematization of some condition can be based on a shift in current evaluative standards, or the introduction of new ones, as occurs when there is a change in comparison group, from downward to upward; a shift from a focus on distributional issues to procedural matters; or an emphasis on threatened losses. In the case of many "rights" movements, for example, procedural rather than distributional issues are problematizied. The claim is not that all folks or groups should necessarily receive an equal share of the pie, but that they should have an equal and fair chance of securing a bigger or better piece of the pie. The unacceptable condition or injustice, then, is that the rules of the game are biased in that they advantage or favor some groups over others. In such scenarios, the rules of the game need to be changed such that the metaphorical playing field is leveled and some social categories are no longer more or less advantaged or disadvantaged than others.[42] The early part of the civil rights movement in the United States is instructive. While there were certainly grievances over distributional inequities, attention was riveted more on procedural inequities, such as the absence of equal educational opportunity for black Americans. Thus, following the famed 1954 Supreme Court decision in *Brown v. Board of Education of Topeka, Kansas*, in which the Court ruled in favor of integration of public schools and thereby overturned the Jim Crow separate-but-equal doctrine established in *Plessy v. Ferguson* fifty-eight years earlier, in 1896, one of the movement's battle cries was for equal educational opportunity.[43] School desegregation—both K through 12 and at the college and university level—became one of the central objectives and prognostic frames of the civil rights movement, with some of the most memorable collective confrontations occurring at schools throughout the South. One of the most memorable examples occurred when President John F. Kennedy federalized National Guard troops and dispatched them to the University of Alabama to force its desegregation on June 10, 1963. Governor George Wallace of Alabama reluctantly yielded to the federal show of force, allowing two African American students to enroll, but he did not give up his battle to preserve Jim Crow segregation as he attempted to block the desegregation of Tuskegee High School in Huntsville in September of the same year. As before, President Kennedy deployed federalized National Guard troops and forced Wallace to relent once again.

What becomes an animating grievance, or set of grievances, for a movement, then, is often a result of framing discussions and/or debates over such issues as appropriate comparisons and procedural inequities. This is true even in the case of some kinds of quotidian disruptions, which are often preceded by framing debates and contests regarding the matter of victimhood and the character of the threat or loss. Such framing contests are evident in the constitution of grievances promulgated by NIMBY (not-in-my-backyard) movements that surfaced in abundance in the United States during the 1980s, as the residents of urban and suburban neighborhoods found themselves "threatened" by the proximate location of facilities for so-called undesirable individuals or activities, such as group homes, halfway houses, restitution centers, homeless shelters and soup kitchens, and toxic waste facilities.

The campaign of the city of Austin, Texas, to relocate and build a new Salvation Army facility primarily for the homeless in the mid-1980s provides an interesting case in point. The existing facility was not only much too small to help meet some of the many needs of the city's rapidly expanding homeless population but was located on property that was coveted by developers associated with the glittering redevelopment of the booming downtown. Consequently, there was dire need for a new facility in a new location.

The relocation effort proved particularly onerous and contentious, however, as it moved from one neighborhood to another, engendering at each prospective site strident, organized community opposition that constituted localized, small-scale NIMBY movements. At the core of the framing efforts of the NIMBY movements in Austin was the portrayal of the neighborhood and its residents as being victimized by the proximate relocation of the Salvation Army. This was not a simple rhetorical task, however, since claiming or establishing victimhood implies the existence of causal agents or perpetrators, thus calling for attribution of blame, which is the second signifying aspect of diagnostic framing.

In the Austin case, attributing blame for the claimed victimization was complicated by the Salvation Army's lofty moral status as an agent of Christian charity and outreach. Thus, a more negatively evaluated target of blame and opposition was needed, which was provided by the growing numbers of transient homeless men who had migrated to Austin and were served by the Salvation Army. As one neighborhood activist revealed: "Everybody believed we couldn't fight the Salvation Army because it is good. But you can make anything look bad. So we focused on the transients, and emphasized how they threatened neighborhood residents, particularly women and children." That was exactly what the neighborhood activists did, repeatedly framing the homeless as criminally inclined, drunken, sex-crazed men who would infiltrate their neighborhoods and "rob their homes" and "rape the women." As the two researchers observed:

> in one prospective neighborhood, signs were hung on doors asking "Do you want your women raped and your children mauled?" In another, residents appeared before the city council carrying placards that read "Vagrance [sic] and kids don't mix" and gave testimony highlighting the threat to women and children posed by the homeless. One neighborhood resident emphasized "how the neighborhoods will be unfit for raising children," and another angrily asked the council whether they understood the "impact these womanless men will have on schoolchildren, on women, and on families." The local Catholic university located adjacent to one of the prospective sites joined the resistance, similarly framing its opposition in terms of the danger the homeless posed to its students. As the chairman of the university's board of trustees emphasized on three different occasions at one board meeting: "We have to be able to reassure the thousand coeds on campus, and I don't think we can."[44]

At the same time that these local NIMBY movements were attempting to mobilize citizens and persuade political officials about the dangers of locating facilities for the homeless next to residential neighborhoods, the Salvation Army and its proponents were not sitting by idly. Rather, they were offering their own counterframings that attempted, in some instances, to deflect attention from homeless men to the many poor and homeless women and children the Salvation Army served and, in other instances, to reframe homeless men as victims rather than potential victimizers. Thus, public hearing after public hearing in city council chambers were essentially framing contests between local NIMBY activists and adherents, on the one hand, and advocates, on the other hand.

In addition to underscoring the relevance of framing activities, particularly diagnostic framing, to the development and crystallization of mobilizing grievances, this case illustrates another important feature of movement framing activities: they generally occur in a contested discursive field consisting minimally of three sets of actors—the protagonists, or activists and advocates, proffering the challenging frame, as represented by the NIMBY movements in the Austin case; the antagonists, including both targets and groups or movements with competing interests who often engage in counterframing, as did the Salvation Army and the Austin city government; and one or more groups of bystanders who may be indifferent or open to being swayed in one direction or the other, as illustrated by the city council members in the above case.[45] Such discursive fields highlight the fact that the construction of mobilizing grievances and the associated framing activities occur in a dynamic, interactive context.

An additional consideration needs to be emphasized: mobilizing grievances are not solely social constructions or merely the products of framing activity; they are constrained, in part, by the material conditions and events that are being framed.

Yet, although there may be empirical substance to the events or conditions in question, it is also the case that they typically lend themselves to differential interpretation and thus invite different framings. Consider, for example, the claims of the Heaven's Gate movement. Recall, as noted in Chapter 1, that nearly forty members of the movement committed mass suicide in San Diego in March 1997 because they believed their deaths would guarantee them heavenly passage aboard a UFO trailing the Hale-Bopp comet streaking through the universe within eyesight of Earth. The claim that a flying saucer was hidden in the tail of the comet was certainly empirically unfounded, but the existence of the comet and its tail of gasses were incontestable empirical facts. For end-of-the-millennium, otherworldly movements like Heaven's Gate, which presaged the end of the world ("Planet Earth About to Be Recycled, Your Only Chance to Survive—Leave with Us"[46]) and was deeply into science fiction ("We watch a lot of *Star Trek,* a lot of *Star Wars* ..."[47]), the coming and passing of Hale-Bopp, which was the last comet of the century and an especially bright one at that, held a special opportunity. But the meaning of this special coincidence of events depended in large measure on how it was framed. The leaders of Heaven's Gate were able to articulate a connection between the comet and the movement's beliefs that was sufficiently compelling to its small band of adherents to warrant mass suicide. The passing of the comet was an empirical event that the movement seized upon and framed in accordance with its purposes and interests. It was the "marker" the movement had been waiting for. Had the comet not passed so close to Earth, it is unlikely that the event would have been framed as it was, and it is unlikely that the movement's final exit would have occurred as it did. The point, then, is that the movement's framings regarding its ending on Earth were constructed in relation to, rather than in spite of, an empirical event, but one that lent itself to being framed in mysterious ways, just as passing comets have always done since ancient times.

Movement frames are not only anchored, in part, to empirical events or conditions but constrained by the cultural contexts in which they are embedded. Cultural contexts provide the interpretive material—the codes, narratives, ideologies, general values, and beliefs—that is drawn on to frame events and conditions. However, these materials are not determinative of the social movement frames. Instead, they constitute resources that can be tapped and articulated in different ways to produce, through framing processes, alternative and often novel understandings of events and conditions, whether past or new. As Sidney Tarrow explained with reference to the civil rights movement:

> The lesson of the civil rights movement is that the symbols of revolt are not drawn like musty costumes from a cultural closet and arrayed before the public. Nor are new meanings unrolled out of whole cloth. The costumes of revolt [or protest or exit] are woven from a blend of inherited and invented fibers into collective action frames in confrontation with opponents and elites.[48]

This interactive connection between cultural materials and movement frames and claims can be seen even with such seemingly bizarre movements as Heaven's Gate. It is highly improbable that its claim that heavenly passage awaited members' spirits would have been contrived in a cultural context in which Christian beliefs, particularly regarding ascension to heaven, were not prominent. However, the commission of suicide as the means to release the spirit to catch a ride, via a flying saucer, through the gates of heaven no doubt struck most Christians as highly incredible given the more traditional and canonized understanding of the final days and "rapture." Consequently, the beliefs and claims of Heaven's Gate stood little chance of striking a responsive chord with large numbers of Americans. This suggests that although movements may draw on extant cultural materials to make their claims, there are serious mobilization costs if they stray too far from their cultural moorings or weave together some of those materials in a way that has little, if any, cultural fidelity. This dilemma speaks to the problem of "resonance," which concerns the effectiveness or mobilizing potency of movement framings. Not only are all movements of all kinds confronted with this problem, but their success depends in part on resolving it, thus indicating again how culture constrains the development of mobilizing grievances and movement mobilization more generally.[49]

To illustrate more fully the character of this dilemma, let us return to Beijing in the spring of 1989 and the student-led Chinese democracy movement (see Chapter 1). According to Jiping Zuo and Robert Benford's analysis of the movement, based in part on firsthand observation:

> student activists walked a dangerous tightrope. On the one
> hand, if they framed their grievances in counter-revolutionary
> terms, they were certain to elicit (almost immediately) a
> violent response from state officials.... On the other hand, if
> students failed to frame their grievances as to strike a familiar
> chord among the masses, in all likelihood their frames would

have been dismissed as the immature whining of impetuous youth. Thus the major framing task was to win sympathy and active support from bystander audiences while earning understanding and tolerance from state authorities, or at least to neutralize the legitimacy of any official pretense to using repressive force.[50]

The students addressed this dilemma by grounding their articulation of the injustices and improprieties resulting from state economic reforms in a blend of ideas about freedom and democracy along with traditional Chinese cultural values and narrations associated with Confucianism, communism, and nationalism. By grounding the movement's grievance framings in these cultural traditions, "activists were able to deflect any state attempts to impugn their collective character, particularly attributions regarding their 'patriotism'" . . . , while simultaneously providing other students and ordinary citizens compelling reasons for supporting their campaign.[51] So the 1989 Chinese student democracy movement helped to generate, through its framing activities, mobilizing grievances that resonated with a segment of the population and forestalled a repressive response by the state, at least for a while.

Although strikingly different movements with strikingly different objectives, Heaven's Gate and the Chinese student democracy movement both illustrate the extent to which movement framing efforts, particularly in regard to the generation of mobilizing grievances, are facilitated and constrained by empirical events and conditions and by cultural contexts. Thus, movement activists and leaders may be free in principle to frame events, conditions, and groups as they choose, but they are not free do so in fact. Activists and leaders and their activities are embedded in an enveloping culture, so to ignore that context in framing efforts is to guarantee nonresonance and thus to doom the movement's mobilizing efforts.

CHAPTER SUMMARY

In this chapter we have distinguished between individual, everyday grievances and mobilizing grievances, which are shared among some number of actors and felt to be sufficiently serious to warrant both collective complaint and corrective, collective action. Arguing that mobilizing grievances provide the primary motivational impetus for organizing social movement campaigns and for engaging in social movement activities, we have sought to identify and elaborate the conditions and/or processes that account for the generation of mobilizing grievances. Since pursuit of this issue has entailed a fairly long expedition, involving the critical assessment of a variety of perspectives and arguments, we now summarize and bring into sharp focus what we have learned.

The first major point that can be culled from this journey is that mobilizing grievances are more like mushrooms after a spring rainfall than weeds; they do not flourish continuously and everywhere but only under specifiable conditions. Thus, the matter of grievances cannot be sidestepped or ignored by invoking the assumption of ubiquity. That assumption not only is misguided but also wrongly implies that routine, individual grievances are equivalent to mobilizing grievances, thus glossing over the generation of the latter.

Second, it is equally clear that there is no automatic or determinant relationship between structural or material conditions—such as social arrangements that stratify aggregations of individuals unequally or dire, immiserating life circumstances—and the formation of mobilizing grievances. Yet, we also learned that some events and conditions—that is, those that disrupt the quotidian (everyday taken-for-granted routines) and accent what one has lost or is likely to lose—are more likely than others to spur mobilizing grievances. Still, even palpable quotidian disruptions do not always speak, or speak clearly, for themselves. Analogically, structural and material conditions and changes are rather like kindling on the forest floor; they increase the prospect of fire, but other contributing factors must be present for combustion to occur. As Bohan Zawadski and Paul Lazarsfeld concluded in their study of unemployed Polish workers during the great depression of the 1930s:

> The experiences of unemployment [read, frustration, discontent, grievance] is a preliminary step for the revolutionary mood, but … they do not lead by themselves to a readiness for mass action. Metaphorically speaking, these experiences only fertilize the ground for revolution, but do not generate it.[52]

In other words, certain structural and/or material conditions may be necessary for the generation of mobilizing grievances, but they alone are not sufficient conditions.

Third, our observations indicate that certain social psychological processes also contribute importantly to the generation of mobilizing grievances. Here we highlighted social psychological processes—comparison processes, assessments of procedural justice, and weighing the prospect of loss—rather than social psychological states—frustration and status dissonance—

because the former constitute the intervening mechanisms that may ignite the fertilized conditions.

Fourth, it has become increasingly clear in recent years that the formation of mobilizing grievances, including the character of the intervening psychological processes, is highly contingent both on the manner in which grievances are interpreted and on the generation and diffusion of those interpretations. The key, in other words, is not merely the presence or absence of grievances but also the process of grievance interpretation, which has been theorized and analyzed empirically in terms of framing processes.

Taken together, these observations suggest that the generation of mobilizing grievances cannot be adequately understood in terms of a single perspective or line of argument. Rather, our journey leads to the conclusion that their generation can best be understood as a function of the confluence and interaction of structural or material conditions, social psychological factors, and interpretive framing processes.

Chapter Three
CONTEXTUAL CONDITIONS

WE ARGUED IN THE previous chapter that it is difficult to imagine the development of social movements in the absence of some number of individuals feeling deeply aggrieved about some condition that is regarded as contrary to the interests, rights, moral principles, or well-being of themselves or others. We also noted that mobilizing grievances are unlikely to congeal out of whole cloth apart from the process of grievance interpretation. Yet the existence of mobilizing grievances does not guarantee the emergence of a social movement or affiliated protest activity. In the language of causal analysis, mobilizing grievances constitute a necessary rather than sufficient condition for movement emergence. Also necessary is the opportunity to redress those grievances through various means of strategic action that involve their articulation to relevant audiences and the capacity to pressure the appropriate authorities to remedy those grievances. Such opportunity, however, is not a simple, one-dimensional phenomenon. Rather, it is multidimensional in the sense that the opportunity to press one's concerns and claims collectively is based on the existence and confluence of a number of overlapping conditions: the opportunity or freedom to express one's grievances publicly and to relevant authorities, whether through the media or by assembling and protesting in various public places; access to sufficient resources to organize and mount a campaign to address those grievances; and relatively safe, spatial enclaves in which the aggrieved can associate in absence of the curious and perhaps watchful eye of their targets or government officials. Considered together, these three sets of factors may be thought of as the necessary contextual conditions for the emergence of social movement activity. The massive Tiananmen Square student-led protest in Beijing, China, in the late spring of 1989 lasted several weeks but ended abruptly and bloodily when the communist government ordered its military to squash the protest. This widely chronicled repressive action effectively slammed shut the window of opportunity for students and their supporters to publicly express their grievances, thus foreclosing one necessary, requisite condition for social movement mobilization and action.

Not surprisingly, social movement scholars have theorized and researched these facilitating or enabling contextual conditions. In *Theory of Collective Behavior*, Neil Smelser hinted some time ago at the importance of such conditions with the concept of "structural conduciveness,"[1] but he did not go as far as subsequent scholars who have conceptually unpacked and elaborated such conditions into three overlapping perspectives on the emergence and functioning of social movements. One perspective focuses broadly on political opportunity and the various factors that affect the opening and closing of the window of opportunity; another directs attention to the importance of various resources, such as money and relevant supplies; and a third accents ecological and spatial factors, such as the proximity of prospective protestors to each other. All of these conditions were at work in the case of the Tiananmen Square protest, as they are in one form or another in the life span of all social movements that manage to get off the ground and press their claims. In this chapter, we discuss and illustrate these three sets of facilitating contextual conditions.

POLITICAL OPPORTUNITY

Whether individuals will act collectively to address their grievances depends in part on whether they have the political opportunity to do so. From a folk standpoint, political opportunity entails the elbowroom or freedom for individuals and collectivities to express their grievances and pursue their interests above ground rather than belowground: that is, publicly through the various communication channels (for example, electronic media, press, Internet) and/or through assemblage in various public and quasi-public places, including not only parks, streets, sidewalks, universities, and colleges, but also the halls and meeting chambers of the relevant authorities. This conception of political opportunity has long been expressed by activist scholars. Writing in *The Class Struggle* in 1910, for example, Karl Kautsky noted that "a free press and the right to communication are absolutely essential." They "are to the proletariat [working class] the prerequisites of life; they are the light and air of the labor movement."[2] Contemporary social movement scholars also acknowledge the importance of such freedoms but see them as contingent on the degree of openness or accessibility of the political system, and thus focus on its "receptivity or vulnerability" to organized challenge.[3]

The point is that social movements have great difficulty reaching out and mobilizing various kinds of support in the absence of a political context that allows for the free and open expression of collective grievances and claims, even when they run counter to the interests of the system of authority being challenged. Recognizing the importance of political opportunity for the emergence and operation of social movements is not terribly helpful alone, however, for a number of interconnected reasons. The first is that political systems—be they local, state or regional, national, or international—can vary considerably in terms of how receptive (open) or unreceptive (closed) they are to challenge. The second is that this variability is not announced, as in the rendering of an edict, but is signaled by aspects of the system's ongoing functioning. The third is that these signals, just as with any signals in social life, are sometimes missed, ignored, or read or interpreted in ways that may unexpectedly facilitate or curtail mobilized dissent and challenge.

In light of these observations, we turn to an examination of three sets of issues: the extent of variability in the openness of political systems to challenge; the dimensions of political systems and the sociopolitical conditions or events that are likely to signal something about its receptivity or openness to challenge; and the sometimes neglected fact that signaling dimensions and events are vulnerable to differential interpretation and associated action or inaction.

Variation in System Accessibility

System accessibility is the shorthand expression for the extent to which a political system and its institutions are open or closed to participation and influence. The degree of access can vary with a host of factors, including decision-making structures, the party or political orientation of officeholders, and the relative status of different groups or categories of claimants. In the case of decision-making structures, governments in which power is concentrated rather than diffused among various branches and actors and in which administrative functions are centrally co-ordinated are likely to be less accessible than are governments wherein power is more diffused and administration is not so heavily coordinated. But even the existence of relatively open and democratic governmental structures does not ensure that all constituents will have equal access. As the political scientist Michael Lipsky asked rhetorically in 1970 in reference to the American political system, "is it not sensible to assume that the system will be more or less open to specific groups at different times and at different places?"[4] Given the historical experiences of women, blacks, Latinos, and gays and lesbians, as well as other underrepresented minorities, in relation to the American political system, Lipsky must have known full well the answer to his rhetorical question. But it was a question that had not been widely researched at the time he broached it. Years of subsequent research on this question has shown that the answer is unequivocally affirmative for the U.S. political system as well as for the political systems of other countries.

The first major empirical examination of Lipsky's question was conducted a few years following Lipsky's query by Peter Eisinger, who investigated the extent to which variation in protest and riot behavior in forty-three American cities in the 1960s was affected by differences across the cities in what he termed "the structure of political opportunity." He defined it as "the degree to which groups are likely to be able to gain access to power and to manipulate the political system," and he found that the "incidence of protest" was indeed "related to the nature of the city's political opportunity structure," but not necessarily in the way one might initially assume.[5] Protest occurred more readily in cities in which the political opportunity structure was neither fully open nor closed but exhibited "a mix of open and closed characteristics,"[6] thus suggesting a curvilinear relationship between opportunities and levels of protest. This curvilinear relationship, which is shown in Figure 3.1, has since become the foundational proposition for political opportunity theorizing and research.

How well does the curvilinear relationship hold up across various incidents of movement protest and political contexts? The answer, as with most phenomena that social scientists investigate, is conditional. It is certainly true that countries that are governed by dictatorial, authoritarian regimes are heavily skewed toward the closed end of the continuum, often characterized by relatively little, if any, protest, either emergent or

Figure 3.1

THE POLITICAL OPPORTUNITY CURVE

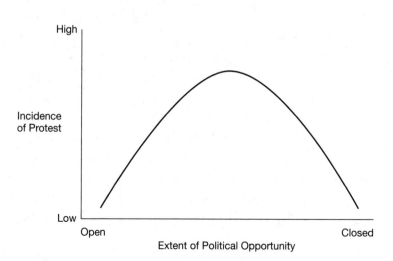

movement-sponsored. That is not to say that collective behavior is absent in these countries; rather, the collective behavior tends to be state-sponsored and celebratory rather than contested or protest-oriented.[7] North Korea, governed for some time by the dictatorial personality cult of Kim Jong-il, provides a glaring example of a country in which protest is virtually absent but celebratory collective behavior is quite common. Not only is protest outlawed, but the means of generating and communicating collective grievances are unavailable to regular citizens: cell phones are illegal, the Internet is inaccessible to all but the elite; newspapers feature only state propaganda, and radios and TVs receive only government channels. Other countries in recent times that similarly have negated the prospect of protest by limiting the means for the generation and dissemination of mobilizing grievances and responding repressively to hints of protest mobilization include China, Cuba, Myanmar, and the former East Germany and Soviet Union. Although these countries vary somewhat in the structures of their governments and repressive impulses, they are or were unquestionably authoritarian and nondemocratic.

In contrast to such regimes are those that are more democratic, generally less repressive, and, therefore, generally skewed toward the open end of the continuum. Examples include, among others, Australia, Canada, the various countries that make up the European Union, and the United States. But these and other democratic countries are neither uniformly nor consistently open to protest. Rather, consistent with Lipsky's point mentioned above, the historical record for each country or set of countries reveals temporal, group-based, and locational variability in their respective openness to movement contestation and challenge. And even across countries that appear quite similar in political structure, there can be noteworthy variation in receptivity to social movements. For example, in a comparative study of the fate of various so-called new social movements in four West European countries (France, Germany, the Netherlands, and Switzerland), Hanspeter Kriesi and his colleagues found that the extent and form of movement mobilization varied according to differences in the political structures of the countries.[8]

Such variability in political opportunity structures is also evident in countries governed by more authoritarian regimes. Moreover, this variability in openness can change very quickly, as in the spring 1989 Beijing student movement and the sudden flowering of protest in the former Soviet Union and in Eastern Europe in the late 1980s.

Both of these now historically memorialized instances of social movement protest[9] are consistent with the political opportunity curve and the observation that partially opened access to some system of authority encourages, or at least allows for, protest, all else being equal. That systems of authority in which access is partial rather than completely open or closed are more generative of collective challenge makes sense. After all, if access is completely closed and external challenge is forbidden, not only is it logistically difficult to organize a collective challenge, but such action is almost certain to invite repression. If, in contrast, access to the system is completely open, such that various classes and status groups are incorporated into the system and have an opportunity to pursue their interests, then challenge in the form of social movement activity is unnecessary. Of course, the existence of such an open system is more of a figment of our utopian imagination than historical reality.

Signaling Dimensions of Political Systems
Variability in system accessibility, and thus the prospect of social movement challenge, can be affected by a host of factors that appear to cluster into three broad categories: (1) the relative stability of the pattern of political alignments within a system; (2) the presence or absence of influential allies; and (3) the repressive capacity or impulse of the state or relevant political entity.[10]

SHIFTING POLITICAL ALIGNMENTS. Changes in the pattern of alignments within a political system can signal prospective changes in system accessibility. When existing alignments are stable, as when there is party unity and leadership continuity, there is less opportunity for marginal or antagonistic groups to mount a challenge to the system. However, shifting alignments may increase the vulnerability of the system to challenges from groups outside the system. Such shifts may be signaled by leadership voids and elite cleavages occasioned by the death of a ruler or president or by a palace scandal; by changes in party support and solidarity; by general electoral volatility; and by regime crises that can result from the confluence of these factors, the mismanagement of economic or international affairs and events, and the manufacturing of contrived events,[11] any or all of which can lead to what has been called a legitimation crisis.[12]

To illustrate more concretely the relationship between this assortment of events and shifting alignments, consider how electoral volatility and shifts in party strength in the United States have been associated with corresponding social movement activity. In an analysis of poor people's movements in the United States through the 1970s, Piven and Cloward note that changes in parties' electoral strength in both the 1930s and the 1960s encouraged organized labor, black Americans, and other marginalized groups to press for changes in party strategies for bringing unrepresented social groups into the political arena.[13] The erosion of the "solid South" of segregationist white voters from the Democratic party in the 1950s and 1960s also prompted Democrats to seek black political support, thus opening up the political process to black America. As Doug McAdam observed with respect to the growing importance of the black vote in his study of the development of the black civil rights movement in the middle third of the twentieth century, "the black vote increasingly became a more volatile political commodity than it had heretofore been, prompting both parties to intensify their efforts to appeal to black voters."[14] Research has also shown that a divided government—divided party control over the House of Representatives, the Senate, and the presidency—in the United States has been positively correlated with African American protest.[15]

Declining political party strength and party instability in the United States have also been found to make both parties more vulnerable to manipulation and control by more extremist views and movements, as demonstrated by the control of party platforms at national conventions by more extremist groups.[16]

Illustrative of this finding is the control of the Democrat platform at the 1968 convention by the Mississippi Freedom Party and the more recent influence of the far "religious right," with its focus on banning abortion and same-sex marriage, on the party platforms of the Republican conventions in early 2000 and 2004. Thus, shifting alignments may not only invite access but also give rise to manipulation and control of the older guard by new players.

INFLUENTIAL ALLIES. The presence or absence of allies who have standing and connection within the power structure can also affect system accessibility. The importance of such allies in relation to movement campaigns and successful outcomes has been theorized by Edwin Amenta and his colleagues in terms of the "political mediation" thesis. The thesis, which holds that movement mobilization typically requires mediation by supportive actors in political institutions or in other institutional contexts,[17] has considerable support in the research literature. For example, William Gamson's research on fifty-three challenging groups in the United States between 1800 and 1945 found that those that secured the support of political allies tended to be more successful.[18] Sarah Soule and her collaborators, moreover, found that the pro–Equal Rights Amendment movement in the fifty U.S. states had more success when there were allies in the state governments.[19] Likewise, Jenkins and Perrow's analysis of the American farm workers' movement in the United States found that the greater success of the movement in the 1960s, compared with the 1940s, was due in part to the receipt of support from three influential allies: urban liberals who boycotted lettuce and grapes in support of the UFW; organized labor;

and a new generation of sympathetic administrators in the U.S. Department of Agriculture.[20] Similarly, McAdam found, in his previously mentioned study of black mobilization in the middle part of the last century, that supportive allies do not necessarily have to be formally embedded in the political power structure but can be positioned to exert pressure on important actors within the structure. Thus, he noted that:

> a variety of external political pressures continued, in the early 1960s, to render the political establishment vulnerable to pressure from black insurgents. Among these pressures were increased public awareness of, and support for, civil rights....[21]

In each of these cases, as well as others, such as the pro-democracy movements in the former Soviet Union and in Eastern Europe, the presence of influential allies accounts for neither the emergence nor the success of these movements. But having such allies can clearly enhance the prospect of movement development and success by functioning as a conveyor of political pressure, as a hedge or buffer against repression, and as a source of legitimation. What is less clear is whether differences in the character of the relationship between allies and a social movement make any difference in whether movement protest increases or decreases. For example, some research suggests that African American congressional representation reduced protest by providing greater access and thereby channeling movement action into more institutionalized politics.[22]

REPRESSIVE CAPACITY OF AUTHORITIES.   A third factor generally thought to signal the degree of accessibility of authorities to challengers is their repressive capacity or inclination to resort to repression, and particularly changes in that capacity or inclination. McAdam's research on the rise of the civil rights movement provides a clear illustration of this relationship, as it shows how the movement surfaced following a decline in the South's tendency to invoke repressive measures to keep black Americans in their place. Using the annual number of lynchings as an indicator of repression, he found a significant decline in lynching during the years preceding the movement. Additionally, he argues that an increase in federal protections of black civil rights and a growth in the support of white liberals for black churches and colleges dampened the repressive inclination of Southern social control agents and thus facilitated the rise of the civil rights movement.[23]

Since governmental authorities, and particularly the national state, tend to monopolize the instruments of repression (legal system, weapons, prisons), scholarly attention has generally focused on the relationship between, on the one hand, the repressive behaviors and appetites of national states and, on the other hand, social movement activity. It is important to keep in mind, however, that not all states or regimes are equally ready or likely to exercise their repressive potential. In general, democratic states are less likely to resort to repression on a consistent basis than are authoritarian states. Whatever the regime type, however, the actual or threatened use of repression can be quite variable over time. In the case of the Chinese student movement in Beijing in the spring of 1989, for example, there was initially a relaxation of the state's iron-fisted social control procedures, with the result that "heterodox views were less subject to sanctions such as denouncement and imprisonment" and "college students ... felt free to participate in authorized political activities on campus."[24] But this restraint proved to be short-lived,

as the state slammed shut the window of opportunity by unleashing its troops in Tiananmen Square in early June 1989,
about a month and a half after the commemorative gatherings
for Hu Yaobang, the former secretary of the Communist General Party whose tolerance of student demonstrations two years
earlier had forced him to resign that post, and the initial student
demands for governmental rehabilitation of Hu's reputation. In
between the initial public outpouring of student sympathy for
Hu on April 16 and the military repression of June 3, the student movement evolved in a pro-democracy direction and the
government's social control efforts vacillated between hardline
measures and a more tolerant approach. As noted in Dingxin
Zhao's analysis of the dynamics of the relationship between the
government and the student movement:

> The government initially tolerated the 1989 Movement, while
> trying to confine it to mourning activities for Hu Yaobang. Af-
> ter Hu Yaobang's state funeral, the government's policy shifted
> to a more hardline approach, as was indicated by the April
> 26 *People's Daily* editorial that labeled the movement anti-
> revolutionary turmoil. When students successfully organized
> April 27 demonstrations that defied the editorial, the govern-
> ment came back with a soft strategy and tried to contain the
> movement through a policy of limited concessions. On May
> 19, however, after a week of the hunger strike, the government
> declared martial law and brought a mass of troops to Beijing,
> first trying to scare the protestors away. When that didn't work
> military repression followed.[25]

Given the highly authoritarian bent of the Chinese regime at
that time, what is surprising was not the eventual repressive reflex of the state but the fact that it allowed the students to protest

at all. Perhaps more surprising is the occasional violent repressive hiccup that surfaces in more democratic countries like the United States. Three memorable examples that occurred during our lifetimes were the skirmishes between student protestors and the police, and the eventual police rioting, in Chicago at the time of the 1968 Democratic Convention, resulting in hundreds of injuries and nearly seven hundred arrests;[26] the shooting of students, resulting in four dead and nine wounded, by Ohio National Guardsmen on the Kent State University campus on May 4, 1970; and again ten days later, on May 14, the police firing on protesting students at Jackson State College in Jackson, Mississippi, leaving two dead and twelve wounded.[27] But these repressive reflexes did not suddenly close the door to student protest across the United States as did the Tiananmen Square massacre. In fact, within days of the Kent State killing, students on campuses across the country were marching to close down their universities to the chant of "Strike! Strike! Shut it down!" As noted in the 1971 *Report of the President's Commission on Campus Unrest*, "[d]uring the four days that followed the Kent killings, there were a hundred or more strikes a day" and, "[b]y the end of May . . . nearly one third of 2,500 colleges and universities in America had experienced some kind of protest activity."[28]

At the nearby University of Akron, for example, around noon a day or two after the Kent State shootings, 150 students were listening to speakers in an outdoor "free speech area" that had been established immediately after the shootings. Following the last speech, there was a pregnant pause, as students seemed to be waiting for another speaker or directions as to what to do next. Out of the blue came a clarion call from the back of the gathering: "Strike! Strike! Shut it down!" Within seconds, that keynote was repeated among other crowd members, and then the entire gathering was chanting the slogan in unison. Within a minute or two, the gathering was marching to the campus's main administration building to "shut it down."[29] So not only do repressive actions by the social control agents sometimes fail to stifle movement protest, such actions, in some places and times, appear even to stimulate it.

The observation that repression that appears to close the doors of opportunity may sometimes stimulate protest rather than dampen it seems to be counterintuitive, but there is considerable evidence of this, especially in countries other than industrialized democracies: for example, in Argentina, Burma, Chile, El Salvador, Iran, the Philippines, and South Africa.[30] Because of such findings, including his own research on revolutionary movements in Central America, Jeff Goodwin stated emphatically:

> Far from being a response to political openings, the revolutionary mobilization that occurred in Central America during the 1970s and 1980s was generally a response to political exclusion and violent repression—the *contraction* of political opportunities and the *closing down* of "political space."[31]

So how are such contradictions to the core political opportunity thesis explained?[32] The answer, as suggested earlier, is that the presence of certain conditions, or their confluence, accounts for the exceptions. One such set of conditions was revealed in Paul Almeida's study of two waves of protest that occurred between 1962 and 1981 in El Salvador. He found that the key to the puzzle resided, at least for El Salvador, in "a sequential model of political opportunity and threat" wherein the organization building that occurred during periods of liberalization and political opportunity provided a durable organizational infrastructure that nurtured protest even in the face of subsequent repression.[33] As he explains:

> The wave of demonstrations and strikes that rocked El Salvador between 1967 and 1972 . . . came to an end when the state held successive fraudulent presidential and parliamentary elections in 1972. Even with this closing in opportunities, the organizational infrastructure founded in the late 1960s endured in both the countryside and cities through the 1970s.[34]

In turn, this organization building and sedimentation provided the base for continuous, and even more radicalized, challenge during the ten-year period prior to El Salvador's civil war in the 1980s.

The other part of the equation that fostered radical mobilization in the face of escalating repression was the broadening and intensification of the grievance base confronting Salvadorans. Almeida discusses these mounting grievances—state attributed economic woes, erosion of rights, and state repression itself—as "threats" without specifying the exact character of the threats. Consistent with our discussion of threats in the previous chapter, we understand the threats confronting Salvadorans to have been the kind that threaten the quotidian or everyday order by making things worse. In effect, Salvadorans were confronted with the threat of loss in terms of rights, freedoms, and economic functioning; as previously discussed, the threat of loss is a particularly potent prod to mobilization. The suggestion, then, is that when grievances associated with the actual or threatened loss of what people already have and believe is rightfully theirs reaches a threshold in which the prospect of taking action to curtail the loss, and perhaps recapture something of what was lost, is less costly than doing nothing, then the probability of mobilization in the face of repression increases. This appears especially to be the case, Almeida explains, when an existing organizational infrastructure is already in place.

Taken together, these observations provide two important reasons that mobilizations sometimes occur in the face of mounting repression. But they also reveal that it is not easy to predict when such mobilizations will occur. The difficulty arises because of variation in the tipping point between the costs of action and the costs of inaction and the presence or absence of a viable organizational infrastructure with associated leadership strengthened by what has been called "iron in the soul."[35] There are other sources of iron in the soul as well, such as moral shock or outrage and even a deep sense of honor that may sometimes motivate collective action in the absence of structural opportunity. This was the case in 1943 when Jews in the Warsaw Ghetto resisted with smuggled weapons and explosives Nazis' efforts to deport them to the Treblinka death camp.[36]

Another factor that can affect the relationship between mobilization against authorities and repression is the character of the repression. Although repression is often discussed as if all repression is much the same, clearly that is not the case. Distinctions have been made recently among different types of repression, or forms of protest control, based on different agents of control, whether the control is direct or indirect, and whether it is publicly visible.[37] Military control and protest policing illustrate a state-based, direct, observable form of repression; in contrast, countermovements, such as the anti-cult movement of the 1970s and the pro-life movement, illustrate grassroots, private sector mobilization seeking to repress adversarial movements or to reverse their successes. For example, the ongoing push to overturn *Roe v. Wade* (the 1973 U.S. Supreme Court decision establishing that abortions are permissible for any reason a woman chooses, up until the "point at which the fetus becomes 'viable,' that is, potentially able to live outside the mother's womb") emerged in response to the pro-choice movement and focuses on halting the efforts of that movement.[38] In addition to appealing to authorities to act on their behalf, countermovements sometimes get authorities to look the other way and countenance indirectly their repressive activities or those of more radical spin-off groups that operate underground and engage in more extreme measures to terrorize and thus repress their targets. This is what the Ku Klux Klan did for years during the Jim Crow era via its lynching campaigns, and what Operation Rescue tried to do for the anti-abortion/pro-life movement.

As in the 1989 Beijing student movement, repression can also be relatively "soft" in contrast to the more conventionally understood "hard" repression illustrated by the unleashing of the military and police at the governmental level or by vigilante groups and terrorizing countermovements at the level of rank-and-file citizens. Besides a pulling back of the police or military, or softening of their repressive tactics, soft repression can also involve the strategic use of nonviolent action to mute or delegitimate oppositional groups and ideas.[39] This is done quite commonly through negative stereotyping or stigmatization, as when 1960 student activists were called "commie, pinko fags," gay and lesbian activists are referred to as "fags" and dykes," and feminists are called "feminazis," a derogatory term popularized by the popular conservative radio talk-show host Rush Limbaugh. Soft repression can also take the form of silencing, as when a movement is denied voice via exclusion from governmental hearings or media coverage. An example of how this can work in the media is provided by Myra Ferree and her colleagues in a study comparing abortion discourse in the United States and in Germany over the twenty-five-year period from 1970 through 1994. Not only were significant differences found in the extent to which nonstate speakers were given voice in the newspapers of the two countries, with the U.S. press being more accommodating than the German press, but the majority of the nonstate voices in Germany were institutionalized representatives of the churches (55 percent) rather than those of social movement speakers (6 percent). In the United States, in contrast, only 17 percent of the nonstate speakers were church-based, and 39 percent of all nonstate speakers were associated with social movements.[40] Hence, the following conclusions:

> Compared to the U.S., the silence of social movements in Germany is deafening.... This is not because there are no feminist or right to life mobilizations in Germany, but because the media have a strong preference against giving voice to less institutionalized speakers.... [Thus] the mobilization potential for social movement mobilization is enhanced in the United States and repressed, softly, in Germany by the institutional form by which movements relate to civil society in media practices.[41]

A final factor affecting the relationship between repression, or protest social control, and mobilization is the fact that repressive behaviors or threats, whether soft or hard, are not always read the same way, if read at all. But this is true for other signaling elements as well and thus warrants a separate discussion.

Reading Political Opportunity

We have noted how the presence or absence of political opportunity may be signaled by shifting political alignments, the coming and going of allies, and by the repressive behavior of authorities. For two fundamental reasons, however, there is no automatic relationship between these signals and mobilization. First, signals are signs that must be noticed, which means that they can be missed or ignored. Second, signals have to be read or interpreted, which means that they are subject to differential interpretation.

Just as signal lights or stop signs at traffic intersections are sometimes overlooked or missed, so signals of changes in a political structure or some authority system can be missed or glossed over. Sometimes the missed opportunity may be the result of internal tensions, debate, and even fragmentation, such that a movement is not sufficiently cohesive to take advantage of existing or emergent political opportunities. Some scholars have argued, for example, that "the women's movement of the 1980s was less effective in achieving its political aims . . . partly because its supporting coalition fragmented, as radical and institutionally oriented wings polarized."[42] Similarly, research has suggested that the nuclear freeze movement stagnated, in part, because of internal debate over whether institutional access would absorb, or co-opt, the movement.[43]

At other times, the missed opportunity may be attributable to a misreading of the situation. In such cases, the opportunity was not glossed over; rather, it was read or interpreted as not being very auspicious. We suspect, however, that it is far more common for movement leaders and activists to exaggerate the extent of openness and, at times, to interpret as an opening what may appear to some observers as an absence of opportunity. This happens because movements are likely to assess opportunity "with a systematic optimistic bias, exaggerating opportunities and underestimating constraints."[44] As noted in Gamson and Meyer's discussion of the "framing of political opportunity,"

> This bias is built into the functional needs of movements which need to sustain a collective action frame that includes the belief that conditions can be changed. Since movement action can sometimes create political opportunity, this lack of realism can produce a self-fulfilling prophecy.[45]

Additionally, dissidents and protesters may sometimes define opportunities in terms of other factors, such as the perceived strength of their oppositional allies. Such perceptions appeared to be operative in the case of the Iranian Revolution of 1979. As Kurzman noted in his study of structural and perceived opportunity associated with the revolution:

> the state was *not*, by several objective measures, particularly vulnerable in 1978 when widespread protest emerged. Instead, Iranians seem to have based their assessment of their opportunities for protest on the perceived strength of the opposition. In other words, Iranians believed the balance of forces shifted, not because of changing state structure, but because of a changing opposition movement [emphasis in original].[46]

Equally important as interpretive bias in assessing the degree or character of opportunity is the extent of passion and outrage shared by activists and their adherents. As noted earlier with respect to Salvadoran mobilization, escalating repression did not keep some citizens from protesting against the state because of the outrage they felt over their mounting grievances. Similarly, the increasing threat of hardline repression by the military in Beijing in the spring of 1989 failed to deter students from engaging in further protest. "Most expected a harsh crackdown, but for many 'the feeling of injustice was too strong for students to succumb to' the prospect of increased repression."[47] Such examples of movement activists and protestors forging ahead in the face of mounting repression are not hard to come by, thus underscoring the observation that presence or absence of political opportunity is not merely an objective matter but also in the eyes of the beholders.

So while the actual presence or absence of political opportunity matters, it is arguable that it matters less than its perception, which is affected by threat-based grievances, moral shock or outrage, the perceived strength of the movement, and the passion generated by those threats, shocks, perceptions and the movement's goals, and, thus, how the structure of opportunity is read and framed.

Conclusions Regarding Political Opportunity

We began our discussion of political opportunity structures with the widely held proposition that varying degrees of political opportunity can facilitate or constrain the prospect of movement emergence and associated protest. There is nothing in our discussion that contradicts this proposition, but we have suggested that the relationship between the structure of political opportunity and movement emergence and protest is highly conditional. One condition, of course, is the political opportunity curve itself (see Figure 3.1). Recall that it posits a curvilinear relationship between movement protest and political opportunity, with most protest occurring in a context in which the window is neither fully open nor closed. Interestingly, it is partly for this reason that some studies testing political opportunity hypotheses against other theories sometimes find that political opportunity measures are not terribly significant.[48] Yet, we have seen that this curve is neither static nor generalizable across time, various groups, location, or place: both regimes that are traditionally open and those that are repressive can oscillate temporally between the two extremes; openness for one status group does not necessarily apply to other groups; and just as there can be variation across countries, so there is often variation across municipalities within the same country. We have also seen that whatever the extent of accessibility, structures of opportunity can be read differently or misread, and that how they are read can be influenced by the character of grievances, associated passions, and framing. We can thus conclude that signaling of some level of political opportunity, or the bypassing of a closing window, constitutes a necessary condition for the emergence and operation of social movements. But such signaling conditions are not sufficient to spark mobilization in the absence of the mobilizing grievances discussed in the previous chapter and the accumulation and deployment of various resources and the organizational space in which to operate. We thus turn to consideration of the facilitating condition of resource mobilization.

RESOURCE MOBILIZATION

The proposition that the emergence and persistence of social movement activity depend on the availability of resources that can be accumulated and channeled into movement mobilization and activity constitutes the orienting premise of the resource mobilization perspective developed principally by John McCarthy and Mayer Zald in the mid-1970s.[49] As McCarthy and Zald hypothesized regarding the link between resource availability and movement emergence, "the absolute and relative amount of resources available to" social movements is contingent on "the amount of discretionary resources of mass and elite publics"; moreover, "the greater the absolute amount of [those] resources available to the SMS" [social movement sector] within a society, "the greater the likelihood that new SMIs [social movement industries] and SMOs [social movement organizations] will develop."[50]

This general hypothesis is noncontroversial today, as it has received wide-ranging support from a variety of empirical studies. For example, a study of the determinants of the founding of U.S. environmental movement organizations between 1895 and 1995 revealed that their founding was positively associated with national prosperity and negatively associated with high rates of business failures.[51] Another study found that protest activity by U.S. feminist groups in the thirty years between 1955 and 1985 similarly increased during prosperous times.[52] Likewise, an examination of the city-level contextual determinants of temporal variation in the frequency of homeless protest across seventeen U.S. cities in the 1980s and early 1990s revealed that the incidence of protest was greatest in those cities with larger monetary resource pools, as measured in terms of per capita income and transfer payments.[53] An assessment of this pattern internationally similarly found that citizen participation in transnational social movement organizations, such as Greenpeace, tends to be positively associated with national wealth.[54]

These and other studies provide compelling support for the core resource mobilization thesis,[55] but they do not address a number of other important questions that are relevant to understanding the relationship between resources and the course and character of social movements. These include: (1) what are the various types of resources of importance to social movements? (2) from where or whence do these resources flow? and (3) does the source affect movement goals and activities?

Types of Resources

Broadly conceived, resources include almost anything that movements, and other organizations, need to mobilize and deploy for the purpose of advancing their interests. This includes, most generally, people and money, and some degree of legitimacy within one or more sets of relevant actors, such as the movement's constituency or the larger public. We could stop here and conclude that movements that are reasonably successful in securing people, money, and legitimacy will be more successful in realizing their interest then movements that are resource poor. But this general conclusion is not very helpful because it also pertains to other collective enterprises, such as political campaigns and the missions of nonprofit organizations. Additionally, resources can vary considerably in terms of how fungible and accessible they are. Money, for example, is highly fungible or portable in the sense that it can be easily converted into other resources (for example, office space and equipment) and is readily transferred from one context to another. In contrast, legitimacy and related symbolic resources, which we discuss below, are typically less fungible and more context or group specific. Similarly, resources can vary in terms of whether access to them is a matter of proprietary control, as with money and human labor, or more generalized, as with such cultural phenomena as tactical repertoires and models of organizing that can be accessed and adopted or imitated by other groups.[56] Rather than merely note the obvious importance of money, people, and some degree of legitimacy for movement mobilization, we offer a more refined typology of the various kinds of resources that can be of varying importance to different social movements or at different points in a movement's career. The typology, presented in Table 3.1, identifies five general kinds of resources and lists sub-types for each, concrete examples of each sub-type, and whether the sub-type is skewed more or less fungible and more or less proprietary.[57]

While it is arguable that all five general resource types are of some importance to all movements, there can be considerable variation in the relative importance of the different sub-types to different movements. To illustrate, let us contrast two quite different movements. Consider first, movements of the homeless that percolated in many American cities in the 1980s and 1990s. A study assessing the viability of fifteen homeless movement organizations across eight American cities (Boston, Denver, Detroit, Houston, Minneapolis, Oakland, Philadelphia, and Tucson) found that the viable SMOs were those that secured nine or more resources out of a repertoire of fifteen sub-types.[58] But SMO viability was not merely a matter of the volume of resources secured, since some resources (such as moral support, leadership, and having a place to meet) were found to be more important than others. In the case of moral support, for example, all of the viable organizations realized both verbal and solidary support. Illustrative of solidary support are the comments of the

Table 3.1

TYPOLOGY OF RESOURCES

General Resources	Sub-Types	Examples	Properties Fungible	Proprietary
Material	Money	Cash donations	Yes	Yes
	Supplies	Paper, telephones	No	Yes
	Physical Space	Meeting and office spaces	No	Yes
	Transportation	Cars, vans, pickups	Partially	Yes
	Employment	Jobs for activists	Partially	Yes
Human	Generalized Labor	Envelope stuffers, marchers, picketers	Partially	No
	Specialized Labor	Computer experts, legal council	Partially	Yes
	Leadership	Organizational and inspirational	Partially	Yes
Social-Organizational	Infrastructures	Sidewalks, streets, postal service	Yes	No
	Social networks	Extra-movement ties to individuals and organizations	Partially	Yes
	Formal organizations		Partially	Yes
Moral	Legitimacy	Positive public opinion	Partially	No
	Solidary support	Joining in the cause	Partially	No
	Celebrity	Celebrities like Bono may do both	Partially	No
Cultural	Repertoires and recipes	Organizational, tactical, and technical schema or models	No	No
	Literature, media, film, Internet, etc.	Use of these sources to frame SMO interests	No	Yes

leader of the Oakland Union of the Homeless, who noted when discussing a Christmas Day protest:

> We had a bunch of ministers from all over the Bay area come and their basic statement was, "I'm not here to say our church can solve homelessness; I'm here to say our church can stand in solidarity with the homeless." And so they all stood there and pledged that night that even though their churches needed them on Christmas, they would commit civil disobedience with us.[59]

Such support was especially important for the homeless because of their pariahlike status and the associated ways in which they are stigmatized. But just as important for homeless SMO viability was having secured space in which to meet and having associated office supplies, which makes sense in light of the severe generalized material resource deficits of the homeless.

Such base material resources, however, are not so critical for many social movements. For movements that are more culturally deviant or idiosyncratic, such as the religious movements that were imported into the United States and Europe from various parts of Asia in the 1960s and 1970s, securing some measure of public legitimacy and respectability via celebrity ingratiation and endorsement seeking is especially important. Two examples include the saffron-robed, Hindu-based Hare Krishna movement exported from India and the Buddhist-based Nichiren Shoshu movement exported from Japan. In the case of Hare Krishna, recall the widespread and favorable publicity it received by Beatle George Harrison in his popular song "My Sweet Lord," with its refrain "Hare Krishna [My sweet lord], Hare Krishna, Krishna Krishna, Hare Hare [My Lord]." While the Nichiren Shoshu movement never received the endorsement of an international celebrity with the status of George Harrison, its leaders persistently sought the endorsement of celebrities which the rank-and-file members could invoke as they went about the business of recruitment, presumably to lend an air of importance and respectability to the mantra—Nam Myoho Renge Kyo (Devotion to the Mystical Law of Cause and Effect through Sound)—they were trying to promote.[60]

The importance of legitimacy to the ongoing operation of movements is also illustrated by the efforts of countermovements and targeted authorities to discredit their adversaries or challengers. This can be done through various forms of reputational stigmatization, including the imputation of negative identities to members or the group as a whole, generalizing from a few "bad apple" members to the entire membership, focusing attention on questionable members or organizational ties, and drawing attention to and highlighting questionable ideological beliefs.[61] In the late 1960s and 1970s when there was a flowering in the United States of off-beat, nontraditional religious movements, for example, it was commonplace for more mainstream and institutionalized religious groups and their adherents to attempt to discredit these movements by referring to them as cults and accusing them of brainwashing.[62] It is partly to ward off such discrediting charges and labels that movements such as Nichiren Shoshu, and Scientology more recently, have sought the endorsement of celebrities and have engaged in various impression management activities so as to generate as much idiosyncrasy credit as possible.[63]

In general, the research strongly supports the proposition that the availability and procurement of resources matters greatly for the emergence and the operation of social movements just as they do for all goal-seeking enterprises. But the research also tells us that not all resources matter in the same way for all movements, with some movements being more interested in securing moral resources, such as a measure of legitimacy, and other movements having a greater need for material resources and specialized labor.

Resource Derivation

Given the centrality of resources to movement emergence and viability, an important question concerns their derivation. From where or whence do resources flow?

Regarding derivation, there are basically three possible sources for general resources: they can be secured from external sources, such as "conscience constituents" (individuals, groups or organizations who support movement activity without benefiting directly from attainment of its objectives); they can be derived indigenously from a movement's constituency; or they can be derived from both. Although there has been debate about the generality and relative importance of externally provided versus indigenously derived resources, we contend that both sources are important but that their importance may vary by the resource base of a movement's constituency, by certain objectives and tactical actions, and by different points in the life span of a movement. The previously mentioned research on fifteen homeless social movement organizations (SMOs) across eight U.S. cities illustrates the importance of a movement's resource base when considering the derivation of its resources. Not only did all but one of the SMOs secure most of their resources (75 percent) from external sources, the range of resource types provided by

external supporters was also one of the key factors distinguishing between viable and nonviable homeless SMOs: viable SMOs
procured an average of 9.7 external resources, while nonviable
SMOs mobilized an average of 4.5 external resources.[64]

That homeless SMOs would be so dependent on external resources is not so surprising given the general impoverishment
and resource deficits of the homeless. But relatively few social
movement constituencies are as deprived as the homeless across
the range of resource types. As a consequence, they are much
more likely to generate a greater proportion of their resources
indigenously: that is, from their constituent base. A case in point
is the civil rights movement. Aldon Morris's study of the black
Southern student sit-in movement of 1960 demonstrated, for
example, the importance of internal organization to the emergence and diffusion of the movement across sixty-nine cities.
Specifically, the organizational infrastructure and much of the
leadership for the movement was in place prior to its emergence.
As Morris concludes, "pre-existing activist groups, formal organizations, colleges, and overlapping personal networks provided
the framework through which the sit-ins emerged and spread."[65]
McAdam's research on the development of black insurgency between 1930 and 1970 not only affirms the existence of a broad-
based organizational infrastructure out of which the civil rights
movement grew in the 1950s and 1960s but also traces its development in the 1930s and 1940s.[66] The point, then, is that the
black civil rights movement was bred and fed, in large part, by
the indigenous black community and institutional infrastructure (black churches, black colleges, and NAACP [National Association for the Advancement of Colored People] chapters) in
which it was embedded. However, such findings do not mean

that the black civil rights movement received no support from external conscience constituents, as it was the recipient of externally based moral support, material resources, and some specialized labor.[67] This suggests a pattern of mixed support, albeit skewed in the direction of indigenous support in contrast to the homeless movement, which was skewed heavily toward external support. So both movements were recipients of external support but were in varying degrees dependent on their preexisting resource base and the moral support their causes generated.

Effects of Externally Derived Resources

Although externally derived resources typically facilitate the operation of movement organizations, they may also come with a cost: a loss of autonomy and moderating influence with respect to movement objectives and tactics. This possibility has prompted concern among movement activists and advocates about the specter of external co-optation or control. Scholars similarly have been concerned with this possibility, asking: Does resource dependency transform SMO goals and tactics? In other words, does the piper call the tune? There is no consensual answer to this question; rather, there are three overlapping arguments. One holds that external resource dependency moderates goals and tactics, thus dampening the prospect of militant or radical tactical action.[68] A second argument holds that external support does not necessarily mute radical dissent but channels it into more professional and publicly acceptable forms.[69] The third argument contends that whether the appropriation of external resources alters an SMO's goals or course of action depends on the degree of correspondence between the perspectives and aims of the resource providers and the movement.[70] When there is close correspondence, as when radical sponsoring organizations support movements inclined toward radical action, it is alignment or correspondence with respect to ideology and tactics (rather than resource dependency per se) that accounts for the parallel behavior.

Interestingly, all three arguments find some support. In the case of the fifteen homeless SMOs mentioned earlier, the correspondence argument seemed to hold, as there was no significant relationship between a resource benefactor relationship and the use of radical tactics (for example, blockades, sit-ins, and housing takeovers): three of the five SMOs that had a resource benefactor engaged in radical action, as did five of the ten SMOs that did not have a benefactor.[71] In these cases, a resource benefactor thus appeared to enhance the viability of the SMOs but did not necessarily moderate tactical actions. In contrast, some research on external support of professional organizations in the civil rights movement found that such support had a tempering effect on tactical action or means but not on goals or ends.[72] Such research findings suggest that while the procurement of external resources can modify the course and character of movement action, there is no automatic, determinative effect of receiving or appropriating those resources. Rather, it appears to be a conditional relationship, depending on where the resource provider is located on a continuum of organizations or actors ranging from elites to non-elites, on timing of the support in a movement's life span, and on the degree of correspondence between the perspectives and goals of the supportive agency and the movement.

Conclusions Regarding Resource Mobilization

In this section, we have emphasized the importance of resource availability and acquisition to the emergence and persistence of social movement activity. We also noted that there are at least five general types of resources: material, human, social-organizational, moral, and cultural. Although each of these resource types may be of some importance to all movements, we observed that there can be considerable variation in the relative importance of the different sub-types to different movements. Additionally, we explored the question of resource derivation, observing that resources may be derived internally from a movement's base or core constituency, from external supporters, or from a combination of support. While there has been debate about which is the most important wellspring of resources, the research indicates that most movements are the beneficiaries of both internally and externally derived resources, even though they may rely more heavily on one source than on another. Finally, we took up the question of the effects of the receipt of externally derived resources, concluding that the effects can be varied and are thus conditional rather than determinative.

Two relevant questions that we did not explore concern the role of social movement organizations in securing and deploying resources, and whether different types of movement organizations operate differently in terms of resource acquisition and deployment. Since the answers to these questions depend on the ongoing dynamics of a movement's operation, we address them in Chapter 5, which focuses on dynamics.

ECOLOGICAL FACTORS AND FREE SPACES

In addition to some degree of political opportunity and the accumulation of some variety of resources, the prospect and character of movement emergence and mobilization are affected by ecological factors and the existence of free spaces. Ecological factors refer to the spatial arrangement of movement-relevant populations and physical places, often called free spaces, conducive to facilitating or sustaining collective challenges to authority.

Ecological Factors

Evidence that ecological factors are important to movement mobilization abounds in the literature on different movements and related protest events. To illustrate the significance of the spatial arrangement of relevant populations and physical structures, let us return to the 1989 Beijing student movement and Tiananmen Square. According Dingxin Zhao's in-depth analysis of the movement, the ecology of Beijing's various universities significantly affected student mobilization. Among the most important ecological factors were the proximate location of most of Beijing's sixty-seven universities in relation to each other, with most being less than thirty minutes apart via bicycle; the separation of most of the universities from the outside world by large brick or concrete walls; the dense campus living conditions, with half a dozen or more students typically living in the same dormitory room for at least four years; the almost "total institution" character of campus life, with each university having "its own restaurants, student dining halls, cinema, hospital, post office, barbershops, grocery stores, sports facilities, recreational areas and other such facilities,"[73] and the campus spatial layouts, which channeled and concentrated student routines and activities. Together, these ecological and spatial characteristics constituted an ecology that affected student mobilization in five overlapping ways:

> (1) It facilitated the spread of dissident ideas in the period before the movement and the transformation of news about particular events during the movement. (2) It nurtured many

student-based networks.... (3) It shaped students' spatial activities on the campus[es], creating a few places that most students had to pass or stay in daily. These places became centers of student mobilization. (4) The concentration of many universities in one district encouraged mutual imitation and inter-university competition for activism among students from different universities. (5) The ecology also facilitated the formation of many ecology-dependent strategies of collective action.[74]

Such observations about the ecological facilitators of the Beijing student mobilization in the spring of 1989 are not peculiar to that movement or ecological context. In fact, the ecological character of university campuses across much of the world has been noted by other scholars as a facilitator of student movements. Two campus ecological factors are especially prominent worldwide: the spatial, or, territorial segregation of youth creating what has been called "youth ghettos,"[75] and spatial arrangements that channel the daily comings and goings of students and often aggregate them in particular places at particular times, such as student unions or centers, campus quads that students crisscross between classes, and the administratively designated and ecologically marked "free speech" areas that were created on university campuses in the United States in the 1970s and 1980s to centralize and control student rallies and protest. At the University of California, Irvine, for example, an area on the main campus walkway, including the steps leading up to the walkway next to the Administration Building, has been established as the rally/protest area. It is here that proponents of various political issues and causes, including various student associations, such as the Muslim Student Association and the Jewish Student Association, aggregate and sometimes confront each other via collective gestures and vocalizations. But they are not free to appropriate this space on a whim or at any time. Rather, it must be reserved and scheduled—and only within a limited span of time, usually between noon and 1:00 P.M.

Such regulatory measures are all part and parcel of the administrative control of protest and collective challenge.[76] Interestingly, these measures can, like the ecology of campuses in Beijing and elsewhere, facilitate the flow of communication and exchange of ideas, the interconnection of networks, and the development of a sense of collective enthusiasm and efficacy. The larger point is that it is difficult for social control agents—whether they are associated with the university, the encompassing community, or the state—to fully stamp out ecologically based contacts and interactions. As Zhao noted in his analysis of the Beijing student movement, "an authoritarian regime may crush intermediate associations, but it cannot destroy ecology-centered human interactions." Instead, he submits, the repressive efforts of the state often unintentionally "strengthen ecology-based human interactions."[77]

The effects of such an unwitting social control error may not be publicly visible,[78] especially when public assemblage and protest is stamped out or banned, but that does not mean that those harboring adversarial sentiments mute those sentiments. Rather, they may disappear into various free spaces.

Free Spaces

Free spaces are small-scale community or movement settings beyond the surveillance and control of institutionalized authorities that are voluntarily frequented by dissidents and system complainants. In such settings, various forms of cultural challenge, such as adversarial narratives and frames, that precede or accompany mobilization are generated or nurtured.[79] Examples of free spaces include, on one hand, quasi-public places, such as coffeehouses, neighborhood bars, student lounges, classrooms, religious facilities (for example, churches and mosques), and, on the other hand, more private places, such as one's home, apartment, dormitory room, and office or place of work. Two factors make spaces relatively free in the sense of being safe or protected: they are typically beyond the direct gaze and earshot of authorities, and they either are controlled by movement sponsors or friends or are appropriated and colonized by the dissidents themselves.

The importance of free spaces to the development and nurturing of adversarial sentiments and mobilization is clearly illustrated by the role of black churches and colleges during the course of the civil rights movement. Morris's previously mentioned analysis of the black student sit-in movement that spread across sixty-nine cities in February and March of 1960, mostly in the South, found that preexisting structures—namely, black colleges and churches—functioned to facilitate the emergence and diffusion of the movement.[80] How so? By providing the organizational infrastructure, associational connections, and free spaces in which to organize, strategize, and aggregate. As Morris concluded regarding these factors:

> Because this internal organization was already firmly in
> place prior to the 1960s, activist groups across the South were
> in a position to quickly initiate sit-ins. This rapidity with
> which sit-ins were organized gave the appearance that they

were spontaneous. This appearance was accentuated because most demonstrators were students rather than veteran Civil Rights activists.

Yet the data show that the student organizers . . . were closely tied to the internal organization of the emerging Civil Rights movement. Prior student/activist ties had been formed through church affiliations and youth wings of Civil Rights organizations. In short, students and seasoned activists were able to rapidly coordinate the sit-ins because both were anchored to the same organization.[81]

Although churches and colleges are not immune from state monitoring and intrusion, the state in nonauthoritarian regimes appears reluctant to inject its control agents and forces into those settings, except on rare occasions, such as the previously mentioned Kent State and Jackson State cases. It is partly for this reason that the churches and colleges, in particular, have functioned as relatively free spaces for mobilization.

Not surprisingly, the church and its sister institution in other religious traditions, such as the mosque for Islam, has functioned as a relatively free space for movement mobilization in various times and contexts. In the case of the Iranian Revolution of the late 1970s, for example, anti-Shah sentiments and frames, as well as plans for mobilization, were generated and nurtured, in part, within the protective shield of the mosque.[82] More recently, some mosques and madrasas (or madrassahs), which are Islamic schools, have served as free spaces or havens for learning, discussing, and spreading militant, Islamic fundamentalism.[83] The madrasas, in particular, have been the focus of attention in "the war on terrorism," especially those in Pakistan and Afghanistan that have been charged with functioning to help breed Islamic militancy. In Pakistan, for example, there are an estimated twelve thousand madrasas, with about one million Pakistani students attending these schools.[84] Although not all of them are seed beds for militancy, government leaders and local officials claim that many madrasas function as such. The mayor of a town in the northern Peshawar region of Pakistan, which is close to the tribal areas where the Taliban and Al Qaeda have reputedly flourished, claimed that "there are many madrasas run by mullahs that train jihadis and get funds from Saudi Arabia, Kuwait." He emphasized that "these jihadists know only jihad" but "should be brought into the mainstream."[85] Similarly, President Karzai of Afghanistan asserted that the source of "the Taliban insurgency lies in training camps and madrasas . . . in Pakistan, and that the insurgents take sanctuary there."[86]

Not all movement-related free spaces are as organizationally formalized or institutionalized as schools, colleges, and places of worship. Perhaps even more common are places like coffeehouses and bars or pubs that are appropriated at particular times by or for dissident groups and their gatherings. A researcher for an ongoing study of radical activists in the United States notes, for instance, that many of his contacts and observations have occurred in a coffee shop where they meet regularly.[87] Even in more autocratic, repressive political systems, coffeehouses often function, as illustrated below, as important spaces for the voicing, sharing, and framing of grievances that may congeal into mobilizing grievances that precede and nurture eventual cultural or system challenge.

Free spaces are likely to be more limited and constrained in authoritarian, totalitarian regimes because of their extensive surveillance and frequent effort to infect interpersonal and organizational networks with spies and informants. Yet, the aggrieved and discontented often secure free spaces and devise means of communication that evade the control tentacles of the regime. A case in point is provided by the subculture of public accommodation and private resistance that developed in Estonia during Soviet rule. Conceptually, accommodative subcultures are characterized by privately held values and opinions that are incongruent with those of the regime or state but not manifested behaviorally in public. In other words, there is a contradictory relationship between what some citizens believe and express in the private realm and how they behave in the public sphere.[88] It is this contradictory relationship—typically reflected in adversarial talk, narratives, songs, and poetry—that sustains the subculture and provides the stuff out of which oppositional movements often grow. In Estonia, such incongruent, oppositional sentiments were expressed and nurtured in coffeehouses; in small groups, such as "local theater troupes, choral societies, local history associations, beekeeping and horticulture societies in rural areas, and small intellectual groups like the English Academic Association and Book Lovers' Club"; in university student organizations; and even carefully in the classrooms of some schoolteachers—all of which constituted free spaces in the sense that they operated in places and in a fashion that evaded the gaze and tentacles of the regime. How this compartmentalization of the private and public worked is nicely illustrated by the following comment of a dissident student:

> I wrote a historical materialist analysis of the father of Estonian nationalism, Ferdinand von Kruetzer. It was terrible. We actually wrote this stuff! We had to in order to get our degrees.

> But when we gathered at the coffee house we could say there
> what it really was. It was pure garbage![89]

In Estonia, this accommodative subculture, which flourished
out of view the state, ultimately functioned as the seedbed for
the subculture of opposition that flowered in the late 1980s in
the wake of Soviet President Gorbachev's policies of glasnost
and perestroika that loosened the Soviet regime's social control
efforts and helped set the stage for the fall of the Berlin Wall.

Estonia is only one case, of course, but Estonians' efforts
to carve out and maintain free spaces within which to nurture a culture of resistance is commonplace across authority-
challenging movements. It would thus appear that the existence
of free spaces, however they are identified, appropriated, and
secured, is a necessary condition for movement emergence.

Conclusions Regarding Ecological Factors and Free Spaces

In this section, we have highlighted the relevance of ecological factors, including free spaces, to the prospect and character
of movement emergence and mobilization. We have illustrated
the importance of these factors by referencing the 1989 Beijing
student movement, the 1960 black student sit-in movement,
student protest gatherings and movements on U.S. college campuses, radical Islamic fundamentalist movements, and the anti-
Soviet, Estonian Independence movement. These movements
vary in a number of ways, including time and place, but they
were all facilitated or constrained by ecological factors. The importance of such factors resides in large part "in the fact that,
other factors being equal, the potential for mobilizing a population will be different if the same population is spatially arranged

in a different way."[90] One final example will suffice to illustrate the point. In a study of the distribution of peasant radicalism in Chile in the 1960s, it was found, among other things, that spatial proximity to highly organized and politically radical mining municipalities located in the countryside functioned as the main determinant of variation in the degree of peasant radicalism. In other words, those peasants most ecologically proximate to the mining municipalities became the most radical because of increased exposure to the miners' leadership and ideology.[91]

CHAPTER SUMMARY

In this chapter, we have argued that the emergence and functioning of social movements are contingent on the confluence of a number of core contextual conditions. These conditions include the actual or perceived political opportunity or freedom to express one's grievances and press one's claims publicly and to relevant authorities; access to sufficient resources to organize, mount, and sustain a campaign and the organizational capacity to deploy those resources in an effective manner; and favorable ecological or spatial arrangements of movement-relevant populations and relatively safe, spatial enclaves (often called free spaces), in which the aggrieved can associate beyond the eyes and ears of their targets or government officials and social control agents.

Each of these three sets of conditions can be thought of as the necessary contextual conditions for the emergence of social movement activity; together, it is arguable, they constitute the sufficient contextual conditions for movement emergence. Another way of thinking about them is as enabling conditions in that their presence enhances the prospect of movement emergence and mobilization, while their absence or foreclosure diminishes that prospect.

But, as noted at the outset of this chapter, even the temporal confluence of these contextual conditions does not ensure movement mobilization in the absence of mobilizing grievances. As concluded in a study by Jenkins et al. that examined the relationship between political opportunity and African American protest from 1948 to 1997: "it is not a question of opportunities alone being important, or grievances or organization alone, but all three contributing to protest."[92] We have argued, moreover, that ecological and spatial factors also matter.

Even the presence of these factors—political opportunity, resource aggregation, favorable ecological conditions, and mobilizing grievances—does not affect alone the course and character of a movement once it is up and running. Equally important are how movements operate strategically and tactically, their internal organizational functioning, and their relations with other movements and organizations within their organizational fields. These and related topics cluster under the conceptual umbrella of movement dynamics, which we examine in Chapter 5. We first consider, however, the issue of participation.

Chapter Four
PARTICIPATION IN SOCIAL MOVEMENTS

IN CHAPTER 1 WE described four primary types of challenges to systems of authority, noting that the focus of this book, as with most research on social movements, is on direct challenges by collective actors. Direct challenges by collective actors encompass movement-organized rallies and demonstrations, lawsuits, marches, and sit-ins as well as activities designed to undermine and seize a state's authority, as in the case of revolutions. Of course, individuals often challenge a system of authority without ever joining a social movement, as when an employee files a grievance against his or her employer for discrimination. While there have been numerous social movements concerned with issues of discrimination in the workplace,[1] an individual filing a claim against his or her employer for discriminatory practices does not necessarily make him or her part of that movement.

The distinction between individual and collective challenges gives rise to one of the most frequently asked questions in the study of social movements: why do individuals sometimes participate in *collective* challenges rather than act alone to challenge a system of authority or not act at all? More pointedly, why do some victims of discrimination decide to challenge their employers directly by themselves, while others join a social movement to address such grievances? More generally, at a national level, why do some citizens participate in social movement activities while others do not? According to the World Values Survey, a rather high percentage of people in the Western world report that they have participated in the activities of social movements (for example, demonstrations, boycotts, unofficial strikes, and building occupation), with around 25 percent of U.S. respondents reporting to have done so at least once during the 1995–1998 period.[2] Why, however, do some citizens participate and not others? One major objective of this chapter is to understand why it is that certain people join and participate in social movements while other similarly situated or aggrieved people do not.

We emphasized in Chapter 2 the importance of shared grievances to mobilization, but even shared grievances among a set of individuals does not mean that they are all equally likely to participate in some movement-sponsored event. This was made very clear in a series of studies, conducted by Bert Klandermans and Dirk Oegema, of the efforts of the Dutch peace movement to mobilize citizens against the deployment of the cruise missile in the mid-1980s.[3] In one study of a community outside Amsterdam, they found that while three-quarters of a random sample of community residents were sympathetic to the movement's goals, not many of them (only 1 out of 20) ended up participating in a protest event for the cause. This high rate of nonparticipation was due to three factors: first, not all of the sympathizers were targeted or recruited (60 percent); second, only one-sixth of those targeted expressed sufficient motivation to participate; and third, only one-third of those who intended to participate actually ended up doing so, largely because of different obstacles that popped up, such as having to work or attend to a sick family member. Such findings underscore the importance of looking beyond shared grievances to understand the determinants of movement participation. Or as Klandermans emphasized with his distinction between "consensus mobilization" (shared grievances and goals) and "action mobilization" (actual participation), the former does not necessarily guarantee the latter.[4] Sympathizing with or identifying with a cause indicates mobilization potential but does not ensure participation. This suggests, then, that participation is a sequential or multistep process entailing, first, the willingness to participate (consensus mobilization) and, then, perhaps, actual participation (action mobilization).

Additionally, once some level of initial participation has occurred, there is no guarantee that it will be repeated or persistent. As shown by a study of participation rates in new religious and parareligious movements in Montreal, Canada, in 1975 and 1980, 75.5 percent of those who participated in these movements were no longer participants at the time of the interviews in 1982.[5] The "typical participant" was thus "a transitory affiliate"—someone who was "involved for a while and then drop[ped] out."[6] While the study does not explain whether the dropouts subsequently participated in some other movement, other research suggests that persistent participation is atypical. For example, in an analysis of panel data from a national representative sample of U.S. high school seniors at four points in time (1965, 1973, 1982, and 1997), Catherine Corrigall-Brown found that while two-thirds participated in some social movement organization or activity in at least one of the four time periods, most did not participate across the four time periods:

29.5 percent participated in one time period, 18.9 percent in two time periods, 10.6 percent in three time periods, and only 6 percent in four time periods.[7]

Taken together, the findings of the above studies of movement participation in three different countries not only emphasize the importance of considering the initial question of what accounts for the participation of some individuals rather than others but also raise the questions of what accounts for persistent participation and what accounts for disengagement. In this chapter, we seek to account for initial participation or engagement, more persistent or sustained participation, and disengagement. Before doing so, however, it is important to clarify what is meant by social movement participation and to consider the obstacles to such participation.

CONCEPTUALIZING SOCIAL MOVEMENT PARTICIPATION

What does it mean to participate in a social movement? Are people who risk their jobs and families and even their lives to participate in revolutionary activity in highly repressive states drawn to do so by the same factors that may lead others to sign a petition or attend a peaceful vigil in less repressive states? In thinking about the various forms of participation in social movement activities, it is useful to think of *the degree of participation*.

The degree of participation can be assessed in terms of the associated *costs* and *risks*, both of which can be thought of as obstacles to participation. Scholars interested in assessing the costs and risks of participation typically assume that individuals engage in a rational calculus, weighing both the costs and the risks of participation.[8] Some forms of participation are more costly than others and require that participants draw on their own resources, such as when participation requires traveling to a capital city, like Washington, D.C., or Austin, Texas, to take part in a protest event directed at lawmakers.

The costs of participating in social movement activity are generated directly and indirectly. *Direct costs* of participation come from travel expenses (including lodging and transportation, if a participant has to travel some distance to take part), costs of child care while attending an event, as well as any costs incurred at the actual social movement activity. For example, activists may purchase materials to make signs and banners for use at a protest event or pay to have a leaflet photocopied so that it may be handed out at the event. *Indirect costs* of participation may occur in the form of lost wages in the case of a participant who attends a social movement event rather than show up for work. Another indirect cost may be receiving a failing grade on a paper or examination, in the case of a student who participates in social movement activity rather than turn in assignments or take scheduled examinations. Finally, another form of indirect cost may be less tagible, such as when an individual is stigmatized for participating in a particular social movement.

In addition, some forms of participation incur risks, such as when a participant is involved in a confrontational protest event at which police are present and are making arrests and using weapons to quell dissent. Risks of participation may be thought of as both direct and indirect. *Direct risks* of participation are those that potentially affect the participant at the moment of participation. For example, participating in any kind of collective challenge directed at a system of authority brings with it the possibility that the system of authority may decide to retaliate against the challengers. One such direct risk comes in the form of police repression of protest activity (see Chapter 3). Film footage of large protest events sometimes shows protesters and police with wounds generated from protester-police interaction, as happened in the previously mentioned 1968 Chicago Democratic Convention and in the "Battle in Seattle" in 1999. As well, countermovement actors have been known to show up at protest events to harass their opponents, sometimes with the consequence that these interactions turn violent. *Indirect risks* are those that typically are not specific to the site and moment of collective challenge. For example, some protesters claim that undercover surveillance by state agents at various collective action events poses an indirect risk in that undercover agents may use surveillance tapes and photos in the future when making a legal case against a particular participant or group of participants.[9]

When thinking about the overall level of cost and risk associated with movement participation, it is possible to cross-classify these facets of participation to develop four different types of participation, as shown in Table 4.1.

Cell 1 includes actions that are, in ordinary times, neither especially risky nor costly. Signing a petition in the United States, for instance, is not likely to incur any costs other than the cost of the ink for the signature or perhaps the cost of a cup of coffee at a café offering free Internet access to its customers in the case of electronic petitions. Under normal conditions, signing a petition is not especially risky. However, there are exceptions, as noted in Cell 2, when signing a petition could be very risky. Signing a pro-Communist petition during the McCarthy era in the United States (from 1949 to 1952), for example, was quite

Table 4.1

TYPES OF COST AND RISK ASSOCIATED WITH

MOVEMENT PARTICIPATION

Type of Risk/ Type of Cost	Low Risk	High Risk
Low Cost	(1) Low Risk, Low Cost Participation (e.g., signing a petition)	(2) High Risk, Low Cost Participation (e.g., signing a pro-Communist petition in McCarthy Era)
High Cost	(3) Low Risk, High Cost Participation (e.g., traveling to Washington, D.C., for large march)	(4) High Risk, High Cost Participation (e.g., Freedom Summer)

risky, as might have been signing a petition against the Iraq war under the Patriot Act era.[10]

Other forms of activity can be costly but of low risk, as depicted in Cell 3, as when activists travel from a western state in the United States to Washington, D.C., for a large, permitted march on the mall. Such demonstrations, when conducted lawfully and peacefully, are not especially risky for individuals but can be quite costly. Finally, an example of participation that is both high cost and high risk would entail participation in an intensive movement campaign that requires both financial commitments and risk of injury and even death. The paradigmatic example of this, as shown in Cell 4, is the Mississippi Freedom Summer campaign of 1964, when college students from around the United States traveled to Mississippi, after first participating in a two-week-long orientation session at the Western College for Women in Oxford, Ohio, to register black voters and to participate in the operation of "Freedom Schools." Within the first few weeks of the campaign, three volunteer student activists were kidnapped and murdered (James Chaney, Andrew Goodman, and Michael Schwerner), and countless other activists were beaten and harassed over the course of the summer-long campaign.[11]

In addition to thinking about how cost and risk affect the degree of movement participation, it is important to also assess how the participant's level of commitment to the movement may affect the degree of participation. We can think of intensity of commitment as falling along a continuum from a very low level of intensity (for example, donating a small amount of money to a social movement organization) to a much higher level of intensity (for example, volunteering for a high-risk social movement activity, such as Freedom Summer).

The level, or intensity, of commitment to a social movement may significantly impact the level of risk and/or costs that an individual may be willing to incur on behalf of the movement. For example, a highly committed individual may be more willing to draw on personal funds to travel long distances to protest and she or he may be more willing to risk injury and arrest once at the event. However, it is also possible that one's level of commitment may be impacted by actual engagement in risky and costly protest. In other words, those who have taken part in high-risk and high-cost activities may become even more committed to the particular cause, in part because of the social reinforcement by other participants at such activities.

ACCOUNTING FOR DIFFERENTIAL RECRUITMENT
AND INITIAL PARTICIPATION

Having established that social movement participation can be quite variable depending on different combinations of costs and risks, we now turn to this chapter's first focal question: why do only certain individuals participate in social movement activity, while other similarly situated individuals sit on the sidelines? If it is true, as noted earlier, that a quarter of Americans have taken part in protest activities, what accounts for this differential recruitment and participation?[12]

While this question has generated a prodigious amount of research, close inspection of much of it highlights the importance of four sets of factors that often interact and combine to account for differential recruitment and initial participation. They include structural factors, such as social networks and organizational affiliations; biographical factors, such as past socialization experiences and role availability; social psychological factors, such as shared identity and a sense of efficacy; and factors that generate incentives to participate, such as motivational framing.

Structural Factors: Social Networks and Organizational Affiliation
Whatever ideological orientations or psychological dispositions might be hypothesized to render some individuals susceptible to the appeals of certain kinds of social movements, such factors do not go very far in predicting participation without the potential participant being informed about and asked to participate in one or more movement activities. Analysis of a 1990 survey of

a cross section of U.S. adults, age eighteen and over, who were asked if they had taken part in a protest, march, or demonstration in the past year, showed that "being asked to" participate "was found to be the strongest predictor of participation."[13] We therefore begin our discussion of the factors that account for differential recruitment by considering the following question: what determines which potential participants are most likely to come into contact with or be recruited by a social movement?

The answer is essentially a structural one, meaning that the probability of initial participation in a movement is, in large part, a function of being linked to one or more movement members through a preexisting or emergent interpersonal or organizational tie. Indeed, it is not an exaggeration to assert that few, if any, factors are more important to understanding differential recruitment and participation than are network linkages, whether they are actual, face-to-face networks or mediated (through radio or television) or virtual networks. Whatever the form, social networks function in two primary ways: as bridges connecting two or more individuals, individuals and organizations, or two or more organizations; and as conduits for the flow of all varieties of information. Both of these functions are operative in the case of movement recruitment, as it is those individuals who are linked to movement members who are most likely to be asked to attend and who actually do so. Recall that 60 percent of the sympathizers with the Dutch peace movement did not participate in some sponsored event, in part because they never learned about it or were not asked to attend.

Evidence of the salience of social networks to differential recruitment comes from studies of engagement in a variety of movements across the globe. These include, for example, studies of recruitment to and participation in religious movements,[14] the civil rights movement,[15] the women's movement,[16] the Dutch peace movement,[17] the environmental movement in Italy,[18] terrorist movements in Italy,[19] and the Beijing student movement of 1989.[20]

Indeed, empirical documentation of the importance of network ties to movement members as a predictor of differential recruitment is so pervasive that it would be easy to conclude that such ties are a necessary condition for movement participation. But that would be incorrect, as there are instances of initial movement participation in the absence of prior network linkages. Some people, for example, are "seekers" or "searchers" in the sense that they are on the lookout for groups or movements that share their lifestyle and/or worldview, or provide an opportunity to realize a particular disposition or identity. A case in point is provided by the participants in the Bo and Peep UFO movement in the late 1970s that eventually morphed into the Heaven's Gate cult. According to research on this movement in the 1970s, new members sought it out rather than being recruited into it via ties to existing members; they sought it out because they "were metaphysical seekers" who defined "their decision to follow the Two" (Bo and Peep) as "a reaffirmation of their seekership . . . as a logical extension of their spiritual quest."[21]

In a somewhat similar vein, some students of identity argue that movements provide people with an opportunity to verify or realize their existing identities and that participation can thus be explained by this identity validation disposition.[22] It is also arguable, both theoretically and empirically, that some events or situations are so provocative morally or emotionally that network ties are more or less rendered irrelevant. This is the "moral shock" argument that the observation of, or direct experience with, some events may be so morally reprehensible and emotionally moving that individuals will be inclined to join the cause irrespective of the presence or absence of ties to movement members.[23] Accordingly, the shock value of some events or happenings is not lost on movement strategists, as with the strategic use of photographs of aborted fetuses by anti-abortion activists and of visualizations of animals used in scientific laboratories by PETA (People for the Ethical Treatment of Animals) to mobilize prospective participants.

Considering that some number of individuals may be genuine seekers or searchers and that exposure to certain events may shock some folks into participation, the inclination to treat social network ties as a necessary condition for participation diminishes. That said, the vast empirical literature prompts the contention that the presence of a network tie to someone already engaged in a movement is one of the strongest predictors of individual participation in that movement.

Although we have focused on interpersonal networks as a key variable accounting for differential recruitment, it is important to understand that such network ties are usually embedded in community and organizational contexts, and that some such contexts may be more facilitative of recruitment and participation than others. Thus, in a study of striking workers at Ohio State University in 2000, Dixon and Roscigno found that those workers who were embedded in a striking unit were more likely to participate in the strike than were other workers because the "workplace networks" functioned as critical conduits for "grievance sharing and identity formation prior to the strike" and influenced "individual decision making and calculations at a pivotal point" in the process.[24]

The fact of "embeddedness" has prompted researchers to go beyond assaying the presence or absence of network ties to examining their structure and multiplexity. In research on the predictors of recruitment to the Mississippi Freedom Summer campaign of 1964, for example, it was found that some universities, such as the University of Wisconsin, contributed a disproportionate share of volunteers. But those volunteers were not randomly distributed across the university; they were students who were in positions of network centrality in a number of the university's various organizations (or, multi-organizational field) and were thus most likely to be recruited.[25] Another example of the relationship between multiplex networks and differential recruitment is provided by Roger Gould's study of mobilization in the Paris Commune of 1871. He found that the key to explaining participation in the movement resided in overlapping neighborhood and National Guard networks. As he put it, "successful mobilization depended not on the sheer number of ties, but on the interplay between socials ties created by insurgent organizations and preexisting social networks rooted in Parisian neighborhoods."[26]

These examples highlight the greater mobilization potential of network ties nested in certain kinds of community contexts, such as universities and neighborhoods, and their overlap with movement organizations. But just as important are the more formalized bureaucratic and voluntary organizations with which most people are associated in varying degrees. Because these organizational forms forge ties among individuals, membership in organizations (both movement-related and nonmovementrelated) may facilitate recruitment into movements and protest. This argument rests, in part, on the assumption that people who hold similar ideologies and/or are similar on some other dimension will join the same organizations. This baseline affinity makes it more likely that ties formed within organizations can be activated for protest, if needed. For example, members of the same church may be mobilized by other parishioners to participate in a protest event, even if the issue of the event is not directly related to the goals of the church itself. Because common membership in the church makes it more likely that the members will agree on issues, the ties formed in the church, as well as in other organizations, may function as important avenues of movement recruitment. However, this connection is not necessarily a direct one in the sense of organizational affiliation automatically leading to participation. Rather, as the above-mentioned analysis of a 1990 survey of a cross section of U.S. adults found, "membership in organizations and the accompanying civic experience obtained therein, increase the probability of being asked to protest, which consequently increases the probability of protesting."[27]

We have seen how social networks, whether interpersonal or organizationally based, constitute a key factor in explaining why individuals come to participate in one movement rather than another, if in any movement at all. Yet it is important to bear in mind that while participation usually is unlikely to occur in the absence of a network tie to a movement member, not all individuals who receive invitations from acquaintances, friends, or family will participate. Recall again that only one-sixth of those citizens who received invitations to participate in a Dutch peace movement event were motivated to do so, and only one-third of those actually did so. Thus, factors other than network ties are necessary to account for differential recruitment.

Social Psychological Factors

In Chapter 2, we identified a number of social psychological processes that contribute in important ways to the generation of mobilizing grievances; the processes included comparison processes, assessments of procedural justice, and weighing the prospect of loss. Taken together, these three processes suggest that individuals who evaluate their situation unfavorably compared with that of relevant others or over time, who believe they have been treated differently and unfairly procedurally, and who are confronted with a loss or devaluation of what they have or value are, all else being equal, likely candidates for participation in movements that address these concerns. We accented these social psychological processes rather than psychological states, such as frustration and status dissonance, because the former constitutes the intervening mechanisms that affect, in conjunction with framing processes, how aggravating conditions are interpreted. But these processes are not the only social psychological factors that influence the likelihood of participation. Also important are a sense of personal and/or collective efficacy and a sense of shared or collective identity.

PERSONAL AND/OR COLLECTIVE EFFICACY. Personal or self-efficacy is a sense that one has the capacity or ability to do what is necessary to produce a desired outcome. In the context of politics and social movements, personal efficacy is the belief that one has the ability to make a difference, especially when it is coupled with little trust in existing authorities. Also in relation to politics and movements, personal efficacy tends to be associated with collective efficacy, meaning that individuals feel not only that they can help make a difference, but that it is possible to create change and realize their interests by working together collectively. Numerous studies support this efficacy hypothesis, ranging from research on participation in the "ghetto riots" in the United States during the 1960s to case-specific studies of participation in a particular movement, to nationally representative studies of participation in social movement activity in general.[28] It is interesting to note that even among constituents who might be thought to have a low sense of efficacy, such as the homeless, research has shown that efficacy measures (for example, a sense that the movement protest would help educate the public) helped distinguish between homeless participants and homeless nonparticipants. For example, those homeless who said they thought protest events educated the public and were beneficial to themselves and others were much more likely to participate in a protest event than were those who felt the events made no difference.[29]

That feelings of personal or collective efficacy would affect the prospect of participation makes good sense. After all, why would one participate in a social movement activity if she felt the event or movement would have no effect in terms of increasing awareness of the issue at hand and perhaps even improving the situation? There are other reasons for participating, of course, such as peer pressure, fun, and curiosity, but for many people there appears to be the associated belief that collective action can make a difference. Perhaps nothing illustrates this point more clearly than the mantra of Barack Obama's 2008 presidential campaign, "Yes we can!"

COLLECTIVE IDENTITY. There has been a great deal of attention paid in recent years to the role of collective identity in the process of mobilizing individuals to participate in the activities of social movements.[30] Although definitions of collective identity vary somewhat, most scholars agree that at issue is a "shared sense of 'one-ness' or 'we-ness' anchored in real or imagined shared attributes and experiences among those who comprise the collectivity and in relation or contrast to one or more actual or imagined sets of 'others.'"[31] Earlier work on collective identity emphasized the way in which collective identities are formed, but more recent work moves beyond the process of collective identity formation to the functions of collective identity in social movement dynamics, such as mobilization and tactical deployment.

Regarding the mobilization function, a growing body of research shows a strong relationship between identification with a particular group or collectivity and movement participation and activism. Examples of such research include studies of shared identification among gay men,[32] Dutch farmers,[33] young women engaging in feminist activism,[34] striking workers,[35] women in such hate movements as the Ku Klux Klan,[36] homeless-movement participants,[37] and even Jewish resistance fighters in the Nazi-occupied Warsaw Ghetto.[38]

When we consider these studies together with the previously mentioned observation that some individuals seek out movements that provide them with an opportunity to affirm their existing identities, it is clear that a relatively strong sense of identification with a particular social category or movement can be a significant determinant of some level of participation in support of that category or corresponding movement. What is not always clear, however, is whether the group/movement identification preceded participation or was a consequence of participation. The same question also holds for personal efficacy. Sometimes movement and protest participation may generate a strong sense not only of identification but also of efficacy; often, however, both senses are the result of prior biographic experiences and framing processes.

Biographic Factors

We use the notion of biographic factors broadly to encompass various aspects of one's past and present life situation and experiences that may affect the likelihood of participation directly and indirectly. We focus specifically on three salient aspects of one's biography: resonant socialization experiences, prior experience with some form of activism or political engagement, and biographical availability (defined below).

RESONANT SOCIALIZATION EXPERIENCES. Socialization involves two overlapping processes: one pertains to learning the values, norms, motives, beliefs, and roles of the groups and society with which one is associated; the other process entails changes in value orientation, beliefs, and identity during one's life course.[39] Here we are concerned with the first type of socialization, directing attention in particular to the intergenerational transmission (for example, from parents to children) of activist values. The relevance of this variety of socialization to movement participation was highlighted by a spate of studies of student activists of the 1960s that found a connection between their activism and their parents' politics: many of the student activists came from liberal to left activist families. Some scholars argued that students active in the 1960 cycle of protest, many of whom were Jewish, were exposed to strong humanitarian values and standards of justice that were transmitted via parental socialization.[40] Others have suggested that Catholics and Jews were more likely to participate in the 1960s social movements because they were more likely to have ancestors who participated in left-leaning movements in Europe.[41] More recently, research has shown that individual's activism for or against the Persian Gulf War is linked to their parents' activism for or against the Vietnam War.[42]

Since so much of the research on the intergenerational transmission of activist values has focused on students on the left in the 1960s, such as those associated with Students for a Democratic Society (SDS), one might conclude, as have too many commentators, that the 1960s were a seedbed out of which only leftist and progressive radicals and movements grew. But that would be an erroneous conclusion, as made clear by Rebecca Klatch's study of the lives of seventy-four activists associated with SDS on the left and YAF (Young Americans for Freedom) on the right, from their political awakenings through their political involvements in the 1960s and into their adult lives.[43] Klatch's findings show not only that aspects of present-day conservatism, including many of its leading figures over the past twenty years, can be traced back to the 1960s and the universities, but also that activists on the right were mightily influenced by their parents and the homes in which they grew up. Klatch notes that although there were "vast differences in the background and orientation" of the students on the right and those on the left, there were also striking similarities in their upbringing compared with that of most other college students of the time. She observes that:

> most youth from both left and right shared the experience of being raised in atypical homes compared to others of their age. Their parents were politically aware and, to one degree or another, engaged and involved in the world. Further, most parents consciously encouraged their daughters and sons to be vocal and active in the political world. Thus, for the majority of these youth their parents provided them with the framework and motivation that gave shape to their identity as activists.[44]

Related to such findings regarding the intergenerational transmission of activist values, some scholars have suggested that some varieties of movement participation are prompted by a "prosocial orientation"—that is, a tendency to think about the general welfare of others and to act in ways that will help others.[45] As with activist values, the degree to which we hold prosocial orientations is related to our parents and thus is also a product of intergenerational socialization processes on both the right and the left.

These research findings suggest that growing up in certain kinds of families and households—wherein there are pronounced political orientations, political participation is seen as important, and participation via social movements is considered appropriate—may nourish not only a predisposition to political engagement and activism but also a sense of efficacy about such engagement.

PRIOR ENGAGEMENT IN POLITICS AND MOVEMENTS. One's disposition toward participating in social movements can also be influenced by whether one has previously engaged in political and movement activity. Individuals who generally are politically unengaged and apathetic are quite unlikely to take part in any form of political participation, especially if it requires incurring costs and risks as does much social movement activity. In contrast, people who are politically engaged are much more likely to participate in various forms of political participation, from voting to protest, as Klatch found with members of SDS (Students for a Democratic Society) and YAF (Young Americans for Freedom).

What does it mean to be politically engaged? There are several dimensions of political engagement, including the level of *political interest, political knowledge,* and *political orientation.*[46] Without some level of political interest, individuals will probably not participate in any political activity, including social movements. As Schussman and Soule found in their analysis of a 1990 survey of a cross-section of U.S. adults, those reporting that they are interested in politics and enjoy political discussion were much more likely to have participated in protest events.[47] Similarly, the research generally suggests that individuals who are informed about politics (political knowledge) via print, media, or Internet news are more likely to be inclined toward some form of political activity.[48]

Political orientation on a left/right or liberal/conservative continuum also seems to influence one's decision to be politically active; typically, research conducted by sociologists and political scientists shows that individuals who self-identify as liberal are more likely than other people to participate in social movement activity.[49] As Dalton notes, protest "is often seen as a tool for liberals and progressives who want to challenge the political establishment and who feel the need to go beyond conventional politics to have their views heard."[50] Clearly it would be a mistake to conclude that only liberals participate in protest activities, but there seems to be an association that has remained over time with respect to political orientation and willingness to protest.

These observations suggest that one's prior experience with and engagement in politics or, by extension, other authority structures enhances the prospect of participation in movement activities challenging such structures. Thus, regarding the determinants of participation, some people are more likely than others either to accept an invitation to participate or to seek participation in some protest events because their prior levels of engagement and awareness increase the odds of their overcoming the associated costs and risks.

BIOGRAPHICAL AVAILABILITY.   Another set of biographic factors theorized to affect the probability of participation includes various life-cycle and life-style characteristics that may alter the costs and risks of movement participation, such as being married, having children, and being employed full time. The absence of such factors, conceptualized as "personal constraints," has been hypothesized to render individuals biographically available for movement participation; the presence of such factors supposedly makes people biographically unavailable.[51] This makes sense intuitively since being married and having children with one or both parents working full time would appear to leave less time for movement participation than, say, being a younger person. After all, younger individuals, on balance, are less invested in their careers—if they even have careers—and are thus more likely to be willing to undertake risks involved in protest. Younger people are also more likely to be in school, unmarried, and free from obligations imposed by careers and families. Moreover, if we consider the role of college students in protest movements throughout history, we can see how the relative freedom from responsibilities of family and careers for most traditionally aged college students could facilitate participation in social movements. Yet empirical research on the effects of various hypothesized indicators of biographical availability (for example, being a student, unmarried, childless, flexibly employed) has been mixed at best and often negative, meaning that these indicators do not go very far in either predicting or increasing the odds of participation.[52]

How might this quandary be explained? The answer resides, in part, in the failure to assess biographical availability or unavailability in relation to the different stages of movement participation. As noted at the outset of this chapter, participation is examined as a sequential process involving several stages or steps: one entails being informed about the occurrence of an event and being willing to participate; the other involves actual participation. Furthermore, recall that Klandermans and Oegema's research on participation in a Dutch peace movement event showed quite strikingly that willingness to participate did not result in actual participation for most of the willing respondents. This disjunction was reported even more graphically in Beyerlein and Hipp's finding that "only a small minority," out of a cross-sectional sample of 1,332 noninstitutionalized U.S. adults eighteen years of age and older, "who were willing to protest" against the government actually did so.[53] Given these findings, Beyerlein and Hipp then examined how the standard measures of biographical unavailability played out in relation to the willingness stage and the actual participation stage. What they found is that the measures of unavailability (marriage, particularly for women, and work) "generally had significant negative effects on *willingness* to participate in protest action, but no effect on actual protest participation...." They concluded that "[b]iographical unavailability therefore *does* constrain people from participating in activism, but it does so only for the first stage of the mobilization, removing people from the pool of potential participants."[54]

Thus, biographical availability or unavailability appears to matter in relation to one's willingness to participate but not as much in determining actual movement participation. We think that participation is likely to be affected by some of the social psychological factors mentioned above, by the generation of various participatory incentives or motivations, and by one's commitment to the cause.

Generating Participatory Incentives: Reflex Emotions, Organizational Structure, Spatial Context, and Motivational Framing

We have discussed a number of factors that can affect one's interest in participating in some movement activity, as well as the prospect of actual participation. These include network linkages to a movement, shared grievances, a sense of identification with the movement and collective efficacy, and various biographical factors and experiences, such as resonant socialization and political engagement experiences. But even if all of these factors align, they may not be sufficient to ensure participation. In fact, from the vantage point of rational choice theory,[55] most prospective participants who are part of a movement's mobilization potential would need added incentives or more motivation before they actually participated because of two considerations. One is that the perceived benefits or gains from participation may not outweigh the perceived costs and risks. The other consideration is the economist Mancur Olson's vaunted "free rider" thesis, which holds that nonparticipation is highly rational when the desired benefit or goal is a "public good" that is available to everyone (it is indivisible and nonexcludable) irrespective of whether a person contributes to its attainment.[56] Consider, for example, the environmental movement and its objective of seeking legislation designed to ensure clean air and clean water. Certainly, environmental activists would not be the sole beneficiaries of such legislation, since all people and animals would stand to benefit from a toxin-free environment. This simple fact raises the question of why any single individual would participate in a movement, such as the environmental movement, designed to secure public or collective goods. Individuals may wonder, Why should I incur the costs and risks associated with activism when others are participating, and if they are successful, I will be one of the recipients of clean air and water anyway? So why not "free ride" on the efforts of others? Even those who may not be inclined to free ride may not be sufficiently motivated to participate in movement activities, despite sharing the movement's grievances and subscribing to its aims. Thus, social movement leaders and activists face the challenge of neutralizing the inclination to free ride and/or to provide additional rationales or motivation for participation. This is the challenge we referred to earlier as the dilemma of "action mobilization"—that is, of moving willing sympathizers from the sidelines to the playing field, from the balcony to the barricades.

Incentives, or motivations, that can be offered to individuals to increase the odds of their participation cluster into three sets: selective, solidary, and moral. *Selective incentives* or benefits, unlike collective goods, are divisible and excludable in the sense that they benefit only those who contribute their time, energy, and/or resources to the cause. *Solidary incentives* are rooted in the affective and emotional attachments that make one feel part of a group or collectivity. Because such incentives flow from group association and identification, they are somewhat selective. *Moral incentives* derive from the principles and values that heighten one's sense of conviction, obligation, and responsibility.

Incentives can be generated through a number of different processes. Some of them are clearly matching processes: for example, the provision of tangible material inducements that constitute a selective incentive for participation, such as the free meals and beverages that are sometimes given to people who attend a demonstration event, as is often done to induce the homeless to participate in movement activities that address their plight. Sometimes movements hand out T-shirts, baseball caps, buttons, and other such items. But these sorts of tangible products are far from being potent inducements except perhaps in the case of the most economically marginalized citizens. There are, however, selective incentives that are promised for future gain and are contingent on present action, as with the seventy-two black-eyed virgins promised to Palestinian suicide bombers, an example to which we will return.

Far more compelling as participatory inducements than most materially based selective incentives are solidary and moral incentives. They are more compelling because passionate identification with a movement's cause is far more likely to be based on affective ties to a group and its moral principles than on instrumental considerations. In other words, a sense of solidarity and

moral conviction regarding distributional and procedural justice and injustice are the stuff that stirs the emotions and helps
forge the "iron in the soul."[57] How are solidaristic and moral
incentives embellished or generated? There are several mechanisms for creating these types of participatory inducement.

Sometimes *reactive* or *reflex emotions* can lead to a sense of
solidarity when those emotions are shared and communicated
among a similarly situated set of individuals. Reflex emotions
are involuntary and do not require cognitive processing. Examples of this type of emotion include anger, fear, and joy.[58]
When someone is afraid of something, he or she may be more
likely to join a movement that aims to do something about the
perceived source of that fear. This is especially so when the fear
is collectively shared, as has been the case with NIMBY (not-in-
my-backyard) movements over the past thirty years. In general,
these neighborhood-based movements have sought to keep "undesirable" folks or facilities—such as shelters for the homeless
and halfway houses for the mentally ill or parolees—out of the
neighborhood.[59]

Certain organizational forms or structures can also generate
intragroup affective bonds. Field studies of the Pentecostal and
Black Power movements in the 1960s, and of some religious
movements in the 1970s, suggest that movement organizations in which members are linked together structurally in a
segmented and reticulated, netlike fashion (see Figure 4.1) are
particularly generative of solidary incentives.[60] *Segmented, reticulated movement structures,* whether centralized or decentralized,
enmesh participants in a set of overlapping and interlocking
relationships that can produce strong, reciprocal, interpersonal
bonds that function to generate fairly powerful incentives to

Figure 4.1

Centralized, Segmented, Reticulated Movement

Organizational Structure

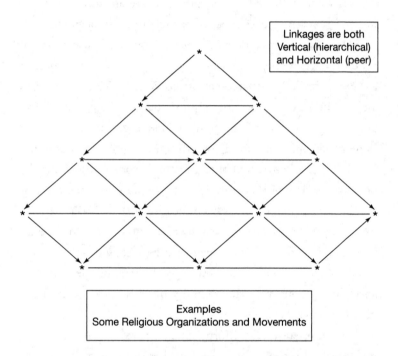

Linkages are both
Vertical (hierarchical)
and Horizontal (peer)

Examples
Some Religious Organizations and Movements

act collectively. In the case of the Nichiren Shoshu/Soka Gak-kai Buddhist movement, for example, participants are associated with a number of age- and gender-based peer groups, like the Young Men's and Young Women's Divisions, that are broken into smaller units and involve members in various activities ranging from traffic control, first aid, and child care to learning how to play musical instruments and marching in drill teams and bands that perform at public and movement-sponsored parades and celebrations.[61]

Solidary incentives are not only a product of segmented, cross-cutting reticulated associations, which were a feature of the Nazi movement of the 1920s and 1930s and are a central characteristic of the modern megachurch. They are also sometimes created by *engagement in social movement protest events,* which can stimulate one's passions, as occurred repeatedly in the 1989 Beijing student movement. The spatial and social ecology of the context also matters. As Zhao observed in the case of the Beijing movement,

> students not only often marched together by school, class, and major, but also by dormitory room. However, they did this not just out of a sense of group solidarity but because the campus ecology and dormitory-based networks were the basis of mutual influence, persuasion, and even coercion among students.[62]

Certain kinds of organizational arrangements and social ecological contexts not only may be particularly generative of solidary incentives but also can sanction free riding by pressuring participation among those who may not feel connected to the movement or the cause.

Motivational framing can also generate solidary incentives and moral incentives—and even some selective incentives. Motivational framing provides a "call to arms," or, rationale for engaging in movement-sponsored collective action that goes beyond the diagnostic and prognostic framing.[63] More concretely, motivational framing entails the construction of vocabularies of motive that provide prods to action by, among other things, amplifying reasons for participation that override feared risks and the free-rider problem. Six sets of vocabularies of motive have been identified. The first four are illustrated in Rob Benford's research on the nuclear disarmament movement. The first vocabulary set emphasizes the *severity,* or seriousness, of the problem (for example, immensity of nuclear dangers); the second accents the *urgency* of taking action now to prevent undesirable consequences that are otherwise likely to follow (for example, the disarmament movement's doomsday clock); the third highlights the probable *efficacy* of collective action (for example, the power of the new movement); and the fourth vocabulary set amplifies the *moral propriety and obligation* of taking action (for example, involvement is needed to save the world from nuclear war).[64]

The remaining two sets of vocabularies of motive can be construed as types of selective incentives in that their receipt is contingent on participation, but they are not materially based. They include the promise of greater tangible benefits and status enhancement to those who engage in certain movement practices. The vocabulary of *greater tangible benefit* seems to be associated mainly with religious or utopian movements that promise physical, relational, spiritual, and even sometimes material benefits to those who engage in particular practices, such as chanting, praying, meditating, making sacrifices, and the like. The vocabulary of *status enhancement* frames participation in terms of being among "the elect" or in the "vanguard of history," a motivational framing practice that is fairly commonplace both in revolutionary political movements and in religious movements.

An illustration of motivational framing in terms of the vocabulary of moral obligation and that of status enhancement is provided by Salehi's analysis of rank-and-file participation in the Iranian revolution. He argued that such participation required that "the fear that had ordinarily prevented people from joining the movement" be neutralized, and that this was done by the motivational framing of clerical leaders who "made the protest a religious obligation by subjecting the political situation to religious definitions and interpretations" such that the struggle was framed as "the equivalent of a holy war" and death as constitutive of "martyrdom."[65] Such appeals to status enhancement have also been evident in the case of Palestinian suicide bombers. Although reference is made to moral obligation, greater weight appears to be placed on the special rewards that await the suicide bomber, or "martyr," as he or she might be called in some parts of the Islamic world, because suicide is generally understood as being contrary to the teachings of Muhammad. Among the special rewards awaiting the martyr, much is made of the previously mentioned "seventy-two black-eyed virgins." But "more basic is the omnibus promise of divine favor rewarding them for righteous deeds."[66] As noted by a member of Hamas[67] involved in the recruitment and training of martyrs:

> We focus attention on Paradise, on being in the presence of Allah, on meeting the Prophet Muhammad, on interceding for his loved ones so that they, too, can be saved from the agonies of Hell, on the houris, and on fighting the Israeli occupation and removing it from the Islamic trust that is Palestine.[68]

In addition to the promise of divine rewards that accompany ascent to paradise, there have been various earthly enticements, such as the enhancement of the martyr's former identity: their pictures have been plastered on public walls; their deaths announced in the press and media as weddings rather than as obituaries; their families have received visits from political officials and sometimes even given money; and they have been praised in mosques and at rallies.[69] Thus, the motivational incentives for martyrdom appear to be multifaceted, involving tangible and more ethereal selective incentives.

Allied Participation Processes: Frame Transformations, Commitment, and Disengagement

The above-mentioned sets of factors invoked to account for initial differential recruitment or action mobilization are not as helpful in explaining consensus mobilization or sustained participation. To better understand what influences agreement or sympathy with the diagnostic framings and goals of a movement and what contributes to more enduring participation, we need to consider the allied participation processes of conversion and commitment. Since participation in most movements is periodic or transitory, we also need to consider the process of disengagement.

FRAME TRANSFORMATIONS. Recall the distinction, discussed above, between consensus and action mobilization: the latter pertains to those who are sympathetic with a movement, and perhaps willing to participate, but who need some coaxing or inducement to do so; the former, in contrast, need to be persuaded about the values and aims of a movement so that they develop a willingness to participate, thus becoming part of the movement's action mobilization potential. Frame transformation can be thought of as the process that produces such a change in cognitive orientation and emotional sensitivities, and it can take a variety of forms and occur at different levels.[70]

The most dramatic type of frame transformation at the level of an individual involves a *conversion*, which entails a seemingly wholesale shift from one way of seeing and understanding an event or issue, or even oneself, to another way. Perhaps the paradigmatic example of such a transformation is found in the refrain of the Christian hymn "Amazing Grace": "Amazing grace! How sweet the sound that saved a wretch like me. I once was lost but now am found; was blind but now I see!" Not all frame transformations are such dramatic, wholesale conversions in the sense of turning away from one worldview and adopting another. Sometimes the transformation involves the *regeneration* of a belief system or orientation that had not been taken seriously or had been abandoned out of skepticism, rebellion, or indifference.[71] This variety of transformation is popularized today by the "born again" phenomenon. A third kind of transformation involves the blending, or *consolidation,* of two contradictory belief systems or worldviews, as in the case of the Jews for Jesus movement.[72] In each case an earlier primary interpretive authority is replaced by a different one—dramatically different, revitalized, or combinatorial. Among the various factors associated with such transformations, the two most important are network linkages (the development of affective ties to other members) and role learning through intensive interaction.[73] Together, these microstructural and social relational factors facilitate (1) reevaluation of one's values and self, often leading to biographical reconstruction,[74] (2) strong identification with the movement, entailing a merging or consolidation of one's personal identity and movement or collective identity,[75] and (3) the development of potent willingness to participate in movement activities. The result is that there is a change, metaphorically, in one's heart and mind; consensus mobilization is thus effected.

Although we have discussed frame transformation primarily at the level of individuals, it is important not to lose sight of the fact that large-scale frame transformations, involving changes in the hearts and minds of a subset of the masses, not only occur on occasion but are sometimes necessary for implementing and sustaining the far-reaching changes of some movements. As Ralph Turner observed, many of the great movements of the past—such as those seeking the abolition of slavery, women's suffrage, and the termination of child labor—sought major legislative changes, but those changes were "unthinkable until [the] tremendous task of altering people's views of reality had been accomplished," which depended "upon reaching the hearts and minds of vast numbers of people."[76]

BUILDING AND MAINTAINING COMMITMENT.   We noted at the outset of this chapter several studies on a variety of movements that indicate that persistent participation is atypical. In a follow-up to one of these studies, Catherine Corrigall-Brown conducted a comparative case study of trajectories of participation in four movements (Catholic Workers, Concerned Women for America, United Farm Workers, and a NIMBY homeowners' movement) that differed in terms of goals and organizational structure. She found that persistent participation was relatively infrequent among the sixty participants interviewed in depth: 17 percent continued participation, in varying degrees, with the same movement; 25 percent disengaged from the initial movement and subsequently became involved in another movement; 13 percent disengaged from the initial movement but resumed participation at some later point in time; and 45 percent disengaged fully from movement participation.[77] Such research findings raise a question that can be asked in two different ways: What accounts for enduring, or persistent, participation? Or, why does movement participation appear to be relatively short-lived or transitory for most participants? The answer to the first question hinges on the concept of commitment; the answer to the second, on disengagement.

Commitment involves the allocation of time, energy, and/or resources to a cause, a group, or a line of action because it is in one's interests to do so, whether those interests are group- or activity-related or side bets.[78] In the context of social movements, to be committed is to engage in actions consistent with the expectations and goals of the movement, not because one is forced to do so, but because one's interests and identity are tied to the movement. Conceptualized in this way, commitment implies the linkage or correspondence of self-interest and group interest. Thus, persistent, or enduring, participation can be understood as a function of commitment. As suggested in our earlier discussion of associated costs and risks, the stronger and more unwavering the commitment, the less relevant those costs and risks; the weaker the commitment, the weightier the costs and risks and the less enduring the participation. What accounts for or generates a strong sense of participant commitment?

Rosabeth Kanter explored this question in her study of the survival viability of nineteenth-century utopian communes. She found that the more successful ones—those lasting thirty-three years or more—were those that successfully developed a greater number of commitment-building strategies and mechanisms.[79] Included among the commitment-building mechanisms indentified by Kanter and others are cultural and social insulation, conversion or consciousness-raising, specific dress, public confession and witnessing, surrendering or donating personal resources, and in-group/out-group polarization.[80] Such mechanisms function, in various combinations and degrees, to accomplish the following: (1) provide gratifications and rewards for participation (instrumental commitment), (2) foster a sense of belongingness and a "we" feeling (affective commitment), and (3) anchor the individual's identity, or worldview, in the movement or cause (moral commitment).

In general, the more effective a movement or organization in generating the above-described commitments, the more successful it should be in retaining its members and the more persistent will be their participation. However, there are several caveats to keep in mind. The first is that movements vary considerably in the extent of commitment required. Some require little more from most members than an occasional donation or petition signature. Others can be exceedingly "greedy," requiring a choice between the movement and a so-called normal life, as with the Hare Krishna movement in the 1970s and 1980s, most communal movements, and radical, violent movements, such as terrorist movements.[81] The second caveat is that movements vary not only in the commitment required but also in their capacity to generate commitment.[82] Third, exiting one movement in favor of another should not necessarily be read as indication of weak or minimal commitment. Some individuals are career activists who are committed to a particular cause that transcends any single movement. They may indeed jump from one movement to another because the latter movement is thought to embrace more fully the cause with which they identify. Or their activist leanings may evolve over time, as exemplified by the activist career of Michael Harrington. From his early twenties on, he was committed to the cause of social justice, but as that commitment evolved toward democratic socialism, for which he was the preeminent advocate, he left the Catholic Workers movement for the Young People's Socialist League.[83] Such longstanding commitment to a particular cause and associated activism is particularly noteworthy because it is far less common than disengagement.

DISENGAGEMENT FROM SOCIAL MOVEMENTS. We have noted at various points throughout this chapter that disengagement is the most common participation trajectory. This is not so surprising given that participation in movements that demand more than an occasional check or signed petition is generally voluntary and requires the coordination of one's everyday life with the varied demands of participation. It is partly for this reason that the question of what accounts for participation has generated far more research than the question of what accounts for disengagement.[84] But in looking back over the sets of factors we have elaborated in trying to account for both initial and persistent participation, we can also infer the reasons for disengagement. Not only is disengagement the flip side of participation, but the factors that account for it are the obverse of some of the determinants of participation. Thus, a decline in the importance of the issues one hoped the movement could address or a decline in one's faith in the efficacy of the movement to address those grievances, a weakening of one's ties to movement members and one's identification with the movement, and an increase in external or countervailing demands and commitments—all, singly or in different combinations, should push or pull one toward disengagement.

In the most systematic attempt to date to theorize disengagement, Bert Klandermans condenses these factors into two sets of precipitants of disengagement: *insufficient gratification* and *declining commitment* to the movement. However, these factors alone seldom prod an individual to defect from a movement; sometimes there has to be a *precipitating event* that acts as a catalyst.[85]

Declining or insufficient gratification from the movement may be caused by a host of factors, ranging from the failure of the movement to achieve its stated goals, to factions and schisms forming in the movement, which can make participation unpleasant for some. Sometimes, moreover, the strategies, tactics, and goals of a movement can change, which can lead some individuals to feel less enthusiastic about supporting a particular movement. Or sometimes a particular goal of a movement can lose its urgency or be replaced by a more pressing need at a particular time. The general point is that social movements are dynamic rather than static entities. As such, they can change in ways in which neither leaders nor participants fully anticipated. This, combined with the fact that a participant's interests and obligations can also change, may lead to significant changes in the level of gratification that people get from movement participation. In turn, this can lead to declining commitment and thus disengagement from the movement. Finally, a precipitating event—such as an argument with another participant, the defection of a close friend, or a turn toward more radical tactics—

can be the proverbial final straw that activates the decision to exit a social movement.

CHAPTER SUMMARY

This chapter has identified and elaborated various sets of factors that influence individuals' decisions to participate in social movement activities. They include social structural factors, such as network linkages; social psychological factors, such as identity correspondence and a sense of efficacy; biographic factors, such as prior socialization experiences; various factors that generate participation incentives; and allied processes, such as frame transformation and commitment. Importantly, it is likely that all of the factors interact and combine in complicated ways to push or pull a person toward social movement participation. We have emphasized that some of these factors matter in different ways and levels of intensity depending on the character or degree of participation. For example, it may be the case that biographical availability or structural connections matter differently in relation to different kinds of movement activity, perhaps depending on the level of cost or risk associated with the activity.

It may also be that some of these factors matter at different stages of the mobilization process. For example, it is possible that although grievances and psychological orientations have a bearing on an individual's initial foray into social movement activity, collective identity, incentives, and certain biographic factors may affect the level of commitment to a movement (which, in turn, affects subsequent activities).

Finally, it is worth noting that these factors may interact with other factors described throughout this book. For example, it might be the case that grievances are critical but will only be successful at bringing people to the movement when the political opportunity structure is favorable, there is a sufficient resource base to draw on, and articulate collective action frames are present.

Chapter Five
DYNAMICS OF SOCIAL MOVEMENTS

IN THE PREVIOUS CHAPTERS, we have concerned ourselves with questions that are, by and large, central to understanding the emergence of social movements and/or the fluctuation in social movement activity. Specifically, we focused on the role of grievances in the emergence of social movements, the effects of the broader political context on movement activity and outcomes, and the role of resources and local ecological factors in facilitating social movement emergence. We have also examined the factors influencing individuals to join or to take part in the activities of social movements, highlighting the importance of both individual and contextual conditions on participation. In this chapter, we switch gears somewhat and ask another question that is central to understanding social movements. That is, once a movement is up and running, what happens to it? In particular, in this chapter we focus on the processes and dynamics that impact the operation of social movement organizations.

Underlying our examination of movement dynamics is the principle of interactive determination. It holds that an understanding of focal objects of analysis—be they self-concepts, identities, organizational practices, or social movements—cannot be fully achieved by attending only to qualities presumed to be intrinsic to the objects or to external factors that impinge on them; rather, such understanding requires consideration of the interactional contexts or webs of relationships in which the objects are ensnared and embedded.[1] This principle means that neither individual nor society, neither self nor other, for example, are ontologically prior but exist only in relation to each other and therefore can be fully understood only in terms of their interaction, whether it be actual, virtual, or imagined. Applied to social movements, this principle directs attention to four orders, or levels, of interaction: those that occur internally, that is, within a social movement; those that occur between a movement and other sets of actors within its ambient environment for which the movement constitutes an object of orientation; those that occur between or within a movement and its cultural context; and the interactions that result because of the dynamic interplay between these internal and external forces and tensions.

The above-described principle of interactive determination, with its four-tiered foci, provides the backdrop for our examination of three key, overlapping domains of social movement dynamics: the function of social movement organizations and the organizational fields in which they operate; movement strategies and tactics; and diffusion processes as they relate to movements.[2]

SOCIAL MOVEMENT ORGANIZATIONS AND THEIR ORGANIZATIONAL FIELDS

In thinking about social movement organizations, it is useful to remind ourselves of the conceptualization of social movements described earlier in the present book. Recall that one of the key facets of social movements emphasized in Chapter 1 is that they are collective enterprises, involving joint pursuit of some common goal or objective. The collective nature of social movements requires some degree of coordination or organization. Of course, there are many different forms that the organization of social movements can take, from loosely networked groups of people to highly bureaucratic and formal social movement organizations. Regardless of the form it takes, however, organization is central to social movements.[3]

We thus begin our discussion by conceptualizing four different vantage points from which to examine social movements and their component organizations. At the most basic level, it is helpful to think of *social movement organizations* (SMOs) as distinct entities. Whether the SMO is a formal organization or a loose group of associates who come together occasionally, we can think of an SMO as a bounded entity of individuals who have come together because of a shared goal concerning one or more grievances. For example, the Santa Cruz chapter of EarthFirst! is a group of people who are joined together by their desire to protect local biodiversity and ecosystems. According to their Web site, the organization is a "... mix of students, teachers, parents, bike activists, organic farmers, contractors, artists, and computer programmers" who are "... bound together by our love and respect for the Earth that we all share, and by a commitment to eradicate all forms of oppression and exploitation of any living being."[4]

We might contrast this chapter of EarthFirst! with a more formal, bureaucratic organization that is also concerned with environmental protection, the National Audubon Society. The National Audubon Society has been known to cooperate in protest directed at the U.S. government by helping to sponsor protest events, letter-writing campaigns, and petition drives, but the organization also actively lobbies Congress, runs gift shops, organizes community bird walks, and coordinates more than five hundred chapters throughout the United States.[5] The general point, of course, is that both the Santa Cruz chapter of EarthFirst! and the National Audubon society are active in environmental protection and both organizations use protest tactics, at least some of the time. However, the two organizations are very different with respect to the specific nature of the goals they articulate, the tactics that they use, and their base of support.

A second vantage point from which to view social movement organizations is the *social movement industry* (SMI) level. A social movement industry is the set of social movement organizations that are working toward change in the same basic area. For example, we can think about all organizations in some geographic area (such as Santa Cruz, California; or Washington, D.C.) working toward environmental change. Or we can think about the coalition of social movement organizations that made up the Austin, Texas, Nuclear Disarmament Movement, studied by Robert Benford in the late 1980s and early 1990s.[6] The advantage of thinking in terms of an SMI is that we can compare and contrast different SMOs within a given area working for change around a given issue. For example, in the Austin, Texas, Nuclear Disarmament Movement, some organizations espoused radical goals and advocated using very disruptive tactics to achieve these goals, but other organizations were more inclined to use tame tactics and espoused goals that were far more moderate. Comparing and contrasting organizations working toward change in a given area allows us to answer questions about how organizational differences account for different organizational outcomes, such as the ability to mobilize individuals or the achievement of other stated goals.

A third vantage point to consider is the *social movement sector* (SMS). The SMS encompasses all extant social movement organizations, associated with all social movements or issues, in a particular time and place.[7] For example, it might be possible to document all social movement organizations active in a given area around all issues areas, as Kevin Everett did.[8] Using newspaper reports of collective action events in our nation's capital, Everett found 308 different social movement organizations engaged in protest activities related to various issues in Washington, D.C., between 1961 and 1983.

The fourth vantage point entails consideration of all organizations that exist beyond the SMI and SMS but have some connection to a given SMO and, as such, have some effect on it. The concept of the *organizational field* is used in organizational sociology, usually to refer to the set of organizations that constitute a recognized area of institutional life; we can consider how this might apply to social movement organizations.[9] We might think of the *social movement organizational field* as that set of organizations that share overlapping constituencies and interests or to which a focal organization is linked, whether this is in a facilitative or antagonistic fashion.[10]

The most obvious members of the organizational field for most movements are the social control agents (for example, police, national guard, military) who not only monitor movement activities but may even try to repress them. But the set of extramovement organizations is almost limitless and ranges from private philanthropic associations that donate money to movement endeavors to civic and religious associations that donate time and personnel to movement causes; from other SMOs within an organization's industry to countermovement organizations; from organizations that a movement may target to lobbying organizations working toward change in the same area.

Overlapping with the movement organizational fields are movement *discursive fields*. They evolve during the course of discussion and debate, sometimes but not always contested, about events and issues of relevance to various sets of actors (for example, targeted authorities, social control agents, countermovements, and media) whose interests are aligned, albeit differently, with the issues or events in question, and who thus have a stake in how those events and issues are framed.[11]

Here we focus on social movement organizations and their dynamics, keeping in mind that these organizations do not exist in a vacuum, that their boundaries tend to be porous, and that it is impossible to understand them without thinking about organizations in relation to the above-discussed entities. We begin with consideration of three organizational processes that are important to the functioning of social movement organizations: organizational trajectories, organizational leadership, and bureaucratization. Following this, we describe two important interorganizational dynamics: cooperation/coalitions and competition/conflict.

Organizational Trajectories

Social movement organizations are in the business of trying to bring about some degree of change by pressuring their targets, educating the public, or mobilizing and sustaining resources. The outcomes of these struggles are discussed in detail in Chapter 6, but that discussion raises the question of what happens to social movement organizations once they have reached their goals. In thinking about the trajectories of social movement organizations, it is useful to recognize that there are several distinct options for such organizations. Some organizations survive over time and grow, others stagnate and die, and others morph into entirely different organizations. Of course, the trajectory of most social movement organizations reflects some combination of these options.

An example of an organization that grew rapidly over time, only to morph into one having different goals and targets, was the U.S.-based Infant Formula Action Coalition (INFACT). INFACT was formed in response to growing concern over the marketing of infant formula in less developed nations, particularly in the 1970s. This concern crystallized in an international boycott that INFACT helped launch of Nestlé, one of the largest producers of infant formula. INFACT, along with other organizations, argued that there were several reasons that infant formula should not be marketed to parents in less developed countries. First, powdered infant formula must be mixed with water and much of the water in these countries is contaminated, leading vulnerable babies to contract water-borne diseases. Second, because of the extreme poverty of many of these nations, parents would often dilute the infant formula, thus causing their children to receive less adequate nutrition. Third, the movement argued that breast-feeding is much healthier for babies. Finally, INFACT and other organizations noted that Nestlé was using unethical marketing strategies for its infant formula, such as using salespeople dressed as nurses to hand out samples of the formula.

INFACT's boycott lasted for about six years, from 1977 to 1983. The organization called off the boycott once it had brokered a deal with Nestlé in which the company would no longer use deceptive means to market its products and would promote breast-feeding.[12] While other anti-infant formula organizations continue to carry the torch of this boycott today (for example, International Nestlé Boycott Committee, Baby Milk Action, International Baby Food Action Network, Infant Feeding Action Coalition), INFACT turned its sights on other issues. In particular, it launched a boycott against General Electric for its production of nuclear weapons and then a campaign against Philip Morris, both of which turned out to be less successful than its Nestlé boycott. Today, the organization still exists, but it has changed its name to Corporate Accountability International and focuses more broadly on corporate abuses, such as the devastation of the environment by oil companies and the privatization of water in less developed nations.[13]

Organizational Leadership

Social movement organizations nearly always have some form of leadership, whether this is embodied in a single person or is shared by group members.[14] We often think of social movements as having charismatic leaders, such as Martin Luther King Jr., Gandhi, or Mao Zedong.[15] The word *charisma* comes from the Greek word that literally means "divine gift." The term refers to a rare human ability to charm and influence people, nearly seamlessly. Charismatic people are often described as magnetic, meaning that others are almost inexplicably drawn to them.

Of course, many qualities of effective leaders have been identified by scholars studying leadership, only some of which are correlated with charisma. For example, effective leaders are said to lead others by example and to possess skills or talents for a particular task at hand. They are said, moreover, to have a clear sense of mission and clearly defined goals and to be optimistic about the chances of success.

In practice, of course, leadership in social movements may take a number of different forms, and it may even be eschewed in some social movement organizations. Because of the sometimes strikingly different tasks that are often required for effective mobilization, there may be two or more significant leaders in a movement who assume these different tasks. This division of labor often centers on the different skill sets associated with administrative and pragmatic leadership versus the ideological or intellectual leadership that engenders enthusiasm and stimulates passion.[16] A classic illustration of the different functions and talents related to leadership is the role of Trotsky versus that of Lenin in the Russian Revolution, with the former providing the intellectual and emotional grist and the latter the organizational leadership. Sometimes individuals may function in an informal leadership capacity, as Belinda Robnett (1996) observed in her study of women in the civil rights movement. Because of their exclusion from formal leadership positions, women operated primarily at the rank-and-file level. But occasionally some would assume the informal role of what Robnett calls bridge leaders, functioning to connect various potential constituents with the movement's SMOs and more formal leaders.

When leadership and decision making are diffuse and participatory, conducted by teams or groups, SMOs may have no clear-cut, definitive leader or leaders. For example, many social movement organizations work as *affinity groups*, which are small collectivities (usually three to twenty people) organized in a nonhierarchical manner that make decisions by group consensus. Typically, affinity groups work together on direct action campaigns, and they are usually based on close friendship ties. The advantage of such groups is that they are small and cohesive, thus decision making can feasibly be accomplished by following democratic principles. The affinity group structure was used by antinuclear groups in the United States and more recently by campaigns against corporate globalization, by movements against the Iraq War, and by movements in favor of animal rights.[17]

Bureaucratization

The discussion of affinity groups leads to our third organizational dynamic: bureaucratization. We have noted that some degree of organization and coordination must be present in social movements, even if such organization is decidedly *not* hierarchical (as in the case of affinity groups). However, many social movement organizations find themselves, over time, becoming more formalized, hierarchical, and professional; in short, they become more bureaucratic.

Bureaucratic movement organizations, like other bureaucratic organizations, in their ideal type have several characteristics. Bureaucratic movement organizations are characterized by a clear, vertical hierarchy of authority and rules, and their procedures of operation are codified. In bureaucratic movement organizations, official business is conducted on a continuous basis following a set of written rules. Individual members occupy positions within the bureaucracy, and these positions are kept separate from the individuals' private lives. Often, members of the bureaucratic movement organization receive a salary for their work. Finally, in bureaucracies there is a clear division of labor; individuals become specialists at the tasks to which they are assigned, and (ideally) these tasks are coordinated to accomplish the ultimate goal.

A good example of a bureaucratic SMO is the National Organization for Women (NOW). At the time of this writing, NOW is led by four national officers: President Kim Gandy, Executive Vice President Olga Vives, Action Vice President Melody Drnach, and Membership Vice President Latifa Lyles. It also is led by a national Board of Directors and by "issues committees" that study and issue policy statements on a variety of issues deemed relevant by NOW.[18] NOW's policies are formulated at the annual National Conference and implemented by the national NOW. These policies are written in a standardized format and exist for members and the general public to read. While much of what the national NOW does is highly bureaucratized, there are also state and local chapters that are loosely coordinated via the national NOW and that vary in degree of bureaucratization.[19] NOW can be contrasted with other, less formal and less bureaucratic organizations, such as the informal groups associated with the "riot grrl" movement of the early 1990s. The riot grrl movement arose out of the alternative or punk rock music scene in the early 1990s and preached, through music and through "zines," feminist political views, including universal female identity and separatism. The riot grrl groups also discussed issues central to the broader feminist movement, such as rape, domestic abuse, sexuality, and female empowerment. Very broadly, the movement focused on increasing the representation of women in alternative music. The broader movement, and the groups associated with it, tended to be highly decentralized and decidedly not bureaucratic, very much unlike NOW.

Interorganizational Dynamics

COOPERATION AND COALITIONS. Beyond organizational-level processes, we can also consider interorganizational processes. As we emphasized earlier, social movement organizations are rarely (if ever) bounded entities. Instead, there are frequent connections between movement organizations within and between different movement industries. Activists talk to other activists in different organizations; activists belong to multiple organizations; and movement organizations often collaborate on different kinds of campaigns. When movement organizations collaborate, we refer to the outcome as a *coalition*, which implies that groups have adopted a shared goal, even if that goal is not the primary goal of one (or all) of the organizations. For example, David Meyer and Catherine Corrigall-Brown note that forty-one different organizations took part in the anti–Iraq War coalition: Win Without War. Of these organizations, only eleven were explicitly anti-war; the other organizations had different primary foci, ranging from the environment, to international politics, to social justice.[20]

Sometimes coalitions may be built on a particular set of ascribed characteristics or social bonds: for example, when feminist organizations collaborate with pro-choice organizations to protest restrictions on abortion rights. But coalitions can sometimes be far more instrumental, such as when multiple groups having no obvious ascribed or solidaristic ties collaborated in staging the Battle of Seattle. At that event (November 1999), groups associated with a wide array of movements (for example, labor, religious, feminist, human rights, environment, and anarchy) collaborated and mobilized tens of thousands of individuals to protest the World Trade Organization.[21]

COMPETITION AND CONFLICT.   One form of interorganizational interaction that is less well understood is *competition for resources*. Although we would like to think that SMOs in an industry cooperate to achieve a common goal by entering into coalitions and collaborating, in reality SMOs are often engaged in competition for limited resources, such as money, time, energy, and skills; and for symbolic goods, like prestige. What effect does competition have on SMIs and SMOs? Some scholars of social movements draw on *organizational ecology* and *resource mobilization* theory to examine how competition between social movement organizations affects the mix of organizations within an industry.[22] The key argument in this literature is that when there are relatively few organizations in a given social movement industry, there are likely to be sufficient resources to support them all. As the number of movement claimants in the field grows, however, the organizations begin to compete for resources, and some organizations will not survive.

Most SMOs constantly appeal to potential members by asking for monetary contributions, mobilizing mass protest events, encouraging letter-writing campaigns, and so on. Yet most of us have limited discretionary resources and limited time to spend on social movement endeavors. We pick and choose our causes and the organizations to which we will donate time and money. The name of the game for SMOs, then, is to figure out how to appeal to certain identity segments of a citizenry. Some choose a more general strategy, hoping to appeal to a mass base. The

Sierra Club, for example, historically has taken part in protest events, promoted outdoor activities, run education campaigns around environmental issues, organized letter-writing campaigns, and lobbied Congress. But other SMOs choose a more narrow approach, hoping to appeal to a more narrowly defined set of actors. For example, the Earth Liberation Front is known for its radical tactics, which include sabotage and vandalism, as when members of this group firebombed SUVs at a car dealership in Oregon or when they took credit for arson at a Vail, Colorado, ski resort. Clearly, the tactics used by the Sierra Club differ markedly from those of the Earth Liberation Front, despite their shared goals regarding environmentalism. The variation in tactics across an SMI is useful, as it allows individuals to take part in a variety of different activities that might appeal to their own identities and beliefs regarding appropriate actions to take.

In addition to competing for funding and time from individuals, organizations also compete for funding from foundations, churches, and other voluntary organizations. This competition can lead organizations to tailor what they do to appeal for funds. For example, Jenkins and Eckert have documented how civil rights organizations changed their tactics to appeal to potential donors. Specifically, movement organizations toned down their tactics and their goals so that mainstream philanthropic organizations would offer them funds—funds that the donors would not be willing to give to social movement organizations that were perceived to be radical.[23]

A classic example of organizational competition (and, in this case, conflict) was when the NAACP Legal Defense and Education Fund (LDF) split off from the NAACP under pressure from the Internal Revenue Service. For a long time, people did not know that the organizations were separate, and donations meant for one often ended up in the coffers of the other. The confusion and competition for resources, especially as funding for the overall civil rights movement began to decline, led to heated conflict between the two organizations.[24]

More recent scholarship by Sarah Soule and Brayden King argues that as competition for resources increases and some organizations begin to fail, successful organizations become larger and more centralized in the SMI.[25] As this happens, however, smaller and more specialized organizations are able to thrive on the fringes of the industry. For example, consider the industry of organizations working toward change in the environment. At the center of that industry might be large organizations (for example, Sierra Club, World Wildlife Federation) that, over the years, out-competed other organizations. However, alongside these large movement organizations are many small environmental organizations that appeal to particular identity segments. Alongside the Sierra Club, for example, we find the Defenders of the Earth and the Earth Liberation Front, both of which use far more radical tactics and espouse more radical goals than does the Sierra Club. These more radical groups appeal to different people than do the larger, more bureaucratic organizations that occupy the center of the SMI.

TACTICS AND STRATEGIES

So far in this chapter, we have alluded to strategies and tactics in passing; now we examine them more closely. Although SMOs often engage in a mixture of institutionalized and noninstitutionalized tactical actions, it is the latter that most readily come to mind when we think of movement tactics. Reflective of this association is the fact that movements have been called politics by other means.

The standard referent for such "other means" are various tactical actions, which are most often dramatic, noninstitutionalized forms of joint action involving two or more people who have appropriated, or received police permission to use, spatial areas (streets, parks, malls) or physical structures (office buildings, theaters, lunch counters) for purposes other than those for which they were intended or designed. Such tactical actions range widely, from silent, public hand-holding vigils commemorating victims of rape, AIDS, or war to lobbing bags of dog feces over barricades of police into marching adversaries; from women lying on the ground naked in the rain to spell out "peace" with their bodies in protest against the war in Iraq to Buddhist monks immolating their bodies in protest against the Vietnam War; from cross-burning associated with such anti-black movements as the Ku Klux Klan to the consciousness-raising efforts of the women's movement; from homeless protestors camping out in front of federal buildings to anti-abortion adherents blocking the entrance to abortion clinics; from large-scale public performances, such as movement-sponsored parades, to no more than two individuals holding up a sign scolding a corporation for discriminatory labor practices. Whether these tactical actions are directed at political authorities or at other institutional or cultural authorities, it is by these actions that movements are best known publicly, for it is these tactical actions that constitute the public face of movements. In other words, what bystanders and targets of protest see or encounter, whether directly or indirectly via the media, is the actual occurrence of tactical actions or some of their immediate dramatic consequences, such as shackled and bloodied participants, cars aflame, and tear gas wafting through the air. But not all movement tactical actions are so graphically behavioral; some are also discursive in that they may entail strategic framing of issues, adversaries, and countermovements, motivational framing, the telling of particular stories in particular ways, and memorable speeches, such as Martin Luther King Jr.'s "I Have a Dream" speech, which he delivered in front of the Lincoln Memorial during the 1963 March on Washington for Jobs and Freedom that attracted more than a quarter of a million participants. These various behavioral and discursive actions, however they evolve, constitute answers to one of the fundamental questions asked about social movements: How do they go about the business of getting their target groups or organizations to do, think, or feel what they want them to?

If tactical actions, whether behavioral or discursive, are the primary means through which social movements attempt to press their claims and advance their interests, what kinds of factors account for or explain the selection and use of different tactical alternatives? We address that question here. More specifically, we want to know what factors constrain or limit and facilitate or enable the selection and use of social movement tactics.[26]

There is no one set of limiting or enabling factors. Rather, there are a number of factors that typically interact and combine to affect the character of tactical actions. Some are internal to the movement and some are external.

Internal Tactical Constraints and Facilitators

STRATEGY. Perhaps the most important determinant of the selection and application of particular tactics is the strategy in which the tactics are enveloped. A strategy is a broad, organizing plan for accomplishing or attaining a particular goal, such as winning a war, exacting concessions from an institutionalized authority, winning an athletic contest, or winning a political election. Tactics are a reflection of strategies in that they are the specific actions or techniques through which strategies are implemented. The relationship between strategies and tactics is clearly illustrated in the game of American football. Both contestants approach the game with offensive and defensive strategies and sets of plays and schemes intended to execute the strategies. These plays and schemes can be regarded as tactics. Thus, an offensive strategy may be to control the ball to keep the competing offensive team off the field by mixing running and short passing plays rather than by throwing long passes for quick-strike touchdowns. In contrast, the defensive strategy may be to curtail an opponent's passing attack by keeping constant pressure on the quarterback through mixing various stunts and blitzes. The point is that the game strategy for the offense and defense suggests some kinds of plays and schemes rather than others. If the chosen schemes and plays do not work so well in the first half, tactical adjustments may be made at halftime that may be more effective, or an alternative strategy may be devised and implemented.

The constraining and enabling effects of strategy on tactical action in the game of football have their parallel in other arenas of social life, such as political campaigns, the lobbying efforts of interest groups, and the campaigns of social movements. Consider the *strategy of nonviolence*, which entails "a self-conscious and collectively disciplined avoidance of violence when the situation is strongly provocative of violence."[27]

The strategy of nonviolence—associated in the United States principally with the civil rights movement in the late 1950s and the 1960s and championed by Martin Luther King Jr. and the Southern Christian Leadership Conference—foreclosed the use of violent tactical actions involving damage to persons and property. The strategy favored, however, other, more congruent tactics, such as sit-ins at white-only lunch counters, boycotts of public transportation, mass marches and demonstrations, and voter registration drives.[28] A sense of how this strategy was applied and refined by King and his adherents is graphically described in the introduction to a firsthand account of the Selma, Alabama, march of 1965:

> Before he came to Selma, King and his Southern Christian
> Leadership Conference (SCLC) had refined their protest
> techniques [read tactics] in civil rights battlefields across the
> segregated South. They would select some notoriously segre-
> gated city, mobilize the local blacks, and lead them in protest
> marches conspicuous for their nonviolent spirit and moral
> purpose. Then they would escalate the marches, increase their
> demands, and even fill up the jails until they brought about a
> moment of "creative tension," when white authorities would
> either agree to negotiate or resort to violence. If they did the
> latter, King would thus expose the brutality inherent in segre-
> gation and so arouse the nation that federal authorities would
> feel obliged to intercede with corrective measures. This tech-
> nique failed in the 1962 campaign in Albany, Georgia, where
> white authorities handled King's marchers with unruffled
> decorum.... But it succeeded brilliantly in Birmingham, Ala-
> bama, in 1963. Here Police Commissioner Eugene "Bull" Con-

> nor went berserk at the spectacle of all those marching Negroes
> and turned police dogs and firehouses on them—in full view
> of reporters and television cameras. Revolted by such scenes
> ... the federal government eventually produced the 1964 Civil
> Rights Act, which desegregated public accommodations—
> what King had demanded all along in Birmingham.[29]

Such nonviolent tactics were also equally successful in Selma
in 1965, when King and his associates led a voting rights campaign that helped bring about the 1965 Voting Rights Act,
which enfranchised American blacks.

In contrast to the strategy of nonviolence and the "creative
tensions" it sometimes generates, the violent *strategy of terrorism* calls for clandestine acts of targeted violence such as kidnap-
ping, blowing up public facilities, and suicide bombing. Terrorism typically excludes more conventional tactical action, such
as public marches and demonstrations, other than in supportive
contexts that constitute safe havens, as was Taliban controlled
Afghanistan for the Al Qaeda terrorist movement prior to the
allied invasion following September 11, 2001.[30]

Just as violence and nonviolence constitute contrasting but
paired movement strategies in that one implies the possibility
of the other, so do the strategies of social transformation versus
personal transformation. Most movements seek to realize their
goals through one of these two broad transformative strategies. The *strategy of social or societal transformation* calls for tactics that bring into sharp focus the inequities and injustices of
social structures and arrangements or various social practices,
such as discrimination, war, and pollution. Movements whose
major tactical practices reflect this strategy include the civil

rights movement, the environmental movement, most anti-war movements, labor movements, both the pro-life and pro-choice movements, and the women's movement in part. In contrast are movements whose tactical practices reflect the *strategy of personal transformation.* Such movements include the various therapeutic and self-help movements that have flourished in the Western world since the 1970s and 1980s, such as the Transcendental Meditation movement and Erhard Seminars Training (known as est); various religious movements and cults, such as Scientology, the Hare Krishna movement, the Moonies, or Unification Church, and Nichiren Shoshu; and various escapist movements that not only seek personal transformation but even believe that it can be maintained or realized only in seclusion or in a protective bubble that shelters adherents from the noises, temptations, and countervailing beliefs and practices of the everyday world in which most of us live. Well-known examples of such escapist movements include the hippies, who retreated to rural, northern California communes to pursue their alternative lifestyle in an uncontaminated fashion;[31] the Jim Jones following who moved from northern California to "Jonestown," Guyana, and eventually disintegrated via a mass suicide and murder resulting in the deaths of 913 communal members in 1978;[32] and the Heaven's Gate cult that sought the ultimate form of escape via mass suicide in San Diego in 1997 (see Chapter 1).[33]

Several caveats about these and other strategies are important to keep in mind. The first is that movement strategies are not irreversible or temporally static; rather, they can change over the life course of a movement as happened with both the Jim Jones and Heaven's Gate cultish movements. Neither began pursuing a fully escapist strategy, and certainly not a suicidal one. The second caveat is that movements rarely act in terms of a single, "pure" strategy. More common, we think, is a blend of two or more strategies. The women's movement, for example, blended social and personal transformation, with an emphasis on eliminating gender discrimination via legal change illustrative of the former and consciousness-raising groups illustrative of the latter; terrorist movements are clearly a blend of social transformative and violent strategies, although personal transformation strategies come into play when there is interest in making martyrs, as with suicide bombers; and "rights" movements have generally social transformative and nonviolent strategies. Additionally, some movements may pursue the same goal, but through different transformative strategies. For instance, most peace movements and the Nichiren Shoshu Buddhist movement pursue some measure of world peace as an ultimate goal, but they do so differently, with Nichiren Shoshu seeing personal transformation, rather than political pressure and change, as the key to world peace.[34]

Last, it is important to note that the existence of a dominant movement strategy, as with nonviolence and terrorism, does not imply consensual support among adherents, especially since strategic, tactical action invites a response by the targets that may call for changes in strategy and corresponding tactics. Returning to the civil rights movement, the strategy of nonviolence, championed by King and the SCLC that he headed, came under increasing scrutiny and challenge in the movement as it encountered police brutality and violence throughout the 1960s. In response, other SMOs in the civil rights movement sought to broaden the movement's strategy beyond nonviolence. A principal voice for a change in strategy was the student-based movement known as SNCC (pronounced *snick*), which changed its name in 1969 from the Student Nonviolent Coordinating Committee to the Student National Coordinating Committee to reflect the change in strategic orientation.[35]

UNDERLYING VALUES. A second important factor that constrains and/or facilitates movement tactical practices, as well as their orienting strategies, are their underlying values. It is difficult to imagine nonviolent protestors engaging in nonviolent action in a persistent and disciplined fashion when confronted almost repeatedly with verbal and physical assaults, as was Martin Luther King Jr. and his many followers in the civil rights movement, in the absence of certain religious and pacifist values. It is certainly arguable from a rational calculus and self-preservation standpoint that the avoidance of violent tactical action makes good sense when the target for one's grievances monopolizes the instruments of violent coercion or when confronted by social control agents who can readily squash protestors when given the right signal. Yet King and Mohandas K. Gandhi, the inspirational leader of India's post–World War I movement for self-rule who provided King and others with a model for nonviolent resistance, often gave principled, value-based rationales for adopting and adhering to a nonviolent strategy. This is not surprising given their backgrounds. In the case of Gandhi, it is said that his guiding principles of "satyagraha" and "ahisma" were based on a mixture of beliefs derived from Hinduism, Buddhism, and Christianity. As noted in one biographic sketch: "While studying in England to be a lawyer, he first read the *Bible* and the *Bhagavad Gita*," which provided him with "a clarion call to the soul to undertake the battle of righteousness. It taught him to renounce personal desires not by withdrawal from the world but by devotion to the service of his fellow man. In the Christian

New Testament, he found the stirring of passive resistance in the words of the Sermon on the Mount."[36]

Even for some terrorist movements, there is often an underlying religious, moral basis for adopting a violent strategy.[37] This is especially the case when the movement frames its constituents as victims embroiled in a holy war in the name of their godhead, as the Al Qaeda movement has done repeatedly. As its leader, Osama bin Laden, declared in a 1998 edict:

> For over seven years the United States has been occupying the lands of Islam in the holiest of places, the Arabian Peninsula, plundering its riches, dictating to its rulers, humiliating its people, terrorizing its neighbors, and turning its bases in the Peninsula into a spearhead through which to fight the neighboring Muslim peoples.... Despite the great devastation inflicted on the Iraqi people by the crusader-Zionist alliance, and despite the huge number of people killed, which has exceeded 1 million ... despite all of this, the Americans are once again trying to repeat the horrific massacres....[38]

These observations regarding the link between movement values and movement strategies and tactics suggest that strategies and associated tactics are either partly derivative of resonant values or moral principles or, at the very least, are rationalized in terms of such ideational factors.

ORGANIZATIONAL CONSTRAINTS. Just as there is often a link between underlying movement strategies and underlying movement values, so organizational structure can affect tactical options. In fact, few questions have generated so much debate historically as that concerning the relationship between the character of movement organizations and their tactical options.

On one side of the debate is the Piven and Cloward argument suggesting that the increased involvement of organizations in movements (at least movements of poor people) leads to a channeling of the movement's energy into organization building and away from disruptive protest, which they see as the only viable tactical recourse available to poor people.[39] Piven and Cloward's argument has a long history in sociology, originating in Michels's argument that large organizations use increasingly conservative tactics as leaders come to value their own interests and the security of their position over the goals of the organization.[40]

Although there is some historical support for the Michels/Piven and Cloward argument, it seems to apply more to large-scale organizations than to movement organizations. Thus, research on social movement organizations has shown that organizations may actually facilitate disruptive collective action. The civil rights movement, for example, emerged when it did partially because of the growing strength of black organizations, including the church, NAACP, and black colleges, with the spread of the highly disruptive sit-in tactic facilitated by many of these same organizations.[41] Other studies similarly demonstrate that organizations facilitated confrontational workers' protests during the 1930s in the United States[42] and the use of confrontational tactics by the women's movement in the United States.[43] Similarly, previously mentioned research on the homeless social movement in the United States has demonstrated the importance of organizational viability for mounting protest campaigns.[44]

Many scholars now agree that while some level of organization facilitates collective action, the involvement of formal, bureaucratic organizations is associated with the use of less confrontational tactics. Indeed, empirical research shows that professional leaders in formal organizations may advocate less confrontational tactics because they are interested in preserving the organization, prefer to work so-called regular hours by using such tactics as lobbying and litigation, and possess the skills necessary for such tactics.[45]

Organizational structure or form can also affect movement tactical options in somewhat ironic ways by privileging some tactics over others. This can be seen in the contrasting recruitment practices of the Hare Krishna and Nichiren Shoshu movements. Both movements were at one time proselytizing movements in the sense that they sought to expand their ranks by recruiting new members, yet Nichiren Shoshu was much larger and grew at a steeper rate than did Hare Krishna. The reason has much to do with the different organizational structures of the two movements. Hare Krishna had a closed, communal organizational structure that compelled members to sever their interpersonal ties with family and friends outside the movement and to focus their recruitment efforts in public places. In contrast, Nichiren Shoshu had a more open, noncommunal structure, which left members' extramovement ties in place and enabled members to recruit among friends and family as well as in public places. This difference in organizational structure thus accounted in part for differences in the size and rate of growth of the two movements.[46]

We have emphasized how organizational structure can affect outward-reaching tactical options, but organizational structure can also influence the kind of tactical decision making that can occur within movements. For movements that are more bureaucratic and hierarchical in terms of having a well-mapped-out or formalized chain of command, or that are headed by a charismatic leader, tactical decision making is likely to be centralized and top-down. For movements that have a more collectivist, nonbureaucratic form of organization, however, tactical decision making is likely to be decentralized and much more participatory and consensus-based.[47] It is not obvious that one form of tactical decision making is better than the other. On one hand, more centralized, authoritative structures certainly are more efficient in the sense of generating faster, unambiguous tactical decisions, but on the other hand, more participatory decision making almost guarantees consideration of a broader array of tactical issues and options. It also is likely to generate more broad-based participant satisfaction. Without a doubt, however, the form of organizational tactical decision making is likely to generate considerable debate.

TACTICAL DEBATES. Internal debates that occur among movement leaders and participants about strategic considerations and tactical options comprise another constraint on developing and exercising movement strategies and associated tactics. Such debates are rarely part of the publicly visible face of movements, but they are no less critical in the determination of tactical practices than are many of the other factors. In her analysis of the aforementioned Student Nonviolent Coordinating Committee (SNCC), Francesca Polletta details the tense debates that occurred among SNCC workers in the mid-1960s over choosing the most strategically and tactically appropriate organizational form for the committee. In the first half of the 1960s, SNCC rejected hierarchies, embraced radical egalitarianism, and "strove for consensus in meetings that often went on all night." But by the middle of the decade, SNCC had become too large and diffuse to "afford the inefficiencies of consensus-based decision making and decentralized administration."[48] Debate ensued to identify the most effective form of organization and decision making for carrying out SNCC's mission in a strategically effective manner. The result was that nonhierarchical, participatory democracy was eventually jettisoned.

Tactical debates can swirl around all sorts of issues, as was made clear by the aforementioned study of the Austin, Texas, Nuclear Disarmament movement, which was rife with "frame disputes."[49] In the course of his participant observation research on the movement in the first half of the 1980s, Benford observed that there were numerous ongoing discussions and disagreements regarding the character of the problems about which the movement was concerned (diagnostic framing), the kinds of actions that the movement should pursue to remedy the problem (prognostic framing), and the ways in which these issues should be presented to prospective adherents to maximize the prospect of adherent mobilization (frame resonance). His analysis of the movement's operation revealed that these various "frame disputes" not only constituted an important aspect of the movement's internal dynamics but also affected the movement's structure, interorganizational relations, and strategic and tactical practices.

Studies like those described above are important not only because they illustrate how tactical practices can be affected by internal debates and disputes, but also because they demonstrate the active role of movement actors themselves in the process of tactical deliberation and selection.

External Constraints and Facilitators

REPERTOIRES OF CONTENTION. Whatever the mixture and relative weight of internal factors in the determination of tactical practices, external factors narrow the range of tactical possibilities. Evidence of this can be found in the clustering or patterning of tactical practices in time and cultural space, such that those tactics that were dominant in one historical period in a particular cultural context may not be dominant or selected, if at all, in another period or context. Charles Tilly coined the concept of "repertoires of contention" to capture this temporal and cultural patterning of protest tactics, thus suggesting a kind of tool kit of established "ways that people act together in pursuit of shared interests."[50]

The "tool kit" conceptualization emerged from Tilly's research on the public expression of grievances in France and Great Britain during the eighteenth and nineteenth centuries and how they differ from more recent forms of protest, which suggested to him two types of repertoires: the "old" and the "new."[51] Whereas the old repertoire included collective actions like food riots and grain seizures triggered by such quotidian disruptions as droughts, famines, and price increases, the new repertoire included what we know today as protest marches, demonstrations, and strikes. The more recent tactical actions are not only different in form, but they are also more "modular" in that they can be readily adopted and executed by movements of all kinds, usually independent of the aims and target of the movement.[52] Thus, we see the appropriation of public spaces (for example, streets, parks, and public squares) for mass marches, rallies, and demonstrations the world over, whether in Beijing in 1989 or in Eastern Europe in 1989 (see Chapter 1); in cities and towns throughout Argentina in 2001 and 2002, as thousands of citizens, principally women, massed in marches and demonstrations to protest the collapse of the Argentine economy;[53] or in Washington, D.C., in October 1997 when reportedly more than one million males gathered on the National Mall for the Christian-based Promise Keepers' "Stand in the Gap" rally,[54] which was reported to be the largest gathering of men in American history, even larger than the Million Man March of African American males in Washington, D.C., in October 1995.[55] These and countless other examples provide illustrative support for the principal repertoire thesis, which states that movement tactical actions are generally derived from and constrained by the historically current repertoire of contention.

Repertoires of contention, however, are not stable, static, or inelastic entities. They are limiting but not determinative of tactical action. This is because of at least three factors that can either precipitate the development of a new repertoire or generate novel tactical actions that are not embedded in the existing repertoire. The first and most general factor associated with repertoire change is an alteration in the broader social structure or in structures of authority. Since there appears to be a kind of "elective affinity" between forms of tactical action and societal organization—as suggested by the occurrence of peasant revolts and food riots in agrarian society, labor strikes in capitalist society, and public demonstrations in democratic societies—it follows that change in socioeconomic and political organizations is likely to open the door to new tactical options and innovations.

A second factor that can lead to tactical innovation is the emergence of new movements that bypass the existing repertoire because the conventional tactics are not suitable for pursuing its interests. A case in point is provided by some right-wing movements in the United States that are opposed to any kind of governmental intrusion into their lifeworlds, and engage in tactical actions that fall outside the now traditional street protest action repertoire. The first author conducted, with a number of former

graduate students, a study of one such anti-government movement organization and found that members were exhorted to
engage in "constitutional confrontations," entailing challenges
to existing laws and legal practices, and "registration refusals or
boycotts," which involve the refusal to heed the registration and
identification-tracking power of governments by throwing away
all varieties of identification, including one's driver's license.[56]
These two types of action indicate that not only are some movement tactical actions not embedded in the currently dominant
repertoire, but perhaps there is no one standard repertoire that
captures or subsumes all forms of tactical collective action in
relatively open democratic societies.

The third factor that can generate tactical innovations and
even refinement or enlargement of an existing repertoire is the
occurrence of technological developments that suggest new tactical possibilities. Examples of technological innovations and
developments that have affected the ways in which movements
have pursued their interests historically include the printing press, radio, television, film, e-mail, and the Internet. The
printing press, for example, played a pivotal role in the spread
of the Protestant Reformation, spearheaded by Martin Luther
beginning around 1517, by enabling and perfecting the development of the pamphlet, which Luther and his adherents used
to agitate against the Catholic Church and to offer an alternative
to Catholicism. According to one scholar writing about the link
between the printing press, propaganda, and the Reformation,

> The Reformation saw the first major, self-conscious attempt to
> use the recently invented printing press to shape and channel a
> mass movement. The printing press allowed Evangelical pub-
> licists to do what had been previously impossible, quickly and

effectively reach a large audience with a message intended to change Christianity. For several crucial years, these Evangelical publishers issued thousands of pamphlets discrediting the old faith and advocating the new.[57]

Luther and the reformists used the printing press, roughly seventy years after its invention in 1450, to spawn tactical innovations that were profoundly consequential not only for the development and spread of Protestant Reformation but also for the spread of subsequent movements.[58] Radio and television have also led to tactical refinements and innovations because they have broadened the scope and character of audiences that can witness indirectly the tactical actions of movements. As the demonstrators in the streets of Chicago chanted in 1968 at the time of the Democratic National Convention, "the whole world is watching."[59] A tactical consequence of such media coverage is that movements have become more self-consciously performative, and thus dramaturgic, in developing or fine-tuning their public tactical displays. Often, demonstrating or celebrating movements are competing with each other for media attention, which itself is a limited kind of resource. Consequently, a premium is placed on novel signage and tactical actions that can capture the camera and/or microphone, as in the case of the previously mentioned women lying on the ground naked in the rain to spell out "peace" in protest against the Iraq War.

As a final example of how tactical repertoires are vulnerable to change, consider how the relatively recent development of the Internet and e-mail has generated new tactical opportunities for participant mobilization and fund-raising and for communication in general. Some of what used to take days and weeks can now be done in minutes or less than a day. Perhaps even more noteworthy are the new forms of activism (such as hacking, strategic voting, online sit-ins, and e-mail floods) and movement organizations (such as MoveOn) that the Internet has spawned.[60] These observations suggest not only a new technologically based repertoire but also that repertories of contention do not always change so slowly or "glacially" as some scholars have argued, and that some tactical innovations are much more significant than merely "innovations at the margins" of existing repertoires.[61]

PUBLIC AND ADVERSARIAL DEFINITIONS OF MOVEMENTS. A second factor external to a movement that can also affect its tactical options is the way in which it is understood and framed by relevant publics—that is, publics for whom the movement is an object of concern and discussion—and by adversarial groups, including those who are in a position of institutional authority. The influence of publics and public opinion on the course and character of social movements was a central concern of movement scholars Ralph Turner and Lewis Killian, who argued that how a movement is viewed publicly "will have more effect than the views and tactics of typical adherents on the sources from which it can recruit adherents and accumulate resources, the type and tactics of opposition and official control with which it must cope, and the degree to which it can operate openly and through legitimate means."[62] The same can be said about how a movement is viewed by authoritative adversaries or targets. The point is that a movement's range of tactical options with respect to various sets of movement functions can be affected by how it is defined or regarded by those in position to react to it either directly, as with social control agents, or indirectly by pressuring official authorities or forming countermovements.

These suppositions are schematized in Table 5.1, which portrays, for heuristic purposes, five types of public definitions of movements, each of which can affect the kind of opposition encountered and tactical options available. Movements that are regarded as publicly respectable, such as Mothers Against Drunk Driving, can appeal for resources and recruit broadly and openly and employ a range of tactics without engendering powerful countermovements and government opposition. This is not to suggest that movements like MADD do not encounter opposition, say from anti-federalist libertarians or the alcohol industry. As long as such movements engage in legitimate movement tactics, however, they are tolerated and regarded as having the right to wage their campaign by virtue of being in a democratic society. For movements that are regarded as the carriers of a respectable challenge or claim but are factionalized, with some SMOs in the movement seen as more militant than others the idea of a "radical flank effect" suggests that public respectability and tolerance are likely to be apportioned differently, with the less militant SMO being favored.[63] The environmental movement provides an example of a factionalized movement, with some SMOs within the movement being more radical in their tactical actions than others. So while there is fairly broad-based support for the environmental movement, not all the associated SMOs are seen in the same light, with the consequence that the more radical ones, like Earth First!, are monitored more closely and given less elbowroom.

Movements that are seen as peculiar and idiosyncratic tend to be offbeat in relation to some dominant set of institutional

Table 5.1

PUBLIC/POLITICAL DEFINITIONS AND TACTICAL IMPLICATIONS

Public/Political Definition	Type of Opposition	Tactics/Means of Action	Movement Examples
Respectable-nonfactional	Disinterest to some support	Legitimate means within within repertoire	Mothers Against Drunk Driving
Respectable-factional	Disinterest to some support for more moderate faction(s)	Legitimate means within repertoire for less-threatening faction(s)	Environmental movement (Sierra Club vs. Earth First!)
Peculiar and Idiosyncratic	Ridicule and guarded interaction	Limited access to legitimate means	Hare Krishna, late 1970s
Threatening	Negative framing, close monitoring, nonviolent suppression	Limited access to legitimate means; protective, cautious measures	Hare Krishna, early 1980s
Revolutionary	Negative framing and violent repression	Driven underground; accepted in safe havens; mainly illegitimate tactics	Black Panthers, Weathermen

Adapted and modified from Turner and Killian (1987: 257).

actors and values. Within the religious arena, it is common for new religious movements to be seen as offbeat or deviant, whether they are groups that have broken away from an established tradition (sects) or are recent cultural imports sometimes framed as cults, which is as much a politically laden, derogatory label as a sociological term. During the late 1960s and the first half of the 1970s, such movement groups flowered in the United States. They included, among others, the previously mentioned saffron-robed Hare Krishna Hindu movement imported from India; the Moonies, nicknamed after their Korean leader, Reverend Sun Yung Moon, of the Unification Church; the Nichiren Shoshu Buddhist movement imported from Japan; and the Children of God, which originated in the United States. Because of being culturally imported and thus relatively foreign, or being offshoots of institutionalized Christianity and/ or blending aspects of their basic religious tenets with the so-called flower children countercultural lifestyle that germinated in the second half of the 1960s, these movements were generally seen as quite peculiar religious movements that were approached at arms length with guarded curiosity and often some disbelief.

Knowing that such a jaundiced view impeded their broader goals and recruitment efforts, some of these movements engaged in various lines of action aimed at generating a positive public image and securing expanded elbowroom in which to operate. Such was the case with the Japanese-based Nichiren Shoshu Buddhist movement that was exported to the United States in the early 1960s. As a culturally transplanted movement engaged in the business of propagating a set of beliefs and practices (for example, repetitively chanting Nam Myoho

Renge Kyo to a scroll that is believed to symbolize the most powerful object in the world) that seemed strange from the standpoint of conventional religious beliefs and practices in the United States, Nichiren Shoshu faced the problem of reducing or neutralizing the stigma attached to its peculiar practices to gain sufficient "idiosyncrasy credit" to pursue its promotion and recruitment activities. Qualitative study of the movement, involving the tracking of its history in the United States from the early 1960s to the mid-1970s, revealed that it attended to this dilemma by engaging in tactical practices suggestive of so-called dramatic ingratiation: that is, "strategically attempting to gain the favor ... of others by conducting and presenting oneself in a manner that projects an image that is reflective of fitting in and deferential regard for certain values, traditions, and proprieties perceived to be important to those whose favor is being courted."[64] More concretely, Nichiren Shoshu did this by "emphasizing that it [was] carrying out the unfinished work of America's founding fathers and early pioneers, by ... deferring to various American traditions and customs, and by actively encouraging members to become 'winners' on the job and 'model citizens'...." Through such ingratiating tactical practices, the movement can be read as having "tried to build up its credit or balance of favorable impressions so that outsiders [would] tolerate or overlook the more idiosyncratic aspects of its philosophy and ritual practices" and grant it sufficient elbow room in which to operate.[65] The fact that the movement, now called Soka Gakkai International, is still thriving in the United States and has established a university in south Orange County, California, named Soka University, suggests some measure of success and perhaps even institutionalization.

Clearly not all movements regarded as peculiar or idiosyncratic engage in such accommodating and tactically ingratiating practices, as evidenced by the changing public perception of some movements over the course of their operation, sometimes with the result that they are seen not merely as peculiar but also as threatening. The operation of the Hare Krishna movement in the United States in the late 1970s and early 1980s provides an instructive example. An in-depth ethnographic field study of the movement during this period found that the public's perception of the movement changed from an initial view of it as being peculiar to a subsequent view of it as threatening and disruptive.[66] This perceptual and definitional change did not materialize out of thin air but was attributable to the conjunction of a number of factors: the growth of the anti-cult countermovement in the mid-1970s, which sought to ban the cults and to deprogram their young adherents, especially those from middle-class families;[67] the movement's assertive recruitment and promotion practices in public places other than the streets, such as in airports and zoos; and media revelations regarding Hare Krishna members' involvement in drugs and storing of weapons.[68] Subsequent internal factionalization and conflict following the death of the movement's charismatic leader also contributed to mounting concern about the Hare Krishna movement.[69] Partly as a result of these factors, the movement's assertive recruitment and promotion tactics in public places (for example, airports, zoos, and other public areas) were increasingly regarded as a nuisance and violation of pedestrian rights, with the consequence that the movement was banned from some of these places and forced to modulate its promotional tactical practices and to begin working on its public image.

Movements like Hare Krishna that are seen as threatening generally still have sufficient elbowroom to operate publicly, albeit with some restraint and greater vigilance by the public and social control agents. Such is not the case, however, with movements that are regarded as revolutionary or terrorist, in the sense that they are perceived as seeking either to displace an existing institutional authority or to generate widespread anxiety and despair among citizens because of the apparent randomness or unpredictability of their violent actions.[70] Movements so perceived, whether rightly or wrongly, generally have limited space to operate above ground, except in relatively cloistered, safe havens. Moreover, their tactical actions are often in accord with the way in which they are perceived, which was clearly the case with the Black Panther Party and the Weatherman organization (known colloquially as the Weathermen) in the United States. The Black Panther Party was a radical African American organization that initially aimed to promote civil rights and self-defense among blacks in the United States between the mid-1960s and mid-1970s. However, their goals became increasingly sidetracked by their militaristic organization; preoccupation with the police, whom they considered to be their oppressors; and brandishing of guns and violent tactics. Their suspicions about the police were not misplaced, however, as the party became a target of the police and the FBI, with several members (including one of its leaders, in 1968) being subsequently killed in gun battles with the police.[71] The Weathermen, which overlapped with the Black Panthers, was a violent, leftist underground movement group with a strong anti–Vietnam War orientation that was born in 1969 out of fragmentation of the Students for a Democratic Society (SDS) and more or less disintegrated in the mid-1970s following the U.S. withdrawal from Vietnam in 1973 and communist North Vietnam's takeover of South Vietnam in 1975. Believing that it was time to move beyond nonviolent anti-war protests, the Weathermen advocated more dramatic, violent actions and engaged in or planned a series of bombings of government buildings, including the plan in 1970 to bomb a U.S. military noncommissioned officers' dance at Fort Dix, New Jersey. Around this time, the Weathermen released its Declaration of a State of War against the U.S. government and changed its name to the Weather Underground Organization.[72]

We see in both cases that increasing friction with the police and a corresponding resorting to violence make violent tactics a kind of self-fulfilling prophecy, with both sides of the conflict identifying each other as combatants and the enemy. We also see, just as with the Nichiren Shoshu and Hare Krishna movements, changes in tactical practices over the life span of the respective movements, thus indicating that movement tactics are not static or etched in stone but change and evolve with changes in the contexts in which movements are embedded.

STYLES OF PROTEST POLICING AND PUBLIC ORDER MANAGEMENT SYSTEMS.   Another external constraint on movement tactical options is the role of formal social control agents who bear primary responsibility for policing public protest. We have already alluded to the role of the police in relation to tactical action for some of the movements mentioned above. Here we briefly explore that interaction in a more general context.

Research on protest policing in Western democracies reveals that historically, policing practices have tended to cluster into two styles: "'hard' police styles, characterized by an escalated use of force in order to implement law and order (with low respect for demonstrators' rights) versus 'soft' polices styles, where negotiations (and protest rights) prevail."[73] Examples of well-known protest demonstrations in the United States in which the escalated-force approach was dominant include "the Birmingham civil rights campaign (May 1963), the 1968 Chicago Democratic convention, and the confrontation between student protestors and National Guard soldiers at Kent State University (May 1970)."[74] In these demonstrations as well as others during the 1960s and first half of the 1970s, force was used to control and disperse protestors. Under the negotiated approach, which began to prevail in the 1980s, police and protestors negotiated in advance of the demonstration to establish ground rules toward the goal of minimizing conflict. Demonstrations occurring under this protest policing style "include thousands each year in Washington, D.C., such as the annual March for Life, the 1993 Lesbian, Gay, and Bisexual March, and the 1995 Million Man March."[75]

The importance of the above-described protest policing styles for movement tactical action is the implication that different protest behaviors may have different consequences. This hypothesis is especially true under the negotiated regime wherein acceptable tactical behaviors are negotiated in advance, thus reducing the likelihood of some protest actions because they would incur greater risks and costs. This does not mean that all movements in the United States negotiate aspects of their demonstrations in advance with some set of social control agents. Sometimes the negotiation mandate is bypassed, which increases the likelihood of conflict and skirmishes between the protesters and the police once the demonstration unfolds. In most cities, small protest marches and demonstrations can be conducted on sidewalks in the absence of prior negotiation and police permits as long as pedestrian traffic is not obstructed. In April 2008, for example, the first author observed an anti-Scientology demonstration (called Operation Reconnect) along both sides of Hollywood Boulevard in Los Angeles. There were a hundred masked demonstrators on the sidewalks on each side of the street carrying signs—such as, "Your mom still loves you! Call Her!" and "Let them speak!"—and chanting "Reconnect!" Throughout the demonstration, protest leaders would yell out to participants to remind them not to block the sidewalk and to let pedestrians through. Two observant police officers confirmed that the non-permitted march was fine as long as it did not impede vehicular and pedestrian traffic.

Such incidents of nonnegotiated movement demonstrations notwithstanding, the general trend in the United States and Europe is toward the development of some kind of public order management system in which protest demonstrations become increasingly standardized and conventionalized, thus reducing the likelihood of strikingly novel and newsworthy tactical innovations.[76]

Tactical Interaction

We have discussed and illustrated three sets each of internal and external constraints on and facilitators of movement tactical options and selection. Throughout the discussion, we have implied or suggested, consistent with the orientation of this chapter, that movement tactical practices are the product of dynamic interaction between various factors both internal and external to any particular movement, and that, therefore, a movement's tactical options and selection cannot be understood apart from these various interactions. To make this point even more clearly, we turn to Doug McAdam's examination of the interactive dynamics that gave rise to new protest tactics, or, what he called "tactical innovation," during the course of the civil rights movement between 1955 and 1979.[77] He found that tactical innovation during this period was largely a function of a tactical chess match involving an interactive process of tactical innovation and adaptation on behalf of the challengers and opponents. As he explains:

> Lacking institutional power, challengers must devise protest techniques that offset their powerlessness. This [can be] referred to as the process of *tactical innovation*. Such innovations, however, only temporarily afford challengers increased bargaining leverage. In chesslike fashion, movement opponents can be expected, through effective *tactical adaptation*, to neutralize the new tactic, thereby reinstituting the original power disparity between themselves and the challenger. To succeed over time, then, a challenger must continue to search for new and effective tactical forms.[78]

Consistent with the principle of interactive determination sketched at the beginning of the present chapter, McAdam's study shows clearly how the actions of movements elicit or provoke responses by external groupings that, in turn, require both strategic and tactical adjustments on behalf of the movements themselves. More generally, this study and the others referenced in this section indicate that the character of a movement's tactical actions is strongly affected by interactions with external sets of actors, such as public and social control agents, with cultural repertoires, and among its own adherents.

DYNAMICS OF DIFFUSION AND SPILLOVER

During the late 1970s, students in the United States began protesting, demonstrating, signing petitions, building blockades, staging sit-ins, building shantytowns, and participating in a movement designed to encourage pension funds, insurance companies, and other organizations to disinvest their South Africa–related securities. This movement, known to most as the student divestment movement, had its roots in earlier student anti-apartheid activism, which began after the Sharpeville Massacre of 1960 in South Africa but fluctuated throughout the 1960s and 1970s, only to rise again in the 1980s.[79]

In the 1980s, students in the United States turned their attention to their own campuses and built shantytowns (or, shanties) to protest their own colleges' and universities' investments in companies doing business in South Africa. Shantytowns were shacks constructed of various building materials (for example, wood, plastic, cardboard, tar paper, and metal), which were built to encourage administrators to reduce or eliminate their capital investment in South Africa–related securities. In many cases, students lived in the shanties, which worried administrators at universities and colleges because of the potential for physical harm of the student activists. From Cornell University to the University of Vermont, UCLA to Middlebury College, the University of Tennessee to New York University, the shantytown tactic diffused across college campuses.[80] At many universities, students had been fighting for divestment for years but did not mobilize large support until the shantytowns were built and until they began to spread. Between 1985 and 1989, forty-six different colleges and universities had shantytowns, with most of them constructed in 1985 and 1986.[81]

Sarah Soule studied the diffusion of shantytowns across campuses, finding that they spread among similar kinds of colleges and universities. Her analysis showed that this innovative protest tactic spread predominantly among liberal arts colleges and research universities. She also found that repressive events, such as when conservative students at Dartmouth College vandalized the shantytown on that campus or when campus police tore down the one at Cornell University, galvanized the movement and sparked diffusion.[82]

The term *diffusion,* as it is used by social movement scholars, refers to the spread or flow of some innovation through direct or indirect channels, across actors in a social system. Diffusion of protest implies that social protest (or some element thereof, such as the shantytown tactic or a collective action frame) is spreading across some set of actors in a social system.[83]

Early treatments of diffusion, like much of social science prior to the 1960s, were framed by an interest in psychology. As such, they tended to view diffusion as motivated by contagion between individuals in groups or crowds—for example, when individuals react to stimuli from others. Maladaptive and aggressive impulses were to be feared, since they were thought to spread from person to person and drive collective action with deleterious consequences. For example, observers of race riots, lynching, Nazism, fascism, McCarthyism, and Stalinism viewed individuals as somehow susceptible to the diffusion of negative influences driving these forms of collective behavior.[84]

With the development of the resource mobilization perspective in the 1970s and its focus on social movement organizations, social movement scholars began to think about diffusion as a function of the connections between different organizations and different individuals, through their organizational memberships. For example, observing the wave of sit-ins that appeared to spread almost spontaneously across the South in the late 1950s and early 1960s, Aldon Morris noted that the spread was actually highly structured and deliberate.[85] He documented the way in which preexisting network connections, structured by student organizations, sporting events, and church groups, facilitated the spread of information about the sit-ins and how this information led students in various locales to stage their own sit-ins. More recently, Kenneth Andrews and Michael Biggs have shown that social movement organizations especially CORE (Congress of Racial Equality), were instrumental in coordinating this wave of sit-ins.[86]

Similar to the above-described treatments of sit-ins, recent studies of the diffusion of social movements recognize that the connections between organizations (movement and other types) facilitate the spread of information across organizational boundaries. As well, movements and movement organizations often overlap, leading to a web of connections between actors and social movement organizations. This web of connections between different movements and movement organizations facilitates the spillover of personnel, ideas, frames, movement cultures, and tactics. Such spillover is clearly illustrated by David Meyer and Nancy Whittier's examination of how the U.S. peace movement in the 1980s borrowed and learned from the feminist movement. They show, for example, that tactical innovations, such as theatrical tactics and peace camps at military bases, spilled over from the feminist movement to the peace movement, and they describe the way in which ideas regarding the connection between militarism and patriarchy spread to the peace movement from the feminist movement.[87] Recent research on the diffusion of protest has gone beyond merely noting the existence of diffusion and has instead tried to better specify the mechanisms by which an innovation diffuses. There are two broad categories of diffusion studies: those that focus on how *direct network channels* facilitate diffusion and those that focus on how *indirect channels* facilitate diffusion.

Direct channels are interpersonal ties, which allow for the easy spread of some item through some form of communication. Sidney Tarrow refers to diffusion via interpersonal connections as "relational diffusion."[88] While many scholars have pointed to the diffusion of the sit-in protest tactics during the civil rights movement as an example of the strength and importance of interpersonal ties to social movements, the aforementioned study by Andrews and Biggs discounts the importance of social networks. They do find, however, that organizations were important to facilitating the diffusion of sit-ins.

More recently, the use of e-mail allows for the very rapid communication of information regarding a protest, campaign, or frame. For example, the Free Burma Coalition (FBC) began primarily as an Internet organization.[89] In fact, the FBC was nothing more than a Web site for a while, combining an e-mail listserv, educational materials about human rights abuses in Burma, and materials (for example, posters, stickers, and leaflets) for organizers on campuses and nationwide. Such a medium facilitates the flow of information between individuals who know each other (or at least belong to the same listservs, chat rooms, and so forth), but as this case illustrates, it also allows for an inexpensive way to reach a mass audience.

Indirect channels are also important to the spread of protest. One form of indirect channel is the mass media, which is often implicated in facilitating the spread of protest. Tarrow refers to this kind of diffusion as "nonrelational diffusion" since, in the case of the media, there is no need for direct or interpersonal connections between individuals.[90] Noting that the urban riots of the late 1960s appeared to cluster in time, Seymour Spilerman hypothesized that riots diffused throughout urban, black areas and were facilitated by television coverage of civil rights activism, which helped create solidarity that went beyond the direct ties of community.[91] To Spilerman, then, the media served as an indirect channel of diffusion by creating a cultural linkage between African Americans in different metropolitan areas. Television, he argued, familiarized individuals all over the country with the details of riots and with the reasons that individuals participated in riots. Similarly, Andrews and Biggs show that the news media were crucial for conveying information about the 1960s sit-ins to students throughout the South and thus were facilitative of the diffusion of the sit-ins.

Of course, in any given instance of diffusion, we can often identify both direct and indirect routes. For example, when considering the diffusion of a strategy of nonviolence from colonial India to the United States during the civil rights movement, Tarrow, drawing on the research of Sean Chabot, identifies Indian exiles, African American theologians, and religious pacifists who spread the word about nonviolence directly to their associates. He also describes the way in which nonviolence was promoted in African American writings and newspapers at the time.[92]

Whether diffusion occurs through direct or indirect channels, the process is not always a straightforward one wherein the
transmitters of the object of diffusion and the adopters share a
mutual understanding.[93] Instead, it is a highly interactive process that can take different forms depending on various characteristics of the two sets of actors, including their relative interest
in the object of diffusion. Such differences can lead to different
types of diffusion processes. In their analysis of cross-national
diffusion in relation to social movements, Snow and Benford
identified four types of social movement diffusion processes
based on whether both object transmitters and adopters are actively or passively engaged in the process.[94] Table 5.2 shows the
different diffusion processes that result when transmitters' and
adopters' orientations are cross-classified according to their level
of engagement in the process. The first cell captures the diffusion process in which both the transmitters and adopters are interested in the object of diffusion and therefore are reciprocally
engaged in the process. The diffusion of the shanty, as a potent
symbol of the South African anti-apartheid movement, across

Table 5.2

TYPES OF SOCIAL MOVEMENT DIFFUSION PROCESSES

Adopter/Importer	Transmitter/Exporter	
	Active	Passive
Active	(1) Reciprocation	(2) Adaptation
Passive	(3) Accommodation	(4) Contagion?

Adapted from Snow and Benford (1999)

U.S. campuses as described earlier is illustrative of this diffusion pattern.

The second cell encompasses the diffusion process in which there is intentional cultural borrowing, such that the adopter, or importer, is an active agent in the process, strategically selecting and adopting the borrowed elements to fit with his culture. In this pattern, there is no deliberate transmission by an exporting agent or reciprocal diffusion. Instead, this adaptive pattern involves the strategic appropriation of specific foreign elements that are adopted in a fashion congruent with cultural values, beliefs, or practices. The previously discussed 1989 Chinese student democracy movement illustrates this adaptive process. Its students selectively imported a few Western movement tactics, slogans, and symbols—the hunger strike, the "Goddess of Democracy" statue, and numerous pro-democracy slogans and framings—and modified them to serve their own interests, in alignment with Chinese cultural narrations, experiences, and accepted forms of protest.[95] In the case of the hunger strike, for example, observers noted that it had been used before but was not a major tactic in the Chinese repertoire until 1980, and that it was probably borrowed from contemporary Western movements.[96] Whatever the exact foreign influences on students' adoption of this tactic, it is clear that students framed it in concert with Confucian moralism and traditional Chinese values.

In the third cell, which encompasses an accommodative diffusion pattern, the transmitter is actively engaged in the spread and promotion of a relatively alien practice and set of corroborating ideas. Not only does interest have to be generated or nurtured in the targeted population or culture, but the ideas and practices have to be fitted to the host culture to enhance the prospect of resonance. Illustrative of this accommodative process is the case of the Nichiren Shoshu Buddhist movement discussed earlier.

In the fourth cell we have the contagion model of diffusion, wherein some idea, behavior, or mood is diffused in the absence of an active agent on one or both sides of the process. While such contagion has been hypothesized to account for the spread of fads and perhaps other forms of collective behavior, there is little empirical demonstration of its occurrence in diffusion processes in the context of social movements.[97] Instead, the preponderance of research indicates that the diffusion of movement symbols, whether material or discursive, or movement practices or tactics is an actor-based or agency-driven process.

Chapter Summary

In this chapter, we have examined the dynamics of social movements by focusing on three key overlapping aspects of movement dynamics: the functioning of social movement organizations within the organizational fields in which they operate, movement strategies and tactics, and diffusion processes. Our examination of movement dynamics via these three focal aspects of movement functioning suggests two general conclusions regarding movement dynamics. First, consistent with the principle of interactive determination discussed at the outset of the chapter, the course and character of a movement once it is up and running can be fully understood only if examined in terms of four levels of interaction: those interactions that occur internally as with decision making and frames disputes; those that occur between movements and other sets of actors within their organizational fields—such as social control agents, targets, the public, and countermovements—for which the movement constitutes an object of orientation; those that occur between movements and their cultural contexts; and those interactions that result because of the dynamic interplay between the internal and external forces and tensions. Taken together, these observations hold that movements qua movements are constituted through ongoing internal and external interactions and the challenge of resolving the tensions that arise because of these interactions.

Second, this chapter also accents the agency-based character of the operation and functioning of social movements. This is not to suggest that movement organizations and their leaders and adherents construct their lines of action independent of the forces around them and the contexts in which they are embedded. Rather, to accent the agentic character of movements is to note that contextual forces and factors are taken into account by movements in constructing their lines of action. Some forces, such as full-blown repression, may be weightier than other contextual factors, but repression, whatever its forms, is not fully determinative of movement action as various kinds of adaptations can be made, as we saw in the preceding pages and in Chapter 3.

That agency-based action should be a characteristic feature of movement dynamics should not be too surprising. After all, it is arguable that few, if any, social contexts are as generative or nurturant of agentic behavior as those commonly associated with social movement activity. To put it more concretely, when taken-for-granted or routinized social life is disrupted, when goal-orientated action is thwarted, when self-identities or collective identities are debased or contradicted, and when a group's treatment and opportunities are seen as injustices, then the issue of agency is especially likely to vault to the foreground as individuals engage in various forms of action aimed at remedying the situation in some fashion or at least retaliating against its presumed perpetrators. On some occasions, the action is individualized in the sense of involving little if any coordination, as in the case of the various forms of indirect, seemingly disconnected resistance behaviors noted in Chapter 1; on other occasions, the action is collective, as when individuals mobilize jointly to press their claims. In either case, agentic action is in the foreground rather than background of the dynamic functioning of social movements.

Chapter Six
CONSEQUENCES OF SOCIAL MOVEMENTS

WE ARGUED IN CHAPTER 1 that a key element of social movements is that they target existing systems of authority. Systems of authority may best be thought of as any structure or system that has influence over citizens or certain groups of citizens. The most obvious system of authority is the state and its agents, but cultural understandings can also wield authority over individuals, as can private, nonprofit, and nongovernmental organizations, and religious denominations. Whether the system of authority is located in the political realm (for example, the state and it agents) or someplace else, social movements almost always target at least one system of authority with their actions.

When women in the United States mobilized during the mid-1800s in favor of their right to vote, they targeted both their state governments and the federal government to encourage the passage and ratification of the Nineteenth Amendment to the United States Constitution. They were also challenging prevailing cultural understandings of the appropriate role of women, which at the time held that women should be confined to the private sphere of the home, engaged in domestic duties, such as child rearing. While the women's suffrage movement had its roots in colonial America, it was not until 1848, when the Seneca Falls Convention was held in the state of New York, that the movement began to take hold. In attendance at the convention were such suffrage activists as Elizabeth Cady Stanton, Lucretia Mott, and Susan B. Anthony, who helped frame the arguments that suffragists would use throughout their seventy-year struggle for the right to vote. Chief among these arguments was the injustice of the fact that the Fourteenth and Fifteenth Amendments to the U.S. Constitution provided African Americans with the right to vote, yet women were still denied that right.[1] Scholarship on the movement points to the success of framing a woman's right to vote in terms of the unique (and gendered) contributions that women make to the political sphere. That is, the broader public and the politicians were more open to arguments about how women, because of their gender, should be allowed to vote because they would offer a distinctive female perspective on political issues, such as war and temperance.[2] It seems strange today to think of it as inappropriate for women to enter the public sphere of politics, but suffragists needed to challenge such deeply held beliefs and attitudes to convince lawmakers to support women's right to vote. In 1920, the Nineteenth Amendment was ratified and American women were finally allowed to vote; the movement had succeeded.

Somewhat implicit in the discussion of the suffrage movement and in our broader discussion of systems of authority is the idea that movements, when making claims against (or in defense of) a particular system of authority, articulate more or less coherent goals. To be sure, some movements are very clear about a particular specific goal, such as in our example of students at the University of California, Irvine, who attempted to halt the demolition of a source of affordable housing near campus or when students at the University of Arizona in October 2003 protested the re-naming of a campus building after César

Chávez. But this is not always the case. Many movements articulate multiple goals, targeting multiple systems of authority, some of which are short-range and some of which may reach far into the future. For example, while the members of the current Lesbian, Gay, Bisexual and Transgender (LGBT) movement may be active in trying to block same-sex marriage bans (a goal that suggests targeting the state, at least some of the time), they also attempt to favorably alter public opinion on same-sex marriage (a goal that suggests challenging cultural perceptions of these groups). Targeting the state in a very specific campaign to block a potential ban on same-sex marriage can be thought of as an immediate or short-term goal, while challenging the prevailing cultural perceptions of LGBT people may be a much farther-reaching, long-term goal. Finally, on top of targeting the state, some specific LGBT movement organizations also attempt to increase solidarity and collective identity among their members; in other words, they target their own organizations and members.[3] When we think about movement goals, it is important to recognize that movements and their organizations often articulate multiple goals that may differ on the level of immediacy and may target different systems of authority.

When we begin to think about "targets" and "goals" of social movements, it is logical also to think about "outcomes" of social movements, as the three concepts are intricately linked. If we are interested in ascertaining whether a particular movement has reached its goals, one place to start would be to examine changes in the targeted system of authority following the movement's emergence and/or specific activities. It would be a fallacy, however, to argue that the only outcomes of social movements are those concessions granted by systems of authority. Instead, outcomes of social movements may better be conceptualized as "consequences," since (as will become clear below) movements often have important consequences that are not tightly coupled with their articulated goals or even their specified target(s).[4] Thus, we begin by discussing two dimensions of movement consequences that are useful as we try to think best about movements and their impacts: intended versus unintended and internal versus external movement consequences.

Conceptualizing Social Movement Consequences

Given that social movements almost always articulate a target (or set of targets) of their actions, it seems reasonable to wonder if the target(s) granted any sort of concession to the movement in question. Did the University of California, Irvine, halt their razing of the near-campus trailer park in 2004, and, if so, did they do so in response to the student protest? Did states ratify the Equal Rights Amendment in the 1970s in response to feminist movement activity? Has public opinion regarding the issue of same-sex marriage changed as a result of LGBT activism? When a system of authority responds positively to a social movement, we consider the outcome to be *intended.*

It is important to note that beyond the attainment of any stated goals of a movement, social movements can have profound *unintended* effects on entities beyond those that they target directly. For example, the organization of the feminist movement in the United States during the late 1960s and early 1970s may, at least in part, be due to the civil rights movement. When considering the effects of the civil rights movement, it is important to emphasize that the master frame of "rights," coupled with interpersonal networks forged in the civil rights movement, facilitated the growth of the wave of feminist activity during the 1960s and 1970s.[5] Similarly, we might argue that an unintended consequence of the Beijing student movement of 1989 was the brutal repression of students in Tiananmen Square in May of that year, as it is difficult to conceive of those student activists wishing for the treatment they received at the hands of the state.[6]

In addition to intended and unintended types of consequences, it is important to recognize that consequences can be primarily internal to the social movement or external to the movement. Implicit in our earlier discussion of systems of authority is that these are often situated externally to a social movement. When students protest at a university about a university issue, they are targeting a system of authority that is external to them. While, obviously, they are part of the organization of the university, students do not typically control the policies and procedures of that university. Thus, any concessions to a social movement that policymakers at the university may make may be thought of as "external consequences" of movement activity.

Of course, sometimes social movement actions directly affect the movement itself; such consequences may be considered internal. Certain types of activities practiced by social movements and directed at a system of authority can also affect the group dynamics of the collectivity. For example, sit-ins and encampments can be effective at bringing about policy change, but they can also serve to increase levels of commitment and solidarity among participants because of the intense and prolonged levels of face-to-face interaction involved in these tactics.[7] Sometimes intense and prolonged interaction can lead to disagreements and disputes, which can be detrimental to the survival or health of a movement organization. For example, the 1969 national convention of the Students for a Democratic Society (SDS) was characterized by a great deal of fragmentation and acrimonious disagreement among the various factions vying for power. Following this meeting, the group disintegrated.[8] In this case, the outcome of years of intense interaction was the death of the organization, yet it is important to note that from the ashes of SDS came the Revolutionary Youth Movement (RYM) and eventually the Weatherman organization (also known as the Weathermen and the Weather Underground); it was a far more radical organization than SDS and took credit for several bombings of federal buildings and banks in 1970 and riots ("Days of Rage") in 1969.[9]

In light of these considerations, it is conceptually useful to cross-classify these two dimensions—intended versus unintended and internal versus external—into four broad types of social movement outcomes, or consequences as shown in Table 6.1.

INTENDED INTERNAL CONSEQUENCES. The first cell concerns the work that movements often to do to affect personal transformation of their recruits or adherents, to increase participant solidarity and commitment, and to forge a collective identity among group members. For example, the therapeutic and quasi-religious self-help movements that flourished in the United States during the 1970s and 1980s, such as Transcendental Meditation, Erhard Seminars Training (also known by its lower-case acronym, est), and Scientology sought to change the habits or characteristics of individual participants, presumably to make them better-functioning or more self-actualized individuals.[10] Religious movements also generally emphasize personal transformation and/or righteousness—but usually as a means to another end, such as eternal salvation, the

Table 6.1

TYPES OF POSSIBLE MOVEMENT CONSEQUENCES

	Consequences Internal to Movement	Consequences External to Movement
Intended Consequence	(1) Intended Internal Consequences (e.g., Consciousness Raising)	(3) Intended External Consequences (e.g., Desired Policy Passed)
Unintended Consequence	(2) Unintended Internal Consequences (e.g., Disputes and Schism)	(4) Unintended External Consequence (e.g., Countermovement and Repression)

attainment of some elevated state of being, such as enlighten-
ment, or even societal transformation. As noted earlier, a large
number of religious movements that flowered in much of the
Western world in the 1970s—such as the Hare Krishna movement,[11] the Moonies, or Unification Church,[12] and the Nichiren
Shoshu Buddhist movement[13]—posited personal transformation
as the key to societal transformation All of these movements are
still active in varying degrees, and they still claim to be interested in transforming the world by bringing about the personal
transformation of their adherents.

Equally important as fostering personal transformation is
maintaining that change and the corresponding commitment to
the group or movement. For some movements, this means that
considerable attention is devoted to sustaining membership
commitment. As we learned in our discussion of commitment
in Chapter 4, this is what Rosabeth Kanter found in her study
of the temporal durability of nineteenth-century separatist utopian communes, all of which were self-sustaining communities

in which relations among members were centrally controlled, and many of which were religiously inspired, like the Oneida community in the northeast, which projected itself as a stellar example of the kingdom of heaven on earth.[14]

Participant commitment to the cause or group is often an equally important consequence of more politically oriented movements. A study of the student anti-apartheid movement at Columbia University in the 1980s, for example, describes the ways that leaders of that movement devoted energies to the education of potential activists—fostering "havens" for ample discussion about the issues of racism and apartheid—and allowed for decision making through consensus. While their chief goal was to get Columbia to divest itself of its South Africa–related stocks and bonds, a secondary goal became maintaining the energy level and managing the emotions of activists during the three-week-long blockade of the administration building on that campus in April 1985.[15]

UNINTENDED INTERNAL CONSEQUENCES. Just as movements often focus on the important task of building solidarity and commitment, there can also be unintended internal consequences, as depicted in the second cell in Table 6.1. Social movements, as we noted in Chapter 1, are collective enterprises and, as such, are composed of people who have come together for a particular reason, presumably to mount a challenge against some system of authority. However, reasonable people can disagree on the strategies and tactics for mounting such a challenge. Or they can disagree on how the issue should be framed, resulting in "frame disputes."[16] Sometimes such disagreements, when particularly acrimonious, can lead to the dissolution of a social movement organization; at other times, factions may defect from the entrenched organization and start a new one more closely aligned with their ideals. Long-standing examples of such schisms include the proliferation of religious sectarian movements, with the history of Christianity providing a plethora of illustrations. These include its fractious birth from the womb of Judaism, the Reformation and the subsequent evolution of various protestant denominations, including Lutheran, Methodist, and Presbyterian, along with more recent divisions within the Baptist church and current potentially schismatic frame disputes among the evangelical Christian right over the environment, the poor, and wealth.[17]

INTENDED EXTERNAL CONSEQUENCES. The third cell includes the consequences that movements explicitly fight for that are external to the movement. One example of an intended external consequence was the successful mobilization in favor of state bans on same-sex marriages. The National Gay and Lesbian Task Force, a pro-LGBT organization, reports that in November of 2004, thirty-three states had statutes banning same-sex marriages. Research by Sarah Soule has shown that conservative interest group mobilization in these states was influential in getting these statutes passed but that pro-LGBT mobilization was successful in slowing the rate of passage of these statutes, and in some cases halting the passage of a statute.[18] In other words, there is evidence that social movements and interest groups on both sides of the issue have been influential to state legislators grappling with the issue of same-sex marriage bans.

Edwin Amenta's research on the Townsend movement provides further illustration of intended external consequences. The

Townsend movement originated in the wake of the Great Depression in the 1930s. It was spearheaded by an elderly Long Beach, California, physician named Francis E. Townsend, who proposed that the government provide all Americans over the age of sixty with a retirement stipend of $200 per month. The movement, or Plan as it was called, managed to recruit and organize some two million older Americans into Townsend clubs, which, among other things, pushed for government approval of the recommended pension plan. Although the movement failed to secure government support, Amenta argues that it did lay the groundwork for the development of Social Security.[19]

But social movements do more than try to influence legislators on policy issues. Social movements also sometimes attempt to obtain acceptance or to formally participate in the policy process. For example, some of the homeless activists studied by Cress and Snow were invited to serve on the boards of homeless service providers, and others were given positions on city task forces designed to address issues central to homeless persons.[20] By seeking formal seats on decision-making boards, activists may be allowed to influence the policy process from within. Cress and Snow refer to this kind of external consequence as *representation*. In addition to obtaining a voice on policy matters, homeless activists also sought resources, such as money, office space, and supplies. Such *material concessions* are another form of external consequence of social movements.

UNINTENDED EXTERNAL CONSEQUENCES.   The fourth cell of Table 6.1 includes unintended external consequences, such as when a countermovement develops in response to a particular social movement. Social movements—because they often address controversial issues regarding the distribution of income, wealth, status, and opportunity in society—frequently spawn countermovements, which mobilize to counter the desired effects of an existing social movement. Examples include the mobilization of social movement groups devoted to the anti-abortion/pro-life cause, which developed after pro-abortion/pro-choice groups began to mobilize to liberalize state and federal laws on abortion. We often think of countermovement groups as a form of backlash against social movements and gains thereof. However, it is important to note that movements influence the development and growth of other movements to which they are not necessarily opposed. For example, "social movement spillover" occurs when movement ideas, personnel, tactics, and frames of one movement are adopted by different social movements.[21] As we discussed earlier, one consequence of the civil rights movement was that it helped mobilize the wave of feminist activity during the late 1960s and early 1970s that in turn may have influenced the development and trajectory of peace activism in the United States.

These four types of movement consequences are helpful in thinking about the variety of effects that social movements may have on systems of authority. But as we conceptualize movement outcomes, it is also important to consider in more detail the targets of social movements, which are usually associated with a system of authority.

Systems of Authority and Movement Consequences

We noted above that most systems of authority are situated externally to social movements. Certainly the most commonly studied targeted system of authority is the state and its many agents, with much of the research on movement consequences focusing on how states react to movements. For example, social movement scholarship has examined the effects of social movements on the Equal Rights Amendment,[22] suffrage legislation,[23] hate crime law,[24] sodomy laws,[25] and various forms of state social spending.[26] All of these are areas around which movements have mobilized in an attempt to get states to pass (or repeal) legislation.

In his well-known study of movement outcomes, William Gamson (1975) argued that two key types of response are *acceptance* and *new advantages*. Acceptance implies that members of the movement are accepted by their targets as legitimate. In practice, this might mean, for example, that movement members are invited to testify during hearings on a particular bill of interest or simply that policy makers take seriously the activities of a social movement. New advantages are those collective benefits that the movement is able to obtain for its members and constituents.[27]

Cross-classifying acceptance and new advantages according to the level of each, Gamson identified four types of state-related outcomes of social movements. First, movements can be met with *full response*, when their targets both accept them as legitimate claimants and provide them concessions and benefits for their constituents. Second, movements can be *preempted* by the state, when some benefits are provided before the movement is actually able to mobilize. Third, the movement can be *co-opted* by the state, when members of the movement are accepted by their targets, but the targets refuse to provide any concessions. Finally, movements can *collapse* when they are provided no new advantages and fail to be accepted by their targets.

One factor that can sometimes lead to collapse of a social movement is repression, such as when states effectively quell a social movement via various forms of repression (including policing of protest). Repression, which we discussed in some detail in Chapter 3, can sometimes effectively stop social movement activists from mobilizing because it can increase the costs and risks associated with protest, thus serving as an effective deterrent of protest. For example, in response to student activism associated with the New Left movement of the late 1960s and early 1970s, the U.S. government implemented a variety of forms of repression. Ranging from investigations by the Justice Department and the FBI, to anti-riot legislation, to brutal forms of policing of protest, repression of the New Left, was, by many accounts, effective at squelching dissent. This is particularly true of the Black Panthers, which was ardently and effectively repressed by the state.[28]

Despite these findings, considerable research has shown (see Chapter 3) that repression does not always serve as a deterrent to mobilization and, instead, can spark future mobilization.[29] Repression can increase the solidarity of movement groups, such as what happened when student anti-apartheid leaders at Columbia were sent letters from the administration threatening expulsion. Rather than ceasing the protest, leaders and activists alike renewed their commitment to their cause and refused to attend disciplinary hearings.[30] Or, when repression is seen as unwarranted or extreme by the broader public, sympathizers can often infuse movement groups with resources, thus increasing the potential for mobilization and decreasing the legitimacy of the repressing agents. This was the case during the many critical events of the civil rights movement, such as those in Birmingham, Alabama, when police officers led by "Bull" Connor routinely used fire hoses and German shepherds to squelch protesters in the 1960s. The media images of the arguably overblown and illegitimate use of repression in Birmingham helped galvanize support for the movement.

Existing research on the precise nature of how repression influences subsequent mobilization has produced mixed findings. This is because the relationship between repression and mobilization is highly conditional and depends on a host of factors, such as the severity of the repression, the characteristics of the protesters, the character of the political opportunity structure, and the length of time between repression and subsequent mobilization.[31]

Thus far in this chapter, our discussion has centered on the most commonly challenged system of authority, the state. Movement actors, however, frequently challenge organizations in which they are embedded.[32] We noted above the example of students at the University of California, Irvine, and at the University of Arizona protesting various administrative decisions and activities. Other examples include student protest around the recycling and divestment policies of universities, as well as the establishment of ethnic and women's studies departments.[33] Illustrative of the latter is Rojas's study of the effects of African American student protest on the creation of African American studies departments at colleges and universities.[34] He found that nondisruptive protest was more effective than violent protest, because sympathetic administrators were better able to work toward change when student activists were seen as more reasoned. More recently, students have organized to encourage their universities to require vendors of sporting and university logo apparel to follow anti-sweatshop guidelines. Duke University was one of the first universities to be targeted by the United Students Against Sweatshops (USAS), which established their own set of anti-sweatshop guidelines designed to ensure that university apparel was made by people earning a living wage in factories with decent working conditions.[35]

While the above-described examples all focus on movements within colleges or universities, other scholars have examined employee activism associated with a number of issue areas (for example, diversity, women's, and lesbian/gay issues) in firms.[36] For example, in the 1991–1999 period, eighty-three Fortune 1000 firms adopted policies of providing benefits for domestic partners of gay and lesbian employees in large part because of gay and lesbian activism.[37] Research on protest directed at publicly traded firms shows that protest decreases the stock price of these firms, something that should capture the attention of corporate leaders.[38] As well, research shows that social movement activities can lead to the development of alternative organizational forms, such as cooperatives and mutuals in several different industries, and can lead to the development of alternative energies, such as wind power.[39]

In addition to systems of authority that are located in the political and organizational realms, some systems of authority are more culturally based and, as such, are also frequently targeted by social movements. One example of cultural outcomes sought by social movements is women campaigning for the right to priesthood in the Catholic Church and for ordination in other religious traditions. In both instances, the challenge is to the cultural authority embodied in the traditions of these religious institutions.[40] Research also has shown that social movements in faith-based institutions may target these institutions for changes in the kinds of services they provide (for example, adoption of Sunday schools, youth groups, and gospel choirs).[41] Another element of the cultural system of authority that is often targeted by social movements is made up of the broader values held by citizens and is often measured by public opinion on various issues.[42]

Cultural practices of organizations and/or the broader society comprise another element of the system of cultural authority. Music is one area of cultural practice that has been affected by social movement activity, as when movements have been instrumental in the creation of new genres of music.[43] For example, VH1 periodically ranks songs with political messages, calling their resulting list the "Top 10 Protest Songs of All Times." Wikipedia, the online free encyclopedia, includes an entry on "protest songs," which lists hundreds of popular (and not so popular) songs that have political messages, sorted by issue area (for example, Abortion, American, War, Terrorism, Slavery, Civil Rights, and so on). The site even includes a subheading for "Protest Songs about Protest Songs."[44]

In addition to influencing music, social movements are capable of influencing literature, as shown in a study of representation of African Americans in children's books. The study shows that representations of African Americans in children's books waxed and waned with levels of civil rights–related protest and violence.[45] When civil rights protest and violence was especially pronounced, book publishers shied away from books portraying African Americans in an effort to not alienate white consumers.

PERSONAL AND BIOGRAPHICAL CONSEQUENCES OF
MOVEMENT ACTIVITY

While many consequences of movement activity are related to external systems of authority or affect the internal dynamics of the movement itself, there are consequences (both intended and unintended) that affect movement participants themselves. Personal and biographical consequences are the effects on the life course of individuals who have participated in movement activities—effects that are at least in part due to involvement in those activities. For example, questioning participants in the 1989 student movement in Beijing might show that these participants' lives have been affected by their participation, more so than other experiences that they have had. In fact, many scholars have attempted to question past activists and compare them with nonactivists from the same birth cohorts in an attempt to discern how social movement activity affects these activists.[46] Most of these studies have questioned Americans who were involved in activism during the 1960s and have turned up some interesting patterns. Most strikingly, it would appear that former activists tend to remain active in current movements and to define themselves as more liberal than do nonactivists. As well, the activists tended to choose employment in the helping professions, such as teaching and social work.

On a less optimistic note, these studies show that the 1960s activists had higher rates of divorce, married at a later age, earned lower incomes, and were more likely to have episodic work histories. Interviews with former members of the New Left show that many of these former activists have had difficulty settling into vocations and often do not make much money.[47]

While most of the studies of biographical outcomes focus on left-leaning activists of the 1960s, some have also examined activists associated with the right. An example is Rebecca Klatch's previously mentioned study comparing the formation of political identity and the biographical consequences of activism among former SDS members with former members of Young Americans for Freedom (YAF).[48] Regarding biographical consequences, Klatch found, with respect to occupation, that former SDS members tended to be in social services, including teaching, while former YAF members were more inclined toward positions in the institutional political arena. This was due in no small part to the fact that, at the time of Klatch's research, the U.S. political system was dominated by conservatives; thus, there were fewer opportunities in institutional politics for left-leaning former SDS members. With respect to marriage, Klatch reports that conservatives were more likely than the left-leaning former activists to be married and to have more children. Thus, Klatch's comparative research suggests that activism can have significant biographical consequences for both those on the right and those on the left, and, moreover, the character of those consequences can be strikingly different.

Thus far, we have focused on conceptualizing movement consequences, emphasizing that these can be immediate or far-reaching in time, intended and unintended, internal or external to the movement, and loosely or tightly coupled to the targets and goals espoused by the social movement and its organizations. We have also highlighted that movements can target and affect more than just the state or the existing political order; they can also affect the broader culture, other movements, workplace environments, organizational phenomena, the internal dynamics of the movement itself, and the biographies of the individual activists. In working to conceptualize movement consequences, we have drawn on a variety of different studies of social movement outcomes. It is useful now to take stock of what kinds of factors this body of literature has found to have an impact on movement outcomes.

FACTORS AFFECTING MOVEMENT OUTCOMES

Above, we distinguished between movement consequences that are internal and those that are external to the movement. When we think about the elements that affect whether or not a movement is able to reach its goals, it is also useful to think about factors that are internal and external to the movement itself. On the internal side, scholars emphasize the role of social movement organizational resources and tactics and the frames articulated by activists during the course of movement activity. On the external side, scholars emphasize the effect of the political opportunity structure or overall political context on the outcomes sought by social movements. As well, many observers now argue for the importance of joint and mediated effects of both sets of factors on movement outcomes. We treat each of these sets of factors in turn.

Internal Factors

One of the most frequently studied internal characteristics of movements is the organizational structure of the social movement and how this impacts the attainment of desired outcomes, either directly or indirectly via the effect of organizational structure on tactical choice. Social movement theory and research emphasize how the strength of supportive social movement organizations can impact policy decisions at the state, local, national, and organizational levels. At the most basic level, social movement organizations mobilize protest, but they also influence policy makers by their use of institutional channels, such as litigation and lobbying. This suggests that movements with a greater organizational capacity, one facet of organizational structure, will be more effective than those lacking a strong organizational infrastructure. This basic model is known as the *access-influence* model.[49]

The access-influence model may be contrasted with the action-reaction model, which holds that movements matter to policy outcomes because they threaten political and corporate elites and disrupt normal operating procedures.[50] The action-reaction model posits that it is not organizational capacity that influences policy makers but protest and other activities of social movements that are disruptive and threatening to those in power. In particular, frequent and vociferous protest is hypothesized to matter (more so than organizational strength) to policy-making elites at the state and organizational levels, as protest can disrupt or threaten to disrupt normal operations of the state or company. For example, the Earth Liberation Front (ELF) has taken responsibility for burning down a McDonald's restaurant in Tucson, Arizona, and several SUVs at a Ford dealership in Detroit, Michigan.[51] Such actions can lead to lost business due to temporary closings; they also can damage the image or reputation of a firm and have ramifications on its stock price, thus being very effective at getting companies to give in to protesters' demands.[52]

Social movement scholars have also argued that, in addition to organizational resources and tactics used by activists, the collective action frames used by social movements can be an important determinant of a movement's outcomes. In examining how frames impact outcomes, some scholars look at the level of specificity of a given frame and make claims about its impact on outcomes. For example, Cress and Snow find that favorable outcomes of the homeless movement across seventeen U.S. cities were more likely when the movement articulated specific frames (for example, shelter conditions) rather than more diffuse frames (for example, homelessness in general).[53] The status and expertise of the person articulating the frame may also influence outcomes, such that more authoritative and higher-status individuals are considered more credible.[54] Finally, the content of a frame matters, such that those frames that resonate more with the existing culture are more likely to be met with success.[55] In the aforementioned case of the women's suffrage movement in the United States, for instance, it was important at that period of history to frame the right to vote in terms of women's unique place in politics as being feminine and thus able to help heal the country's problems, rather than in terms of women's equal rights.[56]

External Factors

Some scholars emphasize the importance of the larger, external environment that shapes both mobilization and chances of success of such mobilization. Central to these arguments when applied to movements targeting the state is the political opportunity structure (see Chapter 3), which has been identified as a salient contextual condition affecting both mobilization of social movements and their outcomes.[57] This work points to the importance of elite allies who are able to help a movement's cause clear the various policy hurdles, as well as the importance of divisions within the elites, which might make some more inclined to support a movement's cause to spite adversaries.

Recent work on the concept of the political opportunity structure has noted that in addition to the domestic opportunity structure, there is also a transnational or international political opportunity structure, which affects how movements operate and whether they attain their desired outcomes.[58] Whereas the political opportunity structure, as described above, refers to characteristics of a given nation state, when we move to the global level, it is necessary also to consider nonstate characteristics that have an impact on social movements, contentious politics, and their outcomes. The international or transnational political opportunity structure, then, may be thought of as the conglomeration of international governmental associations (for example, the United Nations, the European Union, the World Trade Organization, and the World Bank), which establish treaties, agreements, and norms, and structure the impacts that transnational social movements have on their targets.

Joint and Mediated Effects

While some scholars of movement outcomes have focused on either internal or external factors and how these affect whether a movement will have the desired effect, other scholars have pointed to the importance of the contingent and interactive nature of internal and external factors. Building on the insights of the political opportunity approach, the political mediation model argues that although the openings in the political opportunity structure may stimulate protest, these openings also dramatically influence the possibility of the challenger's success.[59] According to this view, movement mobilization and organizational strength provide the necessary, but not sufficient, conditions for social movement activists to achieve their desired outcomes. For example, the political mediation model suggests that successful mobilization by social movement actors depends on the presence of sympathetic elites whose presence is critical in determining policy outcomes of movement activity. Strong versions of the political mediation model hold that movements will only matter to policy outcomes when the political opportunity structure is favorable; weaker versions of the model argue that the effects of movements are intensified when the political opportunity structure is favorable. Soule and Olzak found, for example, that elite allies helped the pro-ERA movement obtain state ratification of the proposed amendment, but that it was not necessary to have elite allies for the amendment to be ratified.[60]

This section has reviewed some of the most recent research on movement outcomes with an eye toward describing the major factors found to impact outcomes sought by various movements. It is helpful to turn now to a discussion of some of the methodological issues involved in studying the consequences, or outcomes, of social movements—issues that this body of literature has both uncovered and made major strides in ameliorating.

METHODOLOGICAL ISSUES IN STUDYING MOVEMENT CONSEQUENCES

Our discussion has highlighted that defining social movement outcomes is a difficult task, since there are many different facets of the concept of outcomes. However, the issue of defining an outcome can get even more complicated when it comes time to measure the outcome.

For studies of state or organizational policy change, the outcome is usually relatively easy to define: did the state or organization adopt a policy within a certain time frame, and, if so, what was the timing of adoption? One chief definitional problem (which also influences measurement) is whether one is concerned with adoption or implementation of a policy. It is typically easier to find data on adoption of a policy than it is on implementation of a policy, which is probably why most studies in this area examine policy adoption and leave questions of implementation unanswered.[61] On top of this, after determining if adoption or implementation of a policy is one's focus, it is important to identify the "risk set" of states or organizations (that is, which states or organizations are actually candidates for adopting/enacting a particular policy), the relevant period of risk, whether each state has adopted/implemented the policy, and (possibly) the timing of the adoption/implementation. Of course, studying a policy outcome as a dichotomous phenomenon is convenient for many sorts of analyses, but most policies (at the state or the organizational level) are passed through a series of stages, significantly complicating what is seemingly a straightforward way to think about an outcome.[62]

Consider the difficulty, however, in measuring cultural change that is believed to have been caused, at least in part, by social movements. Cultural change may involve changing the values, opinions, and beliefs held by individuals. To the extent that public opinion data are available on a particular belief that movements attempt to change, then it is certainly possible to link movement activity to cultural change. For example, the movement to legalize marijuana has recognized that it needs to change how the public views this drug before it is possible to move forward on the legislative front. One strategy of the movement, therefore, has been to teach the public about the benefits of marijuana for the treatment of certain medical conditions (or to ease the side effects of pharmaceuticals used to treat many medical conditions). Teaching the public about industrial uses of hemp also may affect public opinion about marijuana. Finally, challenging commonly held ideas about the recreational use of marijuana is another way that the movement has attempted to change public opinion on the issue of legalization of marijuana.

Other forms of cultural change may be less obviously measurable than are changes in public opinion.[63] The aforementioned study of representations of African Americans in children's literature is an exemplar in the study of cultural change. The researchers developed a complex coding scheme, which they used to ascertain whether African American characters were present in all children's books published between 1937 and 1993 (a total of nearly 2,500 books).[64] While the results are compelling, the amount of work involved in such a study is non-trivial.

Defining and measuring the outcome of interest—whether that outcome is a new policy, a change in public opinion, a change in some cultural form, or a change in the biography of activists—is not as easy as one might expect. Not only do scholars need to think of consistent ways to define outcomes and come up with reliable measures, but they also need to make sure that they can find longitudinal measures (over time) of the outcome. When thinking about some change associated with a social movement, it is critical to be able to demonstrate that there has, in fact, been a change.

On top of the very real methodological issues involved in defining and measuring the very things we expect movements to change (for example, policies, culture, and so on), there are also problems associated with sorting out whether it was the movement or something else that caused the change in which we are interested. In trying to establish a causal connection between a movement and an outcome, researchers must do more than show that changes in movement organization and activity are correlated with some outcome or change; they must also defend their claim against rival claims or arguments. Some quantitative research designs enable such work to be done via the use of statistical controls, for example, when one includes an additional independent variable in a multiple regression model, measuring one of the rival claims. Research on states' ratification of the Equal Rights Amendment, for example, has shown that, in addition to movement activity, public opinion about the amendment was important to state legislators' decisions regarding it.[65]

In studies of movement consequences, the countervailing effects of countermovements in relation to that which movements seek to change should also be taken into consideration. If we believe that movements matter as agents of change, then it follows that the countermovements that a movement engenders should also have some effect on the system of authority. Sometimes it is not easy to discern which of two opposing movements was the initial movement and which was the countermovement. This will vary, moreover, from study to study.[66] It is, however, not clear if this really matters. The point here is that, when considering an outcome of interest, it is crucial to consider the multiple voices that might impact that outcome. For example, regarding the possibility of trying to determine if the movement in favor of legalizing marijuana caused change in public opinion on the legalization issue, it would be ideal to include measures of an anti-legalization movement organization. Clearly the public is susceptible to both sides of any issue. To the extent that we believe movements matter in changing public opinion, we should, then, examine movements on both sides of the issue in question.

In addition to controlling for rival arguments, it is also important to fend off claims of spuriousness. In other words, it is not really enough for researchers to show a time-ordered relationship between a movement and an outcome and thereby offer a viable explanation that can be defended against rival explanations. Researchers also need to show that the movement and the outcome are not both caused by a third factor. For example, in the second half of the twentieth century, many favorable changes in the status of women have been attributed to the women's movement in the United States and especially to the post-1960s wave of feminist activity. However, any analysis of changes in the status of the movement should also examine the rates of female participation in the paid labor force, especially since women in the United States began to enter the paid labor force at unprecedented levels during and after World War II. It is thus possible that changes in the status of women and increases in feminist activity were both caused by increases in women's labor force participation.[67]

Chapter Summary and Conclusions

This chapter began by describing what it is that social movements attempt to change and by noting that sometimes social movements affect change that was not directly intended. To be sure, movements typically have some sort of stated goal or set of goals, and to the extent that these are met, we can talk about social movement outcomes. But movements have effects beyond those they actually intended and beyond those that could even be reasonably predicted by activists and leaders.

Social movements, moreover, can have effects on phenomena that are external as well as internal to themselves. Movements usually target systems of authority and, as such, have potential to change something about that which is challenged. But many movements (either intentionally or unintentionally) also have an impact on the group processes of the collectivity known as the movement or the movement organization. As well, participation in social movements can affect individuals' life courses. Thus, the phenomenon of social movement outcomes is a multifaceted one that can have different meanings for different people.

One issue that we implied in our discussion of movement outcomes is that often social movements can have effects long after their immediate effects. For example, considering the bio-graphical consequences of social movement activity, movement participation may impact an activist's life course. Or, to take another example, it has been argued that one legacy of student protest of the 1960s is that some college campuses are "hotbeds of activism"; that is, campuses that have a history of activism tend to remain active.[68]

Clearly, it would seem, social movements matter in a multi-tude of ways. This may appear to state the obvious, yet the question of whether and how movements matter has been a source of considerable debate, as evidenced by such book titles as *How Social Movements Matter*[69] and *When Movements Matter*.[70] Some scholars used to argue that social movements are epiphenomenal in the sense that they are sideshows to the much more powerful social currents that generate them and that cause the changes that are sometimes attributed to such movements. For example, one might once have argued that the women's movement had no impact on the increase in women's rights, contending instead that both the movement and the new rights were caused by the boost in women's labor force participation.[71] But growing research on movement outcomes or consequences has demonstrated quite convincingly that movements do indeed matter and, as we have shown, often in a multitude of ways. This is not to suggest that movements are the only or even the primary agents of significant change, whatever the institutional or societal domain. But they are often significant players in affecting the lives and careers of classes and clusters of individuals, the public manifestation of certain values (such as equal opportunity), and the character of the organizations and societies in and through which people live their lives. So, yes, movements can and frequently do make a significant difference!

NOTES

CHAPTER 1   CONCEPTUALIZING SOCIAL MOVEMENTS

1. *Time* (June 19, 1989: 14). The above narrative is derived mainly from a descriptive journalistic account by Serrill (1989). For a sense of the chronological development of the 1989 Beijing student demonstrations, also see journalistic accounts by Benjamin (1989) and Birnbaum and Chua-Eoan (1989). For a systematic sociological analysis of the events, see Zhao (2001).

2. Church (1989: 25).

3. See Gleick (1997) for a journalistic account of the "cult" and mass suicide, and Balch (1995) for a sociological account of the group.

4. Cardinale (2004). See also Soule (1997), Van Dyke, Soule, and Taylor (2004), Soule (forthcoming), Davis et al. (2008), and Van Dyke (1998) for other examples of non–state-oriented student movements and protest.

5. Graff (2005: 37).

6. Snow, Vliegenhart, and Corrigall-Brown (2007).

7. Holley (2004: 1).

8. Associated Press (2004).

9. For discussion of the point, as well as other factors affecting newspaper and media coverage of movement protest events, see Earl et al. (2004), McCarthy, McPhail, and Smith (1996), Oliver and Maney (2000), and Oliver and Meyers (1999).

10. Watanabe and Becerra (2006).

11. Cho and Gorman (2006).

12. Meyer and Tarrow (1998).

13. This conceptualization of social movements incorporates elements from other definitions: McAdam, Tarrow, and Tilly (2001), Tarrow (1998), Turner and Killian (1987),

but it is somewhat broader and thus more inclusive. For an elaboration of some these conceptual differences, see Snow (2004a).

14. These and other corporations often are the targets of movement protest. See, for example, Raeburn (2004); King and Soule (2007); and Soule (forthcoming).

15. A "vocabulary of motives" encompasses situationally relevant words and phrases, or accounts, that actors use to rationalize their behavior in or with respect to the contexts in which those vocabularies are relevant. See Mills (1940) and Scott and Lyman (1968).

16. Van Biema (2002).

17. See Keck and Sikkink (1998) and Smith (2004).

18. See Smith (2001) and Thomas (2000).

19. For example, see the discussion of "secondary adjustments" in Goffman (1961); also see Prasad and Prasad (1998) and Scott (1985).

20. Exceptions include the analysis of exit episodes from the German Democratic Republic between 1966 and 1989 by Mueller (1999) and the parallel analysis by Pfaff and Kim (2003). See also, the conceptual elaboration of the exit/voice connection in reference to the German Democratic Republic by Hirschman (1993).

21. See Bergesen (2007), whose conceptualization of terrorism as a three-step process (perpetrator→victim→target) suggests indirect action, and Thornton (1964: 79), who similarly highlights "the differentiation of victims and targets" in appraising terrorism.

22. Berger (1981), Kanter (1972), Zablocki (1980).

23. Bonwick (1991), Kapur (1986), Hall (1977).

24. Barker (1983), Robbins (1988), Wallis (1984).

25. Balch (1995) and Hall (1987, 2000).

26. Some scholars have questioned the analytic utility of distinguishing between interest groups and social movements (Burstein 1998, 1999); others have argued (Gamson 1990, 2004), as we do, that they are sufficiently different theoretically and empirically to justify their retention as separate but overlapping forms of what some scholars call "advocacy organizations." See Andrews and Edwards (2004).

27. Tarrow (1998: 123–24).

28. See McCarthy and McPhail (1998) and Jones et al. (2001), among other works, for discussion and illustration of what might be thought of as the "negotiated calendarization" of social movement demonstrations and other public activities.

29. Balch (1995).

30. Snow (1979, 1987).

31. Rupp and Taylor (1987) and Taylor (1989).

32. Tarrow (1998) and Koopmans (2004).

33. To get a handle on political opportunity theory, see McAdam (1996), Kriesi (2004), and Meyer (2004).

34. For excellent synthetic overviews of resource mobilization theory and research, see McCarthy and Zald (2002) and Edwards and McCarthy (2004).

35. See, for example, Jasper (1997) and Williams (2004) on culture and social movements; Snow (2003) on symbolic interactionsm and social movements; Benford and Snow (2000) and Snow (2004b) on framing and ideology; Polletta and Jasper (2001) and Hunt and Benford (2004) on collective identity; and Goodwin, Jasper, and Polletta (2001, 2004) on emotions and social movements.

CHAPTER 2   MOBILIZING GRIEVANCES

1. Jenkins and Perrow (1977: 250).

2. McCarthy and Zald (1977: 1214–15).

3. See Dahrendorf (1959).

4. See Marx and Engels (1972: 334).

5. For a descriptive distinction, see Marx's discussion of the "small-holding peasants" in *The 18th Brumaire* (1963: 123–25).

6. Lenin (1969).

7. For an overview of the labor movement, particularly in the United States, see Fantasia and Stepan-Norris (2004).

8. See Dahrendorf (1959).

9. Klandermans, Roefs, and Olivier (2001).

10. For comprehensive and insightful analysis of this perspective, see Useem (1998) and Buechler (2004), which inform our discussion.

11. See Coleman (1971) and Kornhauser (1959).

12. Tilly et al. (1975: 4-6).

13. Ibid., 290.

14. See, for example, Snow, Zurcher, and Ekland-Olson's (1980) findings on the role of networks in recruitment to religious movements, McAdam's (1986) research on recruitment to the Freedom Summer campaign, and Gould's (1991) findings on multiple networks in relation to the Paris Commune of 1871.

15. Piven and Cloward (1992) and Useem (1998).

16. See Olzak and Shanahan (1996) and Meyers (1997).

17. See Snow, Soule, and Cress (2005).

18. See Olzak and Shanahan (1996).

19. For an elaboration of this thesis, see Snow, Cress, Downey, and Jones (1998).

20. See Kahneman and Tversky's (1979) discussion of their "prospect theory."

21. See Walsh's (1981) analysis of the grievances and social movement activities associated with the Three Mile Island event.

22. For discussion and illustration of the NIMBY syndrome in the United States, see Takahashi (1998).

23. Scott (1976).

24. Borland and Sutton (2007: 717).

25. Snow, Cress, Downey, and Jones (1998).

26. Useem and Kimball (1991).

27. Snow et al. (1998).

28. Dollard et al. (1939).

29. For a classic examination of different types of relative deprivation, see Gurr (1970).

30. See Lenski (1954) for seminal discussion. Also see Geschwender (1967).

31. Scott (1985: 29).

32. Klandermans, Roefs, and Olivier (2001: 52).

33. See, for example, Hegtvedt and Markovsky (1995).

34. Kluegel and Smith (1986).

35. Klandermans et al. (2001: 49–51).

36. Ibid., 49.

37. Trotsky (1959: 249).

38. See Gamson (1992), Moore (1978), Turner (1969).

39. Snow and Phillips (1980).

40. Blee (2002).

41. Blee (2002: 32).

42. For an historical account and analysis of the minority rights revolution in the U.S. during the 1960s and '70s, which "targeted groups of Americans understood as disadvantaged but not defined by socioeconomic class," see Skrentny (2002: 4). However, the designation of a social category as disadvantaged is not objectively given, but is subject to interpretive contestation and debate, as Skrentny's analysis makes clear. Thus, African Americans constituted the "paradigmatic" disadvantaged, minority group, with Latinos, Americans Indians, women, and the disabled also being categorized as minorities—but not so white ethnics and gays and lesbians.

43. "Jim Crow" is the name given to the racial caste system that evolved around 1877 and persisted primarily but not solely in the Southern and border states until 1954 when the Supreme Court rendered its *Brown v. Board of Education* decision and the mid-1960s when President Johnson signed the Civil Rights Act of 1964 and the Voting Rights Act of 1965. For an incisive and acclaimed account of the Jim Crow era, see *The Strange Career of Jim Crow,* by Woodward (2001).

44. Snow and Anderson (1993: 97).

45. For conceptualization of discursive fields, see Snow (2008).

46. Gleick (1997: 31).

47. Gleick (1997: 29).

48. Tarrow (1998: 118). See also, Rudé (1980) and Steinberg (1999) for parallel discussions of the cultural materials, particularly ideologies, and movement discourse and framings.

49. For more detailed discussion of the problem of resonance in relation to movement framing, see Benford and Snow (2000: 619–23), Ferree (2003), McCammon (2008), Snow and Benford (1988), Snow and Corrigall-Brown (2005), and Williams (2004).

50. Zuo and Benford (1995: 139).

51. Ibid., 139.

52. Zawadski and Lazersfeld (1935: 249).

CHAPTER 3   CONTEXTUAL CONDITIONS

1. Smelser (1962: 15).

2. Kautsky (1910: 184–85). Karl Kautsky (1854–1938) was a leading theoretician of socialism and a significant figure in Marxist history, as he was the editor of the fourth volume of Karl Marx's *Das Kapital*.

3. McAdam, McCarthy, and Zald (1988: 699). Conceptions of political opportunity tend to range between those that sweep any contextual facilitating condition under the political opportunity canopy, thus treating it as a catchall term for all factors external to a movement that affect its mobilization and functioning (see, for example, Meyer 2004: 126), and those that opt for a more restrained view, tying the concept more closely to relevant political systems and their structures (see, for example, McAdam 1996: 25–26). The conception we invoke here is closer to the latter, more restrained end of the conceptual continuum. For reviews of the theorizing and research on political opportunity, see Kriesi (2004), McAdam (1996), Meyer (2004), Tarrow (1998, Ch. 5), and Tilly (1978). It is also important to note that there have been a number of interesting extensions of the concept of "political opportunity structure." For example, some argue for the importance of the "cultural opportunity structure" (Johnston and Klandermans 1995; Taylor 1996); others, for the "legal opportunity structure" (Pedriana 2004); still others, for the "gendered opportunity structure" (McCammon et al. 2001); and yet others, for the "discursive opportunity structure" (Ferree et al. 2002; Koopmans 2004; McCammon et al. 2007). The core insight from these works is that the context that facilitates movements and their outcomes extends beyond the political environment.

4. Lipsky (1970: 14).

5. Eisinger (1973: 25).

6. Eisinger (1973: 23).

7. For an analysis of state-sponsored celebratory collective behavior, see Aguirre's account of Cuba (1984).

8. Kriesi et al. (1995). New social movements, such as the environmental movement and the gay rights and peace movements, are contrasted to older, more materially oriented movements, such as the labor movement and various poverty and welfare rights movements. Whereas the older movements were oriented toward correcting distributional inequities, the so-called newer ones are oriented toward securing procedural rights and lifestyle concerns.

9. For an analysis of the memorialization of instances of protest, see Armstrong and Crage's (2006) examination of the commemoration of Stonewall riots of June 1969 in New York in relation to gay liberation.

10. These clusters are drawn largely from McAdam (1996) and Tarrow (1998, Ch. 5).

11. Boorstin (1961) has called contrived events pseudo-events, which are akin to what Goffman (1974) calls framing fabrications.

12. Habermas (1975).

13. Piven and Cloward (1977).

14. McAdam (1982: 158).

15. Jenkins et al. (2003).

16. Bunis (1993).

17. Amenta, Carruthers, and Zylan (1992); Amenta, Dunleavy, and Bernstein (1994).

18. Gamson (1990).

19. Soule and Olzak (2004), Soule and King (2006).

20. Jenkins and Perrow (1977).

21. McAdam (1982: 160).

22. See Jenkins et al. (2003) and Minkoff (1997).

23. McAdam (1982).

24. Zuo and Benford (1995: 135–36).

25. Zhao (2001: 238).

26. Figures from Walker (1968: 351–58). For analysis of the 1968 Chicago demonstrations and violence, see the full Walker report (1968). Interestingly, but perhaps not coincidentally, the demonstrations and police rioting occurred in the same park in which Barack Obama and many supporters gathered on the night of his presidential election victory on November 4, 2008.

27. For discussion and analysis of these two events, see Scranton (1971). For an up-close analysis of the Kent State shootings, see Hensley and Lewis (1978).

28. Scranton (1971: 17–18).

29. This account is derived from the firsthand observations of the first author, who was employed in a research center at the university at this point in time.

30. See Almeida (2003), de la Luz Inclán (2008), Loveman (1998), Olivier (1990), Raseler (1996), and Schock (1999).

31. Goodwin (2001: 177). Goodwin has been an ongoing critic of the political opportunity thesis. See also, Goodwin and Jasper (1999) and the responses provoked in the same issue of *Sociological Forum* (vol. 14, no. 1, 1999).

32. For a review of the literature on the question of how repression affects subsequent protest, see Davenport (2007).

33. Almeida (2003: 386–87).

34. Almeida (2003: 385–86). The endurance of the mentioned organizational infrastructures can be interpreted as an instance of what Rupp and Taylor (1987) call "survival in the doldrums." See also, the discourse on "abeyance structures" in Taylor (1989).

35. Moore (1978: 89–91). Iron in the soul is defined in terms of three qualities or capacities. One is the moral courage to resist oppressive rules and commands; another is the intellectual ability to recognize what is oppression; and the third is the moral inventiveness to develop so-called new standards of condemnation.

36. Einwohner (2003).

37. See Earl (2003) for an elaboration of these dimensions and the various forms of control that they generate when they intersect.

38. See Werum and Winders (2001) and Soule (2004) for discussions of the movement for gay rights and the active countermovements that this movement spawned.

39. The conceptualization of "soft" repression was developed by Ferree (2004) and illustrated with respect to women's movements.

40. Ferree (2004: 95). For a full accounting of the study, see Ferree et al. (2002).

41. Ferree (2004: 95–96).

42. Sawyers and Meyer (1999: 201).

43. Meyer (1990) and Solo (1988).

44. Gamson and Meyer (1996: 289–90).

45. Gamson and Meyer (1996: 290).

46. Kurzman (1996: 155).

47. Zhao (2001: 256).

48. See, for example, McCammon (2001b) and Snow et al. (2005).

49. McCarthy and Zald (1973 and 1977).

50. McCarthy and Zald (1977: 1224–25).

51. McLaughlin and Khawaja (2000).

52. Soule et al. (1999).

53. Snow, Soule, and Cress (2005).

54. Wiest, Smith, and Eterovic (2002).

55. See Edwards and McCarthy (2004) for discussion of additional research relevant to this perspective.

56. For a more elaborated discussion of the resource attributes, see Edwards and McCarthy (2004: 128–31).

57. This typology is drawn principally from Edwards and McCarthy (2004: 125–31) and Cress and Snow (1996). See also, Williams (1995) for a discussion of cultural resources.

58. In this study (Cress and Snow 1996), viability is assessed in terms of three variables: SMO survival for a year or more; holding two meetings a month; and capacity to conduct action campaigns.

59. Cress and Snow (1996: 1098).

60. In the field notes of the first author, who studied this movement in the first half of the 1970s in the Los Angeles area, there are repeated references in their sidewalk recruitment outings to various members of the Los Angeles Dodgers who reportedly chanted the movement's sacred mantra. For a discussion and analysis of the movement's effort to legitimate itself, see Snow (1979).

61. Fine (2006).

62. See Shupe and Bromley (1980) and Shupe and Darnell (2006) for an analysis of this "anti-cult" movement.

63. See Hollander (1958) for the conceptualization of idiosyncrasy credit and Snow (1979) for its application to social movements.

64. Cress and Snow (1996).

65. Morris (1981: 764).

66. McAdam (1982).

67. For research on externally based resources directed to the civil rights movement, see, for example, Haines (1984) and Jenkins and Eckert (1986).

68. See Haines (1984) and Piven and Cloward (1977).

69. This is known as the "channeling" thesis propounded by Jenkins and Eckert (1986).

70. Cress and Snow (1996).

71. Cress and Snow (1996: 1104).

72. Jenkins and Eckert (1986).

73. Zhao (2001: 244).

74. Ibid., 240.

75. Lofland (1968).

76. For a broader discussion and analysis of protest policing and control, see della Porta and Reiter (1998), della Porta and Fillieule (2004), and Earl et al. (2003).

77. Zhao (2001: 243).

78. Social control errors generally arise when application of some form of control backfires because of its "clumsy and ineffective" use and stimulates rather than controls social movement activity (Gamson 1968: 190).

79. This conceptualization essentially paraphrases Polletta (1999: 1) and her extensive and incisive examination of free spaces. Other parallel terms include "havens" (Hirsch (1993), "submerged networks" (Melluci 1989), "cultural laboratories" (Mueller 1994), and "spheres of cultural autonomy" (Taylor and Whittier (1995). None of these terms is much different than the "free spaces" concept that was originally used by Evans (1979) and was developed more fully by Evans and Boyte (1986). We therefore adopt the free spaces concept.

80. Morris (1981).

81. Morris (1981: 764–65).

82. Snow and Marshall (1984).

83. It should be noted that madrasa means literally a place where learning and teaching occurs and that not all madrasas teach militant, fundamentalist Islam.

84. Sengupta (2007).

85. Perlez (2008).

86. Shah and Gall (2007).

87. Remy Cross, personal communication (2007).

88. See Johnston and Snow (1998), especially pp. 477 and 479–83.

89. Quoted in Johnston and Snow (1998: 481).

90. Zhao (2001: 264). See Tilly (2000) and Zhao (2008) for further discussion of the importance of spatial factors in relation to movement mobilization.

91. Petras and Zeitlin (1967). See, also Stillerman (2003).

92. Jenkins et al. (2003: 293).

CHAPTER 4 PARTICIPATION IN SOCIAL MOVEMENTS

1. See, for example, the studies of Kurtz (2002) and Raeburn (2004).

2. Dalton (2002: 62).

3. Klandermans and Oegema (1987) and Oegema and Klandermans (1994).

4. Klandermans (1984).

5. Bird and Reimer (1982: 5). The religious movements included Western Christian movements and Eastern countercultural movements, such as Hare Krishna and the Divine Light Mission, and parareligious movements such as Transcendental Meditation and Scientology.

6. Bird and Reimer (1982: 1).

7. Corrigall-Brown (2007: 35–36 and Table 2.3). The panel study on which the analysis is based was conducted by Jennings and Stoker (2004).

8. This rational calculus assumption is a key tenet of the rational choice perspective, which gained currency in the study of social movements during the late 1970s and 1980s partly in response to the previous tendency to view participants in social movement as irrational. Analysts of social movement participation today generally assume that movement participants are no more or less rational than participants in other domains of social life. For a succinct summary statement of rational choice theory, see Hechter and Kanazawa. (1997); for a critical overview, see Ferree (1992).

9. For particular cases of government undercover surveillance and counterintelligence, see Cunningham (2004).

10. The McCarthy era refers to a period during the late 1940s and early 1950s in the United States in which there was intense anti-communist suspicion and "witch hunts" stimulated by growing fears about communist influence in American institutions and espionage by Soviet agents. During this period, which was called McCarthyism because of the prominent role of Senator Joe McCarthy, thousands of Americans were accused of being Communists or communist sympathizers and were subjected to aggressive investigations and questioning before government or private-industry panels, committees, and agencies.

11. For a discussion of Freedom Summer and the participants, see McAdam (1988).

12. Sociologists interested in this question use the term "differential recruitment" (Jenkins 1983; McAdam 1986; Zurcher and Snow 1981) to refer to the set of factors that influence individual variation in participation in social movement activity.

13. Schussman and Soule (2005: 1081).

14. Smilde (2005), Snow et al. (1980), Snow and Phillips (1980), and Stark and Bainbridge (1980).

15. See McAdam (1988) and McAdam and Paulsen (1993).

16. See Freeman (1973) and Rosenthal et al. (1985).

17. Klandermans and Oegema (1987) and Oegema and Klandermans (1994).

18. See Diani (1995) and Diani and Lodi (1988).

19. della Porta (1988).

20. Zhao (2001).

21. Balch and Taylor (1978). See also, Straus (1976) for discussion of seekership.

22. See Kaplan and Liu (2000), Klapp (1969), and Pinel and Swan (2000).

23. See Jasper and Paulsen (1995).

24. Dixon and Roscigno (2003: 1321).

25. Fernandez and McAdam (1988–1989).

26. Gould (1991: 716).

27. Schussman and Soule (2005: 1090). A few studies have found no effect of organizational membership on participation in a movement campaign. Nepstadt and Smith (1999), for example, find that while relational ties to activists in the Nicaraguan exchange predicts an individual's participation in the campaign, there is no such direct support for organizational affiliation. This negative finding may be partly due to the indirect influence of such factors as learning civic skills, which encompass organizational and communication skills that are transferable from one organization to another and may be essential to social movement organizations. The point is that in addition to providing network linkages among its members, organizations can also have an important function as a kind of training ground for learning and refining various civic skills. Most people who have spent any time in civic organizations (such as churches, fraternities and sororities, voluntary associations, and social movement organizations) or ever worked in an organization understand that organizations are one venue in which individuals can acquire civic skills. Thus, such skills as public speaking, maintaining

a Web site, and running a meeting that are obtained in a campus organization, for example, can also be used to help run a social movement organization.

28. On the link between efficacy and riot participation, see Forward and Williams (1970) and Paige (1971). On the relationship between efficacy and participation in a nationally representative study, see Corrigall-Brown (2007). For other research findings on the link between efficacy and activism, see Ennis and Schreuer (1987), Paulsen (1991), and Verba et al. (1995).

29. Corrigall-Brown et al. (2010).

30. See, for example, Hunt and Benford (2004), Polletta and Jasper (2001), Melucci (1989), Snow (2001), Snow and McAdam (2000), Taylor and Whittier (1992).

31. Snow (2001: 2213).

32. Simon et al. (1998).

33. Klandermans and de Weerd (2000).

34. Liss et al. (2004).

35. Dixon and Roscigno (2003).

36. Blee (2002).

37. Corrigall-Brown et al. (2010).

38. Einwohner (2006).

39. Gecas (1992).

40. See Flacks (1967), Lewis and Kraut (1972), and Westby and Braungart (1966).

41. See Braungart and Braungart (1990) Rohlinger and Snow (2003).

42. See Duncan and Stewart (1995).

43. Klatch (1999).

44. Ibid., 58.

45. See Penner (2002) and Penner and Finkelstein (1998).

46. Political efficacy, which we discussed earlier, also is often considered a dimension of political engagement.

47. Schussman and Soule (2005: 1089).

48. See Corrigall-Brown (2007) and Schussman and Soule (2005). It is interesting to note that political knowledge secured through various forms of the media may not

be equally potent predictors of participation. Schussman and Soule (2005) found, for example, that daily newspaper readers were more likely to engage in protest than those who watch television news. This is not surprising to us, since newspapers provide more detail, and reading them may reflect greater interest as well as generate more knowledge.

49. See Corrigall-Brown (2007), Dalton (2002), Hirsch (1990), Schussman and Soule (2005), and Verba et al. (1997),

50. Dalton (2002: 67).

51. McAdam (1986) provides the seminal statement of biographic availability in his analysis of Freedom Summer volunteers.

52. See, for example, Barkan et al. (1995), Corrigall-Brown (2007), Kitts (1999), Nepstadt and Smith (2001), Passy and Giugni (2001), Schussman and Soule (2005), and Wiltfang and McAdam (1991).

53. Beyerlein and Hipp (2006: 227).

54. Ibid., 234. See Schussman and Soule (2005) for additional confirmation of the importance of analyzing measures of biographical availability in relation to the different stages of participation.

55. See Hechter and Kanazawa (1997) and Klandermans (1984).

56. Olson (1965).

57. See Moore (1978) and note 33 in Chapter 3 for discussion of "iron in the soul."

58. See Goodwin et al. (2004) for a discussion of reflex emotions and other emotions relevant to social movements.

59. See Takahashi (1998).

60. See Gerlach and Hine (1970) and Snow (1987).

61. Snow 1987.

62. Zhao (2001: 249).

63. Snow and Benford (1988: 202).

64. Benford (1993b).

65. Salehi (1996: 50–51).

66. Lelyveld (2001: 54).

67. Hamas is a militant Palestinian movement born in the late 1980s during the first intifada. It seeks to displace Israel from the land it regards as Palestine's, and it is a major sponsor of suicide bombing, routinely claiming responsibility for a significant number of such bombings. Hamas is more than a militant movement, however. It is also a political party and a provider of social services for citizens living on the West Bank and in Gaza. See Levitt (2007).

68. Hassan (2001: 40).

69. Lelyveld (2001) and Wilkinson (2002).

70. For an elaborated discussion of frame transformation, see Snow (2004: 393–96).

71. For discussion of regeneration, see Lang and Lang (1961) and Nock (1933).

72. See Gordon (1974) for initial discussion of this variety of transformation.

73. For a summary of the factors associated with such transformations, particularly conversions, see Robbins (1988) and Snow and Machalek (1984).

74. Biographical reconstruction is generally regarded as a salient feature of conversion and related frame transformations (see Snow and Machalek 1984). See the section in Chapter 2 on "the neglect of grievance interpretation" for concrete examples of biographical reconstruction.

75. See Snow and McAdam (2000) for discussion of identity correspondence.

76. Turner (1983: 177).

77. Corrigall-Brown (2007: Chapter 4 and Table 4.2).

78. Commitment to a line of action based on a "side bet" is illustrated by a factory worker who does the job not because he or she likes it but because it pays the bills of the family. See Becker (1960) for en elaboration of commitment as a side bet.

79. Kanter (1972).

80. See, in addition to Kanter, Gardner (1978), Hirsch (1990), and Zablocki (1973).

81. See Coser (167) for a discussion of the characteristics of "greedy" organizations.

82. See Hall (1988).

83. See Isserman's (2000) biographic account of Harrington.

84. There is some work on disengagement, but it is quite limited. See Bromley (1988), Corrigall-Brown (2007), Klandermans (2004), and Weiss (1963).

85. Klandermans (2004: 371–74).

Chapter 5   Dynamics of Social Movements

1. This principle of interactive determination is at the core of the symbolic interactionist perspective and has been invoked elsewhere in relation to the analysis of social movements (see Snow 2003). It is also consistent with Rucht's contention that "social movements can be understood only in *relational* terms" (2004: 197).

2. For a more thoroughgoing and wide-ranging discussion of movement dynamics, see McAdam, Tarrow, and Tilly (2001).

3. For focused discussion and analysis of the centrality of organizations to the study and operation of social movements, see Clemens and Minkoff (2004), Davis et al. (2005), and Lofland (1996).

4. http://members.cruzio.com/~cruzef/aboutef.html, accessed on September 8, 2006.

5. www.audubon.org/nas/, accessed on February 25, 2008. Also see, Soule and King (2008) for a broader discussion of the tactical repertoire of environmental movement organizations.

6. Benford (1993).

7. According to McCarthy and Zald (1977: 1218), a social movement organization is a "complex, or formal, organization which identifies its goals with the preferences of a social movement or a countermovement and attempts to implement those goals". An SMI is the collection of all social movement organizations "that have as their goal the attainment of the broadest preferences of a social movement" (McCarthy and Zald 1977: 1219). One might think of the SMI as the organizational analog of a "social movement," which to McCarthy and Zald (1977: 1217) is the "set of opinions and beliefs in a population which represents preferences for changing some elements of the social structure and/or reward distribution of a society." McCarthy and Zald (1977) also define the social movement sector (SMS) as the aggregation of all SMIs in a particular place, at a particular time. Throughout this chapter, we use McCarthy and Zald's (1977) definitions of the social movement organization, social movement industry, and social movement sector.

8. Everett (1992).

9. DiMaggio and Powell (1983).

10. The parallel term "multiorganizational field" was used earlier by some movement scholars in a parallel fashion. See Curtis and Zurcher (1973) and Klandermans (1992).

11. For elaboration of the concept of discursive fields, see Snow (2008). For analysis of the role of the media as an important set of organizational actors in relation to social

movement activity, see Gamson (2004), Gamson and Wolfsfeld (1993), Gitlin (1980), and Rohlinger (2002).

12. Meyer (2007).

13. Meyer (2007).

14. See Morris and Staggenborg (2004) for an extensive review of the literature on leadership in social movements.

15. For assessments of King and Mao as charismatic leaders, see Platt and Lilley (1994) and Andreas (2007).

16. For a discussion such leadership functions and a corresponding division of labor, see Killian (1964), Roche and Sachs (1955), and Wilson (1973).

17. Meyer (2007).

18. Issue committees address the following: Abortion/Reproductive Issues, Violence Against Women, Constitutional Equality, Diversity/Ending Racism, Lesbian Rights, Economic Justice, Affirmative Action, Disability Rights, Family Law, Fighting the Right, Global Feminism, Health, Immigration, Judicial Nominations, Legislation, Marriage Equality, Media Activism, Mothers/Caregivers Economic Rights, Working for Peace, Social Security, Supreme Court, Title IX/Education, Welfare, Women-Friendly Workplace, Women in the Military, Young Feminist Programs. www.now. org/issues/, accessed on April 19, 2008).

19. See www.now.org/chapters/ for a list of state and local chapters (accessed on April 19, 2008).

20. Meyer and Corrigall-Brown (2005).

21. For a descriptive account of the Battle in Seattle, see Thomas (2000).

22. See Hannan and Freeman (1989) on organizational ecology, and McCarthy and Zald (1977) and Edwards and McCarthy (2004) on resource mobilization theory.

23. Jenkins and Eckert (1986).

24. Zald and McCarthy (1987).

25. Soule and King (2008).

26. For a broader discussion of tactics, see Taylor and Van Dyke (2004).

27. Turner and Killian (1987: 303). See Ackerman and Duvall (2000) for an extensive historical accounting of the use of nonviolence worldwide over the past century.

28. For discussion of these tactics, see McAdam (1982), Morris (1984).

29. Quote from Stephen B. Oates in Introduction to Fager (1985).

30. See Thornton (1964) for discussion of the strategic dimensions of terrorism.

31. See Berger (1981).

32. See Hall (1987).

33. See Balch (1995) and Gleick (1997).

34. For an overview of anti-war and peace movements, see Marullo and Meyer (2004).

35. SNCC was born in April 1960 during student meetings at Shaw University in Raleigh, North Carolina, and became a significant organizational actor in the civil rights movement throughout the 1960s. It became increasingly disenchanted with the strategy of nonviolence in the second half of the 1960s and called for a broader and more militant strategy, reflected in the phrase "black power," which became its battle cry. For analysis of SNCC and the context in which it evolved, operated, and mutated, see Claybourne (1981). See also, Carmichael and Hamilton's (1967) discourse on and call for "Black Power."

36. McGeary (1999: 121).

37. For analysis of the link between religion and violence in recent times, see Juergensmeyer (2000).

38. Osama bin Laden (1998:1).

39. Piven and Cloward (1977).

40. Michels ([1911] 1962).

41. Morris (1981, 1984).

42. Vallochi (1990).

43. Soule et al. (1999).

44. Cress and Snow (1996).

45. Staggenborg (1988).

46. Snow et al. (1980).

47. For discussion of these contrasting forms of organization, see Rothschild-Whitt (1979) and Polletta (2006).

48. Polletta (2006: 57).

49. Benford (1993).

50. Tilly (1995: 41).

51. Ibid., 46.

52. See Tarrow (1998: 29–42) for an elaborated discussion of the modularity of movement tactics.

53. Borland and Sutton (2007).

54. See Bartkowski (2004) for an examination of the Promise Keepers.

55. The Million Man March of African American males was organized by Nation of Islam leader Louis Farrakhan and Minister Benjamin Chavis Muhammad to encourage African Americans to register to vote and to increase their involvement in volunteerism and community activism.

56. See Clark-Miller and Murdock (2005) for a description of the study.

57. Edwards Jr. (2005: 1).

58. See Tarrow (1998: 43–47) for further discussion of print and social movement activity, particularly in relation to the French and American revolutions.

59. See Gitlin's (1980) incisive descriptive examination of the relationship between the media and the anti-Vietnam War movement, which is titled *The Whole World Is Watching*.

60. See Earl and Schussman (2002) and McCaughey and Ayers (2003) for more general discussions of the Internet and activism, and see Carty (2009) for a case study of MoveOn.

61. See Tarrow (1998: 31, 102).

62. Turner and Killian (1987: 256).

63. Haines (1984).

64. Snow (1979: 30).

65. Ibid., 38.

66. Rochford (1985).

67. See Shupe and Bromley (1980) and Shupe and Darnell (2006) for analysis of the American anti-cult movement.

68. This latter factor was a particularly poignant trigger of public alarm because of the Jonestown tragedy in 1978, when 913 communal members perished in a "mass suicide/murder" concocted by the commune's leader, Jim Jones, and organized by his

chief lieutenants. The Jonestown event generated increasing fear that other strange and peculiar "cults" might follow the fate of Jonestown. For analysis of Jonestown and Jim Jones and his followers, see Hall (1987).

69. See Rochford (1985) for a discussion of these factors.

70. Terrorist acts, it has been argued, are most effective in generating anxiety, fear, and despair when they are indiscriminate in appearance but highly discriminate in fact (Thornton 1964).

71. For historical discussion and analysis of the Black Panther Party, see Austin (2006) and Hilliard and Cole (1993).

72. For detailed discussion of the Weatherman organization, see Braungart and Braungart (1992), Jacobs (1997), and Varon (2004).

73. della Porta (2004: 219).

74. McPhail, Schweingruber, and McCarthy (1998: 50).

75. Ibid., 51.

76. See della Porta and Reiter (1998), della Porta (2004), McCarthy and McPhail (1998), and McPhail, Schweingruber, and McCarthy (1998) for discussion of protest policies and tendencies throughout Europe and the United States.

77. McAdam (1983).

78. Ibid., 752 (emphasis in original).

79. On March 21, 1960, the Pan African Congress organized a peaceful protest against pass books and pass laws, which were used to limit the movement of nonwhites and were one of the hallmarks of the system of apartheid. In response to the peaceful gathering of several thousand people, police forces opened fire on the crowd and killed sixty-nine people. A wave of protest both within and outside of South Africa followed the massacre, and the South African government declared a state of emergency. The event marks a turning point in South Africa's relationship with the rest of the world, as the international community (including the United Nations) condemned the actions of the police and, more generally, of apartheid. For a complete history of activism directed at South Africa, see Massie (1997).

80. Soule (1997).

81. Ibid.

82. See Soule (1997, 1999). Also see Davenport (2007) for a discussion of how repression can lead to subsequent protest.

83. See Soule (2004) for an extensive discussion of diffusion theorization and research on social movements.

84. See discussion in Garner and Tenuto (1997).

85. Morris (1981).

86. Andrews and Biggs (2006).

87. Meyer and Whittier (1994). Also see, Whittier (2004).

88. Tarrow (2005).

89. Danaher and Mark (2003).

90. Tarrow (2005).

91. Spilerman (1976).

92. Tarrow (2005) and Chabot (2002).

93. Note that Tarrow (2005) also discusses "mediated" forms of diffusion, which occur through a third party. One example that Tarrow discusses is the Highlander Folk School, which taught nonviolent tactics to activists, thus facilitating the diffusion of nonviolence.

94. Snow and Benford (1999).

95. Zuo and Benford (1995).

96. Esherick and Wasserstrom (1990).

97. For a critique of the contagion thesis, see McPhail (1991) and Turner and Killian (1987).

Chapter 6   Consequences of Social Movements

1. In actuality, the right to vote extended to black Americans by the Fifteenth Amendment, passed during Reconstruction in 1870, was only a de jure (rather than a de facto) right, as a number of Supreme Court decisions early on in the Jim Crow era ruled that while states could not exclude voters on account of race, they could set up standards that would restrict who could vote. Such rulings opened the door to the use of poll taxes and literacy tests to disenfranchise blacks. (See *Reese v. United States*, 1896, and *Williams v. Mississippi*, 1898). The threats posed by such terrorist groups as the Ku Klux Klan were also a persistent reminder to black Americans of the danger of voting. So the de jure right enshrined in the Fifteenth Amendment did not become a de facto (in fact) right for some time—ninety-five years later, to be exact, with the passage of the 1965 Voting Rights Act.

2. See McCammon (2001b).

3. See Taylor and Raeburn (1992) and Hirsch (1990).

4. We use the terms *outcomes, impacts,* and *consequences* interchangeably throughout this chapter. These terms refer to the effects that social movements have on something else, the terms avoid the more narrow meanings of *success* and *failure,* since, of course, not all of the effects of movements are about the realization (or nonrealization) of stated goals.

5. See Evans (1980). Note also that the feminist movement, in turn, had an impact on the peace movement as we discussed in Chapter 5.

6. Our use of this example does not mean to imply that social movements never *intend* for repression to occur. In fact, many movements attempt to provoke a repressive response, sometimes to clog up the legal system of a particular locale and at other times to get media attention. Repression, especially when viewed as unjust, can win the sympathies of the broader public, as occurred at times during the course of the civil rights movement in the 1960s. When this occurs, such repression constitutes what can be thought of as a social control error (see Chapter 3, note 78). Because of this possibility, movement activists sometimes seek to foster social control errors. Nonetheless, it is hard to conceive of the students in Beijing in 1989 intending the repression that was meted out by their government.

7. See Hirsch (1990).

8. See Sale (1974).

9. See Ibid.

10. For thumbnail sketches of a host of such groups, including these, see Lande (1976).

11. See Rochford (1985).

12. See Bromley and Shupe (1980) and Barker (1984).

13. See Snow (1979, 1987) and Wilson and Dobbelaere (1994).

14. Kanter (1972).

15. See Hirsch (1990).

16. See Benford (1993).

17. Here we have accented the role of conflicting perspectives and frame disputes in intramovement fractionalization and the generation of sectarian religious movements,

but the history of religion points to the role of power and class differences as often being even more fundamental. As Gillin noted as far back as 1910, "Almost every sect of Protestant Christendom has originated in the lower classes as a protest against what they felt was oppression by the superior classes" (1910: 245). See also, Niebuhr (1957).

18. See Soule (2004).

19. Amenta (2006).

20. Cress and Snow (2000).

21. See Meyer and Whittier (1994).

22. See Soule and Olzak (2004) and Soule and King (2006).

23. See McCammon, Campbell, Granberg, and Mowery (2001).

24. See Soule (2004).

25. See Kane (2003).

26. See Amenta (2006) and Andrews (2001).

27. Note that our earlier discussion of representation and various material concessions that were granted to homeless activists in various U.S. cities are examples of what Gamson calls acceptance and new advantages.

28. See Goldstein (1978: 429–545) and Cunningham (2004) on state repression of the New Left. See Hoover and Kowalewski (1992), Opp and Roehl (1990), Churchill (1994), and Fantasia (1988) for examples of other social movements that states have effectively repressed.

29. See Opp and Roehl (1990) and Hirsch (1990) for examples of research showing that repression can ignite future mobilization of repressed groups. See Davenport (2007) for a recent review of research on this topic.

30. See Hirsch (1990).

31. On these points, see Koopmans (1997), Earl and Soule (2006), and Davenport (2007).

32. See contributions in Davis, Morrill, Rao, and Soule (2008).

33. See Lounsbury (2001), Rojas (2006), and Soule (1997).

34. Rojas (2006).

35. See Manheim (2004).

36. See Raeburn (2004), Scully and Segal (2002), Kurtz (2002), and Taylor and Raeburn (1995).

37. See Raeburn (2004) and Baker et al. (1995).

38. King and Soule (2008) and Soule (forthcoming).

39. On cooperatives and mutuals, see Schneiberg et al. (2008). On wind power, see Sine and Lee (2008).

40. See Katzenstein (1998) and Chaves (1997).

41. See Chaves (2004).

42. See Rochon (1998) and d'Anjou (1996).

43. See Eyerman and Jamison (1995).

44. http://en.wikipedia.org/wiki/List_of_protest_songs, accessed on November 27, 2006.

45. See Pescosolida et al. (1997).

46. See review in Giugni (2004a).

47. See Whalen and Flacks (1989). When such findings have been suggested by a number of studies, it is probably best to regard these findings as tentative in the absence of closer investigation of possible contributing factors that may have preceded social activisim.

48. Klatch (1999).

49. See Andrews (2001, 2004).

50. See Andrews (2001, 2004), Piven and Cloward (1977), and Gamson (1990).

51. See Rosebraugh (2004).

52. King and Soule (2008).

53. Cress and Snow (2000).

54. See Benford and Snow (2000).

55. See McCammon (2001).

56. See McCammon (2001).

57. See Jenkins and Perrow (1977); Kitschelt (1986); Kriesi, Koopmans, Duyvendak, and Giugni (1995); Soule et al. (1999); Andrews (2001); and McCammon et al. (2001).

58. See Kay (2005).

59. See Amenta et al. (1992, 1994), Cress and Snow (2000), Giugni (2004b), and Soule and Olzak (2004).

60. Soule and Olzak (2004). Also see Soule and King (2006) and Agnone (2007).

61. Note, though, that Andrews (2001) and Amenta and his colleagues (1992, 1994) study levels of spending associated with particular policies; levels of spending may be considered one form of implementation.

62. See Burstein et al. (1995) and King, Cornwall, and Dahlin (2005).

63. See Earl (2004).

64. See Pescosolida et al. (1997).

65. See Soule and Olzak (2004) on the ERA, and Soule (2004) on same-sex marriage bans, for a similar point.

66. Consider, for example, the pro-Life and pro-Choice movements. It is not always clear which of these is the movement and which the countermovement, and it probably depends on the context of the study at hand. See discussion of movements and countermovement in Werum and Winders (2001).

67. See Soule et al. (1999) who show that one type of change, congressional hearings and votes on bills related to women's issues, was related to women's participation in the labor force.

68. See Van Dyke (1998).

69. Giugni, McAdam, and Tilly (1999).

70. Amenta (2006).

71. See discussion in Earl (2000).

REFERENCES

Ackerman, Peter, and Jack Duvall. 2000. *A Force More Powerful: A Century of Nonviolent Conflict.* New York: Palgrave.

Aguirre, Benigno E. 1984. "The Conventionalization of Collective Behavior in Cuba." *American Journal of Sociology* 90: 541–566.

Almeida, Paul D. 2003. "Opportunity, Organizations and Threat-Induced Contention: Protest Waves in Authoritarian Settings." *American Journal of Sociology* 109: 345–400.

Amenta, Edwin. 2006. *When Movements Matter: The Townsend Plan and the Rise of Social Security.* Princeton, NJ: Princeton University Press.

Amenta, Edwin, Bruce G. Carruthers, and Yvonne Zylan. 1992. "A Hero for the Aged? The Townsend Movement, the Political Mediation Model, and U.S. Old-Age Policy, 1934–1950." *American Journal of Sociology* 98: 308–339.

Amenta, Edwin, Kathleen Dunleavy, and Mary Bernstein. 1994. "Stolen Thunder? Huey Long's Share Our Wealth, Political Mediation, and the Second New Deal." *American Sociological Review* 59: 678–702.

Amenta Edwin, Neal Caren, and Sheera Joy Olasky 2005. "Age for Leisure? Political Mediation and the Impact of the Pension Movement on Old-Age Policy." *American Sociological Review* 70: 516–538.

Andreas, Joel. 2007. "The Structure of Charismatic Mobilization: A Case Study of Rebellion during the Chinese Cultural Revolution." *American Sociological Review* 72: 434–458.

Andrews, Kenneth T. 2001. "Social Movements and Policy Implementation: The Mississippi Civil Rights Movement and the War on Poverty, 1965–1971." *American Sociological Review* 66: 71–95.

———. 2004. *Freedom Is a Constant Struggle: The Mississippi Civil Rights Movement and Its Legacy.* Chicago: University of Chicago Press.

Andrews, Kenneth T., and Michael Biggs. 2006. "Dynamics of Protest Diffusion: Social Movement Organizations, Social Networks, and News Media in the 1960 Sit-Ins." *American Sociological Review* 71: 752–777.

Andrews, Kenneth T., and Robert Edwards. 2004. "Advocacy Organizations in the US Political Process." *Annual Review of Sociology* 30: 479–506.

Armstrong, Elizabeth A., and Suzanna M. Crage. 2006. "Movements and Memory: The Making of the Stonewall Myth." *American Sociological Review* 71: 724–751.

Associated Press. 2004. "Angry Mob Kills 2 Police Officers in Mexico." *Los Angeles Times*, November 24: A9.

Austin, Curtis J. 2006. *Up Against the Wall: Violence in the Making and Unmaking of the Black Panther Party.* Fayetteville: University of Arkansas.

Baker, Daniel B., Sean O'Brien Strub, and Bill Henning. 1995. *Cracking the Corporate Closet. The 200 Best (and Worst) Companies to Work For, Buy From, and Invest In If You're Gay or Lesbian—and Even If You Aren't.* New York: HarperBusiness.

Balch, Robert W. 1995. "Waiting for the Ships: Disillusionment and the Revitalization of Faith in Bo and Peep's UFO Cult." In *The Gods Have Landed: New Religions from Other Worlds*, ed. James R. Lewis, 137–166. Albany: State University of New York Press.

Balch, Robert W., and David Taylor. 1978. "Seekers and Saucers: The Role of Cultic Milieu in Joining a UFO Cult." In *Conversion Careers*, ed. James Richardson, 43–65. Beverly Hills, CA: Sage.

Barkan, Steven E., Steven F. Cohn, and William Whitaker. 1995. "Beyond Recruitment: Predictors of Differential Participation in a National Antihunger Organization." *Sociological Forum* 10: 113–134.

Barker, Eileen. 1984. *The Making of a Moonie.* New York: Basil Blackwell.

Barker, Eileen, ed. 1983. *Of Gods and Men: New Religious Movements in the West.* Macon, GA: Mercer University Press.

Bartkowski, John P. 2004. *The Promise Keepers: Servants, Soldiers, and Godly Men.* New Brunswick, NJ: Rutgers University Press.

Becker, Howard. 1960. "Notes on the Concept of Commitment." *American Journal of Sociology* 66: 32–40.

Benford, Robert D. 1993a. "Frame Disputes within the Nuclear Disarmament Movement." *Social Forces* 71: 677–701.

———. 1973b. "'You Could be the Hundredth Monkey': Collective Action Frames and Vocabularies of Motive within the Nuclear Disarmament Movement." *The Sociological Quarterly* 34: 195–216.

Benford, Robert D., and Snow, David A. 2000. "Framing Processes and Social Movements: An Overview and Assessment. *Annual Review of Sociology* 26:611–639.

Benjamin, Daniel. 1989. "State of Siege." *Time*, May 29: 36–41, 43–45.

Berger, Bennett M. 1981. *The Survival of a Counterculture: Ideological Work and Everyday Life Among Rural Communards.* Berkeley: University of California Press.

Bergesen, Albert J. 2007. "Three-Step Model of Terrorist Violence." *Mobilization* 12: 111–118.

Beyerlein, Kraig, and John R. Hipp. 2006. "A Two-Stage Model for a Two-Stage Process: How Biographical Availability Matters for Social Movement Mobilization." *Mobilization* 11: 219–240.

Bird, Frederick, and Bill Reimer. 1982. "Participation Rates in New Religious and Para-Religious Movements." *Journal for the Scientific Study of Religion* 21: 1–14.

Birnbaum, Jesse, and Howard G. Chua-Eoan. 1989. "Despair and Death in a Beijing Square." *Time*, June 12: 24–27.

Blee, Kathleen M. 2002. *Inside Organized Racism: Women in the Hate Movement*. Berkeley: University of California Press.

Bonwick, Colin. 1991. *The American Revolution*. Charlottesville: University of Virginia Press.

Boorstin, Daniel J. 1961. *The Image: A Guide to Pseudo-Events in America*. New York: Harper Colophon Books.

Borland, Elizabeth, and Barbara Sutton. 2007. "Quotidian Disruption and Women's Activism in Times of Crisis, Argentina 2002–2003." *Gender and Society* 41: 700–722.

Braungart, Richard G., and Margaret M. Braungart. 1990. "The Life-Course Development of Left- and Right-Wing Youth Activist Leaders from the 1960s."*Political Psychology* 11: 243–282.

————. 1992. "From Protest to Terrorism: The Case of the SDS and the Weathermen." *International Social Movement Research* 4: 45–78.

Bromley, David G., ed. 1988. *Falling from the Faith: The Causes and Consequences of Religious Apostasy*. Newbury Park, CA: Sage.

Buechler, Steven M. 2004. "The Strange Career of Strain and Breakdown Theories of Collective Action." In *The Blackwell Companion to Social Movements*, ed. David A. Snow, Sarah A. Soule, and Hanspeter Kriesi, 47–66. Malden, MA: Blackwell.

Bunis, William K. 1993. *Social Movement Activity and Institutionalized Politics: A Study of the Relationship Between Political Party Strength and Social Movement Activity in the United States*. Unpublished dissertation, University of Arizona.

Burstein, Paul. 1998. "Interest Organizations, Political Parties, and the Study of Democratic Politics." In *Social Movements and American Political Institutions*, ed. Anne N. Costain and Andrew S. McFarland, 39–56. Lanham, MD: Rowman & Littlefield.

————. 1999. "Social Movements and Public Policy." In *How Social Movements Matter*, ed. Marco Giugni, Doug McAdam, and Charles Tilly, 3–21. Minneapolis: University of Minnesota Press.

Cardinale, Matthew. 2004. "Affordable Housing and UCI's Trailer Park." Paper presented at Community Forum at UCI's Cross-Cultural Center, April 19.

Carmichael, Stokely, and Charles V. Hamilton. 1967. *Black Power: The Politics of Liberation in America*. New York: Vintage Books.

Carty, Victoria. 2009. "Bridging Contentious and Electoral Politics: MoveOn and the Digital Revolution." *Research in Social Movements, Conflict and Change:*30.

Chabot, Sean. 2002. "Transnational Diffusion and the African-American Reinvention of the Gandhian Repertoire." In *Globalization and Resistance: Transnational Dimensions of Social Movements*, ed. Jackie Smith and Hank Johnston. Lanham, MD: Rowman & Littlefield.

Chaves, Mark. 1997. *Ordaining Women: Culture and Conflict in Religious Organizations.* 1997. Cambridge, MA: Harvard University Press.

———. 2004. *Congregations in America.* Cambridge, MA: Harvard University Press.

Cho, Cynthia H., and Anna Gorman. 2006. "Massive Student Walkout Spreads Across Southland." *Los Angeles Times,* March 28: A1, A10.

Church, George J. 1989. "Freedom!" *Time,* November 20: 24–30, 33.

Churchill, Ward. 1994. "The Bloody Wake of Alcatraz: Political Repression of the American Indian Movement during the 1970s." *American Indian Culture and Research Journal* 18: 253–300.

Clark-Miller, Jason, and Jennifer Murdock. 2005. "Order on the Edge: Remedial Work in a Right-Wing Political Discussion Group." In *Together Alone: Personal Relationships in Public Places,* ed. Calvin Morrill, David A. Snow, and Cindy H.White, 201–224. Berkeley: University of California Press.

Claybourne, Carson. 1981. *In Struggle, SNCC and the Black Awakening of the 1960s.* Cambridge, MA: Harvard University Press.

Clemens, Elisabeth S., and Debra C. Minkoff. 2004. "Beyond the Iron Law: Rethinking the Place of Organizations in Social Movement Research." In *The Blackwell Companion to Social Movements,* ed. David A. Snow, Sarah A. Soule, and Hanspeter Kriesi, 155–170. Malden, MA: Blackwell.

Cohn, Norman. 1961. *The Pursuit of the Millennium.* New York: Harper & Row.

Corrigall-Brown, Catherine. 2007. *After the Protest: Trajectories of Participation in Social Movements.* Unpublished dissertation, University of California, Irvine.

Corrigall-Brown, Catherine, David A. Snow, Kelly Smith, and Theron Quist. 2009. "Explaining the Puzzle of Homeless Mobilization: An Examination of Differential Recruitment." *Sociological Perspectives,* forthcoming.

Coser, Lewis A. 1967. "Greedy Organizations." *Archives Européenes de Sociologie* 8: 196–215.

Cress, Daniel M., and David A. Snow. 1996. "Resources, Benefactors, and the Viability of Homeless SMOs." *American Sociological Review* 61: 1089–1109.

———. 2000. "The Outcomes of Homeless Mobilization: The Influence of Organization, Disruption, Political Mediation, and Framing." *American Journal of Sociology* 105: 1063–1104.

Cunningham, David. 2004. *There's Something Happening Here: The New Left, The Klan, and FBI Counterintelligence.* Berkeley: University of California Press.

Curtis, Richard L., and Louis A. Zurcher. 1973. "Stable Resources of Protest Movements: The Multi-Organizational Field." *Social Forces* 52: 53–61.

Dahrendorf, Ralf. 1959. *Class and Class Conflict in Industrial Society.* Stanford, CA: Stanford University Press.

Dalton, Russell. 2002. *Citizen Politics: Public Opinion and Political Parties in Advanced Industrial Democracies.* 3rd ed. New York: Chatham House.

Danaher, Kevin, and Jason Mark. 2003. *Insurrection.* New York: Routledge.

d'Anjou, Leo. 1996. *Social Movements and Cultural Change: The First Abolition Campaign Revisited*. New York: Aldine De Gruyter.

Davenport, Christian. 2007. "State Repression and Political Order." *Annual Review of Political Science* 10: 1–23.

Davis, Gerald, Doug McAdam, W. Richard Scott, and Mayer Zald. 2005. *Social Movements and Organization Theory*. New York: Cambridge University Press.

Davis, Gerald, Calvin Morrill, Hayagreeva Rao, and Sarah A. Soule. 2008. "Introduction: Social Movements in Organizations and Markets." *Administrative Science Quarterly* 53: 389–394.

de la Luz Inclán, María. 2008. "From the ¡*Ya Basta!* to the *Caracoles*: Zapatista Mobilization under Traditional Conditions." *American Journal of Sociology* 113: 1316–1350.

della Porta, Donatella. 1988. "Recruitment Processes in Clandestine Political Organizations: Italian Left-Wing Terrorism." *International Social Movement Research* 1: 155–169.

———. 1995. *Social Movements, Political Violence, and the State: A Comparative Analysis of Italy and Germany*. New York: Cambridge University Press.

della Porta, Donatella, and Olivier Fillieule. 2004. "Policing Social Protest." In *The Blackwell Companion to Social Movements*, ed. David A. Snow, Sarah A. Soule, and Hanspeter Kriesi, 217–241. Malden, MA: Blackwell.

della Porta, Donatella, and Herbert Reiter, eds. 1998. *Policing Protest: The Control of Mass Demonstrations in Western Democracies*. Minneapolis: University of Minnesota Press.

Diani, Mario. 2004. "Networks and Participation." In *The Blackwell Companion to Social Movements*, ed. David A. Snow, Sarah A. Soule, and Hanspeter Kriesi, 339–359. London: Blackwell.

Diani, Mario, and Doug McAdam, eds. 2003. *Social Movements and Networks: Relational Approaches to Collective Action*. New York: Oxford University Press.

DiMaggio, P. J., and W. W. Powell. 1983. "The Iron Cage Revisited: Institutional Isomorphism and Collective Rationality in Organizational Fields." *American Sociological Review* 48: 147–160.

Dixon, Marc, and Vincent J. Roscigno. 2003. "Status, Networks, and Social Movement Participation: The Case of Striking Workers." *American Journal of Sociology* 108: 1292–1327.

Dollard, John, Leonard Doob, Neal Miller, Herbert Mower, and Robert Sears. 1939. *Frustration and Aggression*. New Haven: Yale University Press.

Duncan, Lauren E., and Abigail J. Stewart. 1995. "Still Bringing the Vietnam War Home: Sources of Contemporary Student Activism." *Personality and Social Psychology Bulletin* 21: 914–924.

Earl, Jennifer. 2000. "Methods, Movements, and Outcomes: Methodological Difficulties in the Study of Extra-Movement Outcomes." *Research in Social Movements, Conflicts, and Change* 22: 3–25.

―――. 2003. "Tanks, Tear Gas and Taxes: Toward a Theory of Movement Repression." *Sociological Theory* 21: 44–68.

―――. 2004. "The Cultural Consequences of Social Movements." In *The Blackwell Companion to Social Movements*, ed. David A. Snow, Sarah A. Soule, and Hanspeter Kriesi, 508–530. Malden, MA: Blackwell.

Earl, Jennifer, and Alan Schussman. 2003. "New Site of Activism: Online Organizations, Movement Entrepreneurs, and the Changing Location of Decision Making in Social Movements." *Research in Social Movements, Conflicts, and Change* 24: 165–187.

Earl, Jennifer, and Sarah A. Soule. 2006. "Seeing Blue: A Police-Centered Explanation of Protest Policing." *Mobilization* 11: 145–164.

Earl, Jennifer, Sarah A. Soule, and John D. McCarthy. 2003. Protest Under Fire: Explaining the Policing of Protest." *American Sociological Review* 68: 581–606.

Earl, Jennifer, Andrew Martin, John D. McCarthy, and Sarah A. Soule. 2004. "Newspapers and Protest Event Analysis." *Annual Review of Sociology* 30: 65–80.

Edwards Jr., Mark U. 2005. *Printing, Propaganda, and Martin Luther*. Minneapolis: Fortress Press.

Edwards, Robert, and John McCarthy. 2004. "Resources and Social Movement Mobilization." In *The Blackwell Companion to Social Movements*, ed. David A. Snow, Sarah A. Soule, and Hanspeter Kriesi, 116–152. London: Blackwell.

Einwohner, Rachel L. 2003. "Opportunity, Honor, and Action in the Warsaw Ghetto Uprising of 1943." *American Journal of Sociology* 109: 650–675.

―――. 2006. "Identity Work and Collective Action in a Repressive Context: Jewish Resistance on the 'Aryan Side' of the Warsaw Ghetto." *Social Problems* 53: 38–56.

Eisinger, Peter K. 1973. "The Conditions of Protest Behavior in American Cities." *American Political Science Review* 67: 11–28.

Ennis, James G., and Richard Schreuer. 1987. "Mobilizing Weak Support for Social Movements: The Role of Grievance, Efficacy, and Cost." *Social Forces* 66: 390–409.

Esherick, J. W., and J. N. Wasserstrom. 1990. "Acting Out Democracy: Political Theater in Modern China." *Journal of Asian Studies* 49: 835–865.

Evans, Sara M. 1979. *Personal Politics: The Roots of Women's Liberation in the Civil Rights Movement and the New Left*. New York: Knopf.

Evans, Sara M., and Harry C. Boyte. 1986. *Free Spaces: The Sources of Democratic Change in America*. New York: Harper & Row.

Everett, Kevin D. 1992. "Professionalization and Protest: Changes in the Social Movement Sector, 1961–1983." *Social Forces* 70(4): 957–975.

Eyerman, Ron, and Andrew Jamison. 1998. *Music and Social Movements: Mobilizing Traditions in the Twentieth Century*. Cambridge: Cambridge University Press.

Fager, Charles E. 1985. *Selma 1965: The March That Changed the South*. Boston: Beacon Press.

Fantasia, Rick. 1988. *Cultures of Solidarity: Consciousness, Action and Contemporary American Workers.* Berkeley: University of California Press.

Fantasia, Rick, and Judith Stepan-Norris. 2004. "The Labor Movement in Motion." In *The Blackwell Companion to Social Movements,* ed. David A. Snow, Sarah A. Soule, and Hanspeter Kriesi, 555–575. London: Blackwell.

Fernandez, Roberto M., and Doug McAdam. 1988. "Social Networks and Social Movements: Multiorganizational Fields and Recruitment to Mississippi Freedom Summer." *Sociological Forum* 3: 357–382.

Ferree, Myra Marx. 1992. "The Political Context of Rationality: Rational Choice Theory and Resource Mobilization." In *Frontiers in Social Movement Theory,* ed. Aldon D. Morris and Carol McClurg Mueller, 29–52. New Haven: Yale University Press.

———. 2003. "Resonance and Radicalism: Feminist Framing in the Abortion Debates of the United States and Germany." *American Journal of Sociology* 109: 304–344.

———. 2004. "Soft Repression: Ridicule, Stigma, and Silencing in Gender-Based Movements." In *Authority in Contention: Research in Social Movements, Conflict, and Change,* vol. 25, ed. Daniel J. Meyers and Daniel M. Cress, 85–101. London/New York: Elsevier.

Ferree, Myra M., William A. Gamson, Jürgen Gerhards, and Deiter Rucht. 2002. *Shaping Abortion Discourse: Democracy and the Public Sphere in Germany and the United States.* New York: Cambridge University Press.

Fine, Gary F. 2006. "Notorious Support: The America First Committee and the Personalization of Policy." *Mobilization* 11: 405–426.

Flacks, Richard. 1967. "The Liberated Generation: An Exploration of the Roots of Student Protest." *Journal of Social Issues* 23: 52–74.

Forward, J. R., and J. R. Williams. 1970. "Internal-External Control and Black Militancy." *Journal of Social Issues* 26: 75–92.

Freeman, Jo. 1973. "The Origins of the Women's Liberation Movement." *American Journal of Sociology* 78: 192–811.

Gamson, William A. 1969. *Power and Discontent.* Homewood, IL: Dorsey Press.

———. 1990. *The Strategy of Social Protest.* 2nd ed. Belmont, CA: Wadsworth.

———. 1992. *Talking Politics.* New York: Cambridge University Press.

———. 2004. "Bystanders, Public Opinion, and the Media." In *The Blackwell Companion to Social Movements,* ed. David A. Snow, Sarah A. Soule, and Hanspeter Kriesi, 242–261. London: Blackwell.

Gamson, William A., and David S. Meyer 1996. "Framing Political Opportunity." In *Comparative Perspectives on Social Movements: Political Opportunities, Mobilizing Structures, and Cultural Framings,* ed. Doug McAdam, John D. McCarthy, and Mayer N. Zald, 275–290. Cambridge: Cambridge University Press.

Gamson, W. A., and G. Wolfsfeld. 1993. "Movements and Media as Interacting Systems." *Annals of the American Academy of Political and Social Science* 528: 114–125.

Gardner, Hugh. 1978. *The Children of Prosperity: Thirteen Modern American Communes*. New York: St. Martin's Press.

Garner, Roberta, and John Tenuto. 1997. *Social Movement Theory and Research: An Annotated Bibliographical Guide*. Metuchen, NJ: Scarecrow Press.

Gecas, Viktor. 2000. "Value Identities, Self-Motives, and Social Movements." In *Self, Identity, and Social Movements*, ed. Sheldon Stryker, Timothy J. Owens, and Robert W. White, 93–109. Minneapolis: University of Minnesota Press.

Gerlach, Luther P., and Virginia H. Hine. 1970. *People, Power, Change: Movements of Social Transformation*. Indianapolis: Bobbs-Merrill.

Geschwender, James A. 1967. "Continuities in Theories of Status Inconsistency and Cognitive Dissonance." *Social Forces* 46: 160–171.

Giugni, Marco. 2004a. "Personal and Biographical Consequences." In *The Blackwell Companion to Social Movements*, ed. David A. Snow, Sarah A. Soule, and Hanspeter Kriesi, 489–507. Malden, MA: Blackwell.

———. 2004b. *Social Protest and Policy Change: Ecology, Antinuclear, and Peace Movements in Comparative Perspective*. Boulder, CO: Rowman & Littlefield.

Giugni, Marco, Doug McAdams, and Charles Tilly. 1999. *How Social Movements Matter*. Minneapolis: University of Minnesota Press.

Gillin, John L. 1910. "A Contribution to the Sociology of Sects." *American Journal of Sociology* 16: 236–252.

Gitlin, Todd. 1980. *The Whole World Is Watching: Mass Media and the Making & Unmaking of the New Left*. Berkeley: University of California Press.

Gleick, Elizabeth. 1997. "The Marker We've Been Waiting For." *Time*, April 7: 28–36.

Goffman, Erving. 1961. *Asylums*. Garden City, NY: Anchor.

———. 1974. *Frame Analysis*. New York: Harper.

Goldstein, R. J. 1978. *Political Repression in Modern America: From 1870 to the Present*. Cambridge, MA: Schenkman.

Goodwin, Jeff. 2001. *No Other Way Out*. New York: Cambridge University Press.

Goodwin, Jeff, and James M. Jasper. 1999. "Caught in a Winding, Snarling Vine: The Structural Bias of Political Process Theory." *Sociological Forum* 14: 27–54.

Goodwin, Jeff, James M. Jasper, and Francesca Polletta, eds. 2001. *Passionate Politics: Emotions and Social Movements*. Chicago: University of Chicago Press.

———. 2004. "Emotional Dimensions of Social Movements." In *The Blackwell Companion to Social Movements*, ed. David A. Snow, Sarah A. Soule, and Hanspeter Kriesi, 413–432. London: Blackwell.

Gordon, David F. 1974. "The Jesus People: An Identity Synthesis." *Urban Life* (now *Journal of Contemporary Ethnography*). 3: 159–178.

Gould, Roger V. 1991. "Multiple Networks and Mobilization in the Paris Commune, 1871." *American Sociological Review* 56: 716–729.

Graff, James. 2005. "Why Paris Is Burning." *Time*, November 14.

Gurr, Ted. 1970. *Why Men Rebel*. Princeton, NJ: Princeton University Press.

Habermas, Jürgen. 1975. *Legitimation Crisis*. Boston: Beacon Press.

Haines, Herbert H. 1984. "Black Radicalization and the Funding of Civil Rights: 1957–1970." *Social Problems* 32: 31–43.

Hall, John R. 1987. *Gone from the Promised Land: Jonestown in American Cultural History*. New Brunswick, NJ: Transaction.

———. 2000. *Apocalypse Observed: Religious Movements and Violence in North America, Europe, and Japan*. London: Routledge.

Hall, J., ed. 1977. *Black Separatism and Social Reality: Rhetoric and Reason*. New York: Pergamon Press.

Hannan, Michael T., and John Freeman. 1989. *Organizational Ecology*. Cambridge, MA: Harvard University Press.

Hassan, Nasra. 2001. "An Arsenal of Believers: Talking to 'Human Bombs'." *The New Yorker* November 19: 36–41.

Hasso, Frances S. 2001. "Feminist Generations? The Long-Term Impact of Social Movement Involvement in Palestinian Women's Lives." *American Journal of Sociology* 107: 586–611.

Hechter, Michael, and S. Kanazawa. 1997. "Sociological Rational Choice Theory." *Annual Review of Sociology* 23: 191–214.

Hegtvedt, Karen, and Barry Markovsky. 1995. "Justice and Injustice." In *Sociological Perspectives on Social Psychology,* ed. K. Cook, G. Fine, and J. House, 257–280. Boston: Allyn & Bacon.

Hensley, Thomas R., and Jerry M. Lewis. 1978. *Kent State and May 4th: A Social Science Perspective*. Dubuque, IA: Kendall/Hunt.

Hilliard, David, and Lewis Cole. (1993). *This Side of Glory: The Autobiography of David Hilliard and the Story of the Black Panther Party*. Chicago: Lawrence Hill Books.

Hirsch, Eric. L. 1990. "Sacrifice for the Cause: Group Processes, Recruitment, and Commitment in a Student Social Movement." *American Sociological Review* 55: 243–254.

Hirschman, Albert O. 1993. "Exit, Voice, and the Fate of the German Democratic Republic—An Essay in Conceptual History." *World Politics* 45: 173–202.

Hollander, E. P. 1958. "Conformity, Status, and Idiosyncrasy Credit." *Psychological Review* 65: 117–127.

Holley, David. "Ukainian Leader Calls for Talks to Solve Crisis." *Los Angeles Times* November 24: A1, A12.

Hoover, Dean, and David Kowalewski. 1992. "Dynamic Models of Dissent and Repression." *Journal of Conflict Resolution* 36: 150–182.

Hunt, Scott A., and Robert D. Benford. 2004. "Collective Identity, Solidarity, and Commitment." In *The Blackwell Companion to Social Movements*, ed. David A. Snow, Sarah A. Soule, and Hanspeter Kriesi, 433–457. Malden, MA: Blackwell.

Hunt, Scott, Robert D. Benford, and David A. Snow. 1994. "Identity Fields: Framing Processes and the Social Construction of Movement Identities." In *New Social Movements: From Ideology to Identity,* ed. E. Larana, H. Johnson, and J. R. Gusfield, 185–208. Philadelphia: Temple University Press.

Isserman, Maurice. 2000. *The Other American: The Life of Michael Harrington*. New York: Public Affairs.

Jacobs, Ron. 1997. *The Way the Wind Blew: A History of the Weather Underground*. New York: Verso.

Jasper, James M. 1997. *The Art of Moral Protest: Culture, Biography, and Creativity in Social Movements*. Chicago: University of Chicago Press.

———. 2006. *Getting Your Way: Strategic Dilemmas in the Real World*. Chicago: University of Chicago Press.

Jasper, James M., and Jane Poulson. 1995. "Recruiting Strangers and Friends: Moral Shocks and Social Networks in Animal Rights and Animal Protest." *Social Problems* 42: 49–512.

Jenkins, J. Craig, and Craig M. Eckert. 1986. "Channeling Black Insurgency: Elite Patronage and Professional Social Movement Organizations in the Development of the Black Movement." *American Sociological Review* 51: 812–829.

Jenkins, Craig, and Charles Perrow. 1977. "Insurgency of the Powerless: Farm Worker Movements (1946–1972)." *American Sociological Review* 42: 249–268.

Jenkins, Craig, David Jacobs, and Jon Agnone. 2003. "Political Opportunities and African American Protest, 1948–1997." *American Journal of Sociology* 109: 277–303.

Jennings, M. Kent, and Laura Stoker. 2004. "Youth-Parent Socialization Panel Study, 1965–1997: Youth Wave IV, 1997." Data set. Ann Arbor: University of Michigan.

Johnston, Hank, and Bert Klandermans. 1995. *Social Movements and Culture*. Minneapolis: University of Minnesota Press.

Johnston, Hank, and David A. Snow. 1998. "Subcultures and the Emergence of the Estonian Nationalist Opposition, 1945–1990." *Sociological Perspectives* 41: 473–497.

Jones, Andrew W., Richard N. Hutchinson, Nella Van Dyke, Leslie Gates, and Michele Companion." 2001. "Coalition Formation and Mobilization Effectiveness in Local Social Movements." *Sociological Spectrum* 21: 207–231.

Juergensmeyer, Mark. 2000. *Terror in the Mind of God: The Global Rise of Religious Violence*. Berkeley: University of California Press.

Kahneman, D., and A. Tversky. 1979. "Prospect Theory: An Analysis of Decision Under Risk." *Econometrica* 47: 263–291.

Kane, Melinda D. 2003. "Social Movement Policy Success: Decriminalizing State Sodomy Laws, 1969–1998." *Mobilization* 8(3): 313–334.

Kanter, Rosabeth. 1972. *Commitment and Community: Communes and Utopias in Sociological Perspective*. Cambridge, MA: Harvard University Press.

Kaplan, Howard, and X. Liu. 2000. "Social Movements as Collective Coping with Spoiled Identities. Intimations from a Panel Study of Changes in the Life Course Between Adolescence and Adulthood." In *Self, Identity and Social Movements*, ed. Sheldon Stryker, Timothy Owens, and Robert White, 215–238. Minneapolis: University of Minnesota Press.

Kapur, Rajuv. 1986. *Sikh Separatism: The Politics of Faith.* London: Allen & Unwin.

Katzenstein, Mary F. 1998. *Faithful and Fearless: Moving Feminist Protest Inside the Church and the Military.* Princeton, NJ: Princeton University Press.

Kautsky, Karl. 1910. *The Class Struggle.* Chicago: Charles H. Kerr.

Kay, Tamara. 2005. "Labor Transnationalism and Global Governance: The Impact of NAFTA on Transnational Labor Relationships in North America." *American Journal of Sociology* 111: 715–756.

Keck, Margaret E., and Kathryn Sikkink. 1998. *Activists Beyond Borders: Advocacy Networks in International Politics.* Ithaca, NY: Cornell University Press.

Killian, Lewis M. 1964. "Social Movements." In *Handbook of Modern Sociology*, ed. Robert E. Faris, 426–455. Chicago: Rand McNally.

King, Brayden, and Sarah A. Soule. 2007. "Social Movements as Extra-Institutional Entrepreneurs: The Effect of Protest on Stock Price Returns." *Administrative Science Quarterly* 52: 413–442.

King, Brayden, Keith Gunnar Bentele, and Sarah A. Soule. 2007 "Congressional Agenda-Setting and Fluctuating Attention to Civil and Political Rights, 1960–1987." *Social Forces* 86: 137–163.

Kitschelt, Herbert. 1986. "Political Opportunity Structures and Political Protest: Anti-Nuclear Movements in Four Democracies." *British Journal of Political Science* 16: 57–85.

Kitts, James A. 1999. "Not in our backyard: Solidarity, social networks, and the ecology of environmental mobilization." *Sociological Inquiry* 69: 551–574.

Klandermans, Bert. 1984. "Mobilization and Participation: Social Psychological Expansions of Resource Mobilization Theory." *American Sociological Review* 49: 583–600.

———. 1992. "The Social Construction of Protest and Multiorganizational Fields". In *Frontiers in Social Movement Theory*, ed. Aldon D. Morris and Carol M. Mueller, 77–103. New Haven: Yale University Press.

———. 2004. "The Demand and Supply of Participation: Social-Psychological Correlates of Participation in Social Movements." In *The Blackwell Companion to Social Movements*, ed. David A. Snow, Sarah A. Soule, and Hanspeter Kriesi, 360–379. Malden, MA: Blackwell.

Klandermans, Bert, and Marga de Weerd. 2000. "Group Identification and Political Protest." In *Self, Identity, and Social Movements*, ed. Sheldon Stryker, Timothy J. Owens, and Robert W. White, 68–90. Minneapolis: University of Minnesota Press.

Klandermans, Bert, and Dirk Oegema. 1987. "Potentials, Networks, Motivation, and Barriers: Steps Toward Participation in Social Movements." *American Sociological Review* 52: 519–531.

Klandermans, Bert, Marlene Roefs, and Johan Olivier. 2001. "Grievance Formation in a Country in Transition: South Africa, 1994–1998." *Social Psychology Quarterly* 64: 41–54.

Klapp, Orrin. 1969. *Collective Search for Identity.* New York: Holt, Rinehart and Winston.

Klatch, Rebecca E. 1999. *A Generation Divided: The New Left, the New Right, and the 1960s.* Berkeley: University of California Press.

Kluegel, James R., and Eliot R. Smith. 1986. *Beliefs About Inequality: American's Views of What Is and What Ought to Be.* New York: Aldine de Gruyter.

Koopmans, Ruud. 1997. "The Dynamics of Repression and Mobilization: The German Extreme Right in the 1990s." *Mobilization* 2: 149–165.

———. 2004. "Protest in Time and Space: The Evolution of Waves of Contention." In *The Blackwell Companion to Social Movements,* ed. David A. Snow, Sarah A. Soule, and Hanspeter Kriesi, 19–46. London: Blackwell.

Koopmans, Ruud, and Susan Olzak. 2004. "Discursive Opportunities and the Evolution of Right-Wing Violence in Germany." *American Journal of Sociology* 110: 198–230.

Kriesi, Hanspeter. 2004. "Political Context and Opportunity." In *The Blackwell Companion to Social Movements,* ed. David A. Snow, Sarah A. Soule, and Hanspeter Kriesi, 67–90. London: Blackwell.

Kriesi, Hanspeter, Ruud Koopmans, Jan Willem Duyvendak, and Marco Giugni. 1995. *New Social Movements in Western Europe: A Comparative Analysis.* Minneapolis: University of Minnesota Press.

Kurzman, Charles. 1996. "Structural Opportunity and Perceived Opportunity in Social Movement Theory: The Iranian Revolution of 1979." *American Sociological Review* 61: 153–170.

Kurtz, Sharon. 2002. *Workplace Justice: Organizing Multi-Identity Movements.* Minneapolis: University of Minnesota Press.

Lande, Nathaniel. 1976. *Mindstyles, Lifestyles.* Los Angeles: Price/Stern/Sloan.

Lang, Kurt, and Gladys Engel Lang. 1961. *Collective Dynamics.* New York: Crowell.

Lelyveld, Joseph. 2001. "All Suicide Bombers Are Not Alike." *The New York Times Magazine* October 28: 49–53, 62, 78–79.

Lenin, V. I. 1929. *What Is to Be Done? Burning Questions of Our Movement.* New York: International Publishers.

Lenski, Gerhard. 1954. "Status Crystallization: A Non-Vertical Dimension of Status." *American Sociological Review* 32: 405–413.

Levitt, Matthew. 2007. *Hamas: Politics, Charity, and Terrorism in the Service of Jihad.* New Haven, CT: Yale University Press.

Lewis, Steven H., and Robert E. Kraut 1972. "Correlates of Student Activism and Ideology." *Journal of Social Issues* 28: 131–149.

Lipsky, Michael. 1970. *Power in City Politics.* Chicago: Rand McNally.

Lofland, John. 1968. "The Youth Ghetto: Age Segregation and Conflict in the American Sixties." *Journal of Higher Education* 39: 121–143.

——. 1996. *Social Movement Organizations: Guide to Research on Insurgent Realities.* New York: Aldine de Gruyter.

Lounsbury, Michael. 2001. "Institutional Sources of Practice Variation: Staffing College and University Recycling Programs." *Administrative Science Quarterly* 46: 29–56.

Loveman, Mara. 1998. "High-Risk Collective Action: Defending Human Rights in Chile, Uruguay, and Argentina." *American Journal of Sociology* 104: 477–525.

Manheim, Jarol B. 2004. *Biz-War and the Out-of-Power Elite: The Progressive-Left Attack on the Corporation.* Mahwah, NJ: Lawrence Erlbaum Associates.

Marullo, Sam, and David S. Meyer. 2004. "Anti-War and Peace Movements." In *The Blackwell Companion to Social Movements*, ed. David A. Snow, Sarah A. Soule, Hanspeter Kriesi, 641–665. Oxford, UK: Blackwell.

Marx, Karl. 1963. *The 18th Brumaire of Louis Bonaparte.* New York: International Publishers.

Marx, Karl, and Friedrich Engels. 1948. *Manifesto of the Communist Party.* New York: International Publishers.

Massie, Robert Kinloch. 1997. *Loosing the Bonds: The United States and South Africa in the Apartheid Years.* New York: Doubleday.

McAdam, Doug. 1982. *Political Process and the Development of Black Insurgency, 1930–1970.* Chicago: University of Chicago Press.

——. 1983. "Tactical Innovation and the Pace of Insurgency." *American Sociological Review* 48: 735–754.

——. 1986. "Recruitment to High-Risk Activism: The Case of Freedom Summer." *American Journal of Sociology* 92: 64–90.

——. 1988. *Freedom Summer.* New York: Oxford University Press.

——. 1996. "Political Opportunities: Conceptual Origins, Current Problems, and Future Directions." In *Comparative Perspectives on Social Movements: Political Opportunities, Mobilizing Structures, and Cultural Framings*, ed. Doug McAdam, John D. McCarthy, and Mayer N. Zald, 23–40. New York: Cambridge University Press.

McAdam, Doug, and Ronnelle Paulsen. 1993. "Specifying the Relationship Between Social Ties and Activism." *American Journal of Sociology* 99: 640–667.

McAdam, Doug, and Yang Su. 2002. "The War at Home: Antiwar Protests and Congressional Voting, 1965–1973." *American Sociological Review* 67: 696–721.

McAdam, Doug, John McCarthy, and Mayer N. Zald. 1988. "Social Movements." In *The Handbook of Sociology*, ed. Neil Smelser, 695–737. Newbury Park, CA: Sage.

McAdam, Doug, Sidney Tarrow, and Charles Tilly. 2001. *Dynamics of Contention.* New York: Cambridge University Press.

McCammon, Holly J. 2001. "Stirring Up Suffrage Sentiment: The Formation of the State Woman Suffrage Organizations, 1866–1914." *Social Forces* 80: 449–480.

——. 2008. "Beyond Frame Resonance: The Argumentative Structure and Persuasive Capacity of Twentieth-Century U.S. Women's Jury Rights Frames." *Mobilization* 14: 45–64.

McCammon, Holly J., Karen E. Campbell, Ellen M. Granberg, and Christine Mowery. 2001. "How Movements Win: Gendered Opportunity Structures and U.S. Women's Suffrage Movements, 1866–1919." *American Sociological Review* 66: 49–70.

McCammon, Holly J., Courtney Sanders Muse, Harmony D. Newman, and Teresa M. Terrell. 2007. "Movement Framing and Discursive Opportunity Structures: The Political Successes of the U.S. Women's Jury Movements." *American Sociological Review* 72: 725–749.

McCarthy, John D., and Clark McPhail. 1998."The Institutionalization of Protest." In *The Social Movement Society*, ed. David S. Meyer and Sidney Tarrow, 83–110. Boulder, CO: Rowman & Littlefield.

McCarthy, John, and Mayer Zald. 1973. *The Trend of Social Movements in America.* Morristown, NJ: General Learning Press.

———. 1977. "Resource Mobilization and Social Movements: A Partial Theory." *American Journal of Sociology* 82: 1212–1241.

———. 2002. "The Enduring Vitality of the Resource Mobilization Theory of Social Movements." In *Handbook of Sociological Theory*, ed. Jonathon H. Turner, 533–565. New York: Kluwer Academic/Plenum.

McCarthy, John, Clark McPhail, and Jackie Smith. 1996. "Images of Protest: Dimensions of Selection Biasis in Media Coverage of Washington Demonstrations, 1982– 1991." *American Sociological Review* 61: 478–499.

McGeary, Johanna. 1999 "Mohandas Gandhi." *Time* December 31: 118–123.

McLaughlin, Paul, and Khawaja Morgan. 2000. "The Organizational Dynamics of the U.S. Environmental Movement: Legitimation. Resource Mobilization, and Political Opportunity." *Rural Sociology* 65: 422–439.

McPhail, Clark. 1991. *The Myth of the Madding Crowd.* New York: Aldine de Gruyter.

McPhail, Clark, David Schweingruber, and John McCarthy. 1998. "Policing Protest in the United States: 1960–1995." In *Policing Protest: The Control of Mass Demonstrations in Western Democracies*, ed. Donatella della Porta and Herbert Reiter, 49–69. Minneapolis: University of Minnesota Press.

Melucci, Alberto. 1989. *Nomads of the Present: Social Movements and Individual Needs in Contemporary Society,* ed. John Keane and Paul Mier. Philadelphia: Temple University Press.

Meyer, David S. 1990. *A Winter of Discontent: The Nuclear Freeze and American Politics.* New York: Praeger.

———. 2004. "Protest and Political Opportunities." *Annual Review of Sociology* 30: 125–145.

———. 2007. *The Politics of Protest.* New York: Oxford University Press.

Meyer, David S., and Catherine Corrigall-Brown. 2005. "Coalitions and Political Context: U.S. Movements Against Wars in Iraq." *Mobilization* 10: 327–344.

Meyer, David S., and Sidney Tarrow, eds. 1998. *The Social Movement Society: Contentious Politics for a New Century.* Boulder, CO: Rowman & Littlefield.

Meyer, David S., and Nancy Whittier. 1994. "Social Movement Spillover." *Social Problems* 41: 277–298.

Michels, Robert. 1949. *Political Parties: A Sociological Study of the Oligarchical Tendencies of Modern Democracy*. Glencoe, IL: Free Press.

Mills, C. Wright. 1940. "Situated Actions and Vocabularies of Motive." *American Sociological Review* 5: 904–913.

Minkoff, Debra. 1997. "The Sequencing of Social Movements." *American Sociological Review* 62: 779–799.

Moore Jr., Barrington. 1978. *Injustice: The Social Basis of Obedience and Revolt*. White Plains, NY: M.E. Sharpe.

Morris, Aldon D. 1981. "Black Southern Student Sit-In Movement: An Analysis of Internal Organization." *American Sociological Review* 46: 744–767.

———. 1984. *The Origins of the Civil Rights Movement: Black Communities Organizing for Change*. New York: Free Press.

Morris, Aldon D., and Suzanne Staggenborg. 2004. "Leadership in Social Movements." In *The Blackwell Companion to Social Movements*, ed. David A. Snow, Sarah A. Soule, and Hanspeter Kriesi, 171–196. Malden, MA: Blackwell.

Mueller, Carol 1994. "Conflict Networks and the Origins of Women's Liberation." In *New Social Movements: From Ideology to Identity*, ed. E. Larana, H. Johnson and J. R. Gusfield, 234–263. Philadelphia: Temple University Press.

———. 1999. "Escape from the GDR, 1961–1989: Hybrid Exit Repertoires in a Disintegrating Leninist Regime." *American Journal of Sociology* 105: 697–735.

Myers, Daniel J. 1997. "Racial Rioting in the 1960s: An Event History Analysis of Local Conditions." *American Sociological Review* 62: 94–112.

Nepstadt, Sharon Erikson. 2004. "Persistent Resistance: Commitment and Community in the Plowshares Movement." *Social Problems* 51: 43–60.

Nepstadt, Sharon Erickson, and Christian Smith. 1999. "Rethinking Recruitment to High-Risk/Cost Activism: The Case of the Nicaragua Exchange." *Mobilization* 4: 25–40.

Niebuhr, H. Richard. 1957 (1929). *The Social Sources of Denominationalism*. New York: Meridian Books.

Oegema, Dirk, and Bert Klandermans. 1994. "Why Social Movement Sympathizers Don't Participate: Erosion and Nonconversion of Support." *American Sociological Review* 59: 703–722.

Oliver, Pamela E., and Daniel J. Meyers 1999. "How Events Enter the Public Sphere: Conflict, Location, and Sponsorship in Local Newspaper Coverage of Public Events." *American Journal of Sociology* 105: 38–87.

Oliver, Pamela E., and Gregory M. Maney 2000. "Political Processes and Local Newspaper Coverage of Protest Events: From Selection Biasis to Triadic Interactions." *American Journal of Sociology* 106: 463–505.

Olivier, Johan. 1990. "Causes of Ethnic Collective Action in the Pretoria-Witwatersrand-Vaal Triangle, 1970–1984." *South African Sociological Review* 2: 89–108.

Olson, Mancur. 1965. *The Logic of Collective Action: Public Goods and the Theory of Groups*. Cambridge, MA: Harvard University Press.

Olzak, Susan, and Suzanne Shanahan. 1996. "Deprivation and Race Riots: An Extension of Spilerman's Analysis." *Social Forces* 74: 931–961.

Opp, Karl-Dieter, and Wolfgang Roehl. 1990. "Repression, Micromobilization, and Political Protest." *Social Forces* 69: 521–547.

"Osama bin Laden World Islamic Front Statement Against Jews and Crusaders." 1998. www.fas.org/irp/world/para/docs/980223-fatwa.htm. Accessed on February 23, 1998.

Paige, Jeffrey M. 1971. "Political Orientation and Riot Participation." *America Sociological Review* 36: 810–820.

Passy, Florence, and Marco Giugni. 2001. "Social Networks and Individual Perceptions: Explaining Differential Participation in Social Movements." *Sociological Forum* 16: 123–153.

Paulsen, Ronnelle. 1991. "Education, Social Class, and Participation in Collective Action." *Sociology of Education* 64: 96–110.

Pedriana, Nicholas. 2006. "From Protective to Equal Treatment: Legal Framing Processes and Transformation of the Women's Movement in the 1960s." *American Journal of Sociology* 111: 1718–1761.

Penner, Louis A. 2002. "The Causes of Sustained Volunteerism: An Interactionist Perspective." *Journal of Social Issues* 58: 447–468.

Penner, Louis A., and Marcia A. Finkelstein. 1998. "Dispositional and Structural Determinants of Voluntarism." *Journal of Personality and Social Psychology* 74: 525–537.

Perlez, Jane. 2008 (January 18). "Frontier Insurgency Spills into Peshawar." *New York Times,* www.nytimes.com/2008/01/18/world/asia/18peshawar.html, accessed on February 5, 2009.

Pescosolido, Bernice A., Elizabeth Grauerholz, and Melissa A. Milkie. 1997. "Culture and Conflict: The Portrayal of Blacks in U.S. Children's Picture Books Through the Mid- and Late-Twentieth Century." *American Sociological Review* 62: 443–464.

Petras, James, and Maurice Zeitlin. 1967. "Miners and Agriculture Radicalism." *American Sociological Review* 32: 578–586.

Pfaff, Steven, and Hyojoung Kim. 2003. "Exit-Voice Dynamics in Collective Action: An Analysis of Emigration and Protest in the East German Revolution." *American Journal of Sociology* 109: 401–444.

Pinel, Elizabeth C., and William B. Swann Jr. 2000. "Finding the Self through Others: Self-Verification and Social Movement Participation." In *Self, Identity and Social Movements,* ed. Sheldon Stryker, Timothy Owens, and Robert White, 132–152. Minneapolis: University of Minnesota Press.

Piven, Frances Fox, and Richard Cloward. 1977. *Poor Peoples' Movements.* New York: Vintage Books.

Platt, Gerald M., and Stephen J. Lilley. 1994. "Multiple Images of a Charismatic: An Interpretive Conception of Martin Luther King Jr.'s Leadership." In *Self, Collective*

Behavior and Society: Essays Honoring the Contributions of Ralph H. Turner, ed. Gerald M. Platt and Chad Gordon, 55–74. Greenwich, CT: JAI Press.

Polletta, Francesca. 1999. "'Free Spaces' in Collective Action." *Theory and Society* 28: 1–38.

———. 2006. *It Was Like a Fever: Storytelling in Protest and Politics.* Chicago: University of Chicago Press.

Polletta, Franscesca, and James M. Jasper. 2001. "Collective Identity in Social Movements." *Annual Review of Sociology* 27: 283–305.

Prasad, Anshuman, and Pushkala Prasad. 1998. "Everyday Struggles at the Workplace: The Nature and Implications of Routine Resistance in Contemporary Organizations." *Research in Sociology of Organizations* 15: 225–257.

Raeburn, Nicole C. 2004. *Changing Corporate America from Inside Out: Lesbian and Gay Workplace Rights.* Minneapolis: University of Minnesota Press.

Rasler, Karen. 1996. "Concessions, Repression, and Political Protest in the Iranian Revolution." *American Sociological Review* 61: 132–152.

Robbins, Thomas. 1988. *Cults, Converts & Charisma: The Sociology of New Religious. Movements.* Newbury Park, CA: Sage.

Robnett, Belinda. 1996. "African American Women and Leadership in the U.S. Civil Rights Movement." *American Journal of Sociology* 101: 1661–1693.

Roche, John P., and Stephen Sachs. 1965. "The Bureaucrat and the Enthusiast: An Exploration of the Leadership of Social Movements." *Western Political Quarterly* 8: 248–261.

Rochford, E. Burke Jr. 1985. *Hare Krishna in America.* New Brunswick, NJ: Rutgers University Press.

Rochon, Thomas R. 1998. *Culture Moves: Ideas, Activism, and Changing Values.* Princeton, NJ: Princeton University Press.

Rohlinger, Deana A. 2002. "Framing the Abortion Debate: Organizational Resources, Media Strategies, and Movement-Countermovement Dynamics." *The Sociological Quarterly* 43: 479–507.

Rohlinger, Deana, and David A. Snow. 2003. "Social Psychological Perspectives on Crowds and Social Movements." In *Handbook of Social Psychology*, ed. John DeLamater, 503–527. New York: Kluwer Academic/Plenum Publishers.

Rojas, Fabio. 2006. *From Black Power to Black Studies.* Baltimore: Johns Hopkins University Press.

Rosebraugh, Craig. 2004. *Burning Rage of a Dying Planet: Speaking for the Earth Liberation Front.* New York: Lantern Books.

Rosenthal, Naomi, M. Fingrutd, M. Ethier, R. Karant, and D. McDonald. 1985. "Social Movements in Network Analysis: A Case of Nineteenth-Century Women's Reform in New York State." *American Journal of Sociology* 90: 1022–1054.

Rothschild, J., and J. A. Whitt. 1986. *The Cooperative Workplace: Potentials and Dilemmas of Organizational Democracy and Participation.* New York: Cambridge University Press.

Rucht, Dieter. 2004. "Movement Allies, Adversaries, and Third Parties." In *The Blackwell Companion to Social Movements*, ed. David A. Snow, Sarah A. Soule, and Hanspeter Kriesi, 197–216. Oxford, UK: Blackwell.

Rudé, George. 1980. *Ideology and Popular Protest*. New York: Knopf.

———. 1964. *The Crowd in History: A Study of Popular Disturbances in France and England, 1730–1848*. New York: John Wiley and Sons.

Rupp, Leila J., and Verta Taylor. 1987. *Survival in the Doldrums: The American Women's Rights Movement, 1945 to the 1960s*. New York: Oxford University Press.

Sale, Kirkpatrick. 1974. *SDS*. New York: Vintage Books.

Salehi, M. M. 1996. "Radical Islamic Insurgency in the Iranian Revolution of 1978–1979." In *Disruptive Religion*, ed. Christian Smith, 47–63. New York: Routledge.

Sawyers, Traci M., and David S. Meyer. 1999. "Missed Opportunities: Social Movement Abeyance and Public Policy." *Social Problems* 46: 187–206.

Schneiberg, Marc, Marissa King, and Thomas Smith. 2008. "Social Movements and Organizational Form: Cooperative Alternatives to Corporations in the American Insurance, Dairy, and Grain Industries." *American Sociological Review* 73: 635–667.

Schussman, Alan, and Sarah A. Soule. 2005. "Process and Protest: Accounting for Individual Protest Participation." *Social Forces* 84: 1081–1106.

Scott, James C. 1985. *Weapons of the Weak: Everyday Forms of Peasant Resistance*. New Haven: Yale University Press.

Scott, Marvin B., and Stanford M. Lyman. 1968. "Accounts." *American Sociological Review* 33: 46–62.

Scranton, William M. 1971. *The Report of the President's Commission on Campus Unrest*. New York: Avon Books.

Scully, Maureen, and Amy Segal. 2002. "Passion with an Umbrella: Grassroots Activists in the Workplace." *Research in the Sociology of Organizations: Social Structure and Organizations Revisited* 19: 125–168.

Sengupta, Somini. 2007 (July 24). "Red Mosque Fueled Islamic Fire in Young Women." *New York Times*, www.nytimes.com/2070/07/24/world/asia/24madrasa .html, accessed on February 5, 2009.

Serrill, Michael S. 1989. "Beijing Spring." *Time*, May 8: 36–38.

Shah, Taimoor, and Carlotta Gall. 2007 (August 13). "Afghan Rebels Find Aid in Pakistan, Musharraf Admits." *New York Times*, www.nytimes.com/2007/08/13/ world/asia/13afghan.html, accessed on February 5, 2009.

Schock, Kurt. 1999. "People Power and Political Opportunities: Social Movement Mobilization and Outcomes in the Philippines and Burma." *Social Problems* 46(3): 355–375.

Shupe, Anson, and David G. Bromley. 1980. *The New Vigilantes: Deprogrammers, Anti-Cultists, and the New Religious*. Beverly Hills, CA: Sage.

Shupe, Anson, and Susan E. Darnell. 2006. *Agents of Discord: Deprogramming, Pseudo-Science, and the American Anticult Movement*. New Brunswick, NJ: Transaction.

Simon, Bernd, Michael Loewy, Stefan Sturmer, Ulrike Weber, Peter Freytag, Corinna Habig, Claudia Kampmeier, and Peter Spahlinger. 1998. "Collective identification and social movement participation." *Journal of Personality and Social Psychology* 74: 646–658.

Sine, Wesley D., and Brandon H. Lee. 2009. "Tilting at Windmills? The Environmental Movement and the Emergence of the U.S. Wind Energy Sector." *Administrative Science Quarterly* 54: 123–155.

Skrentny, John D. 2002. *The Minority Rights Revolution.* Cambridge, MA: Harvard University Press.

Smelser, Neil. 1962. *Theory of Collective Behavior.* New York: Free Press of Glencoe.

Smilde, David. 2005. "A Qualitative Comparative Analysis of Conversion to Venezuelan Evangelicalism: How Networks Matter." *American Journal of Sociology* 111: 757–96.

Smith, Jackie. 2001. "Globalizing Resistance: The Battle of Seattle and the Future of Social Movements." *Mobilization* 6: 1–21.

———. 2004. "Transnational Processes and Movements." In *The Blackwell Companion to Social Movements,* ed. David A. Snow, Sarah A. Soule, and Hanspeter Kriesi, 311–335. London: Blackwell.

Snow, David A. 1979. "A Dramaturgical Analysis of Movement Accommodation: Building Idiosyncrasy Credit as a Movement Mobilization Strategy." *Symbolic Interaction* 2: 23–44.

———. 1987. "Organization, Ideology, and Mobilization: The Case of Nichiren Shoshu of America." In *The Future of New Religious Movements,* D. G. Bromley and P. E. Hammond, 153–172. Macon, GA: Mercer University Press.

———. 2001. "Collective Identity and Expressive Forms." In *International Encyclopedia of the Social and Behavioral Sciences,* ed. Neil Smelser and Paul D. Baltes, 2212–2219. Oxford, UK: Pergamon Press.

———. 2003. "Social Movements." In *Handbook of Symbolic Interactionism,* ed. Larry Reynolds and Nancy Herman, 811–833. Walnut Creek, CA: Altamira Press.

———. 2004a. "Social Movements as Challenges to Authority: Resistance to an Emerging Conceptual Hegemony." In *Authority in Contention: Research in Social Movements, Conflict, and Change,* vol. 25, ed. Daniel J. Meyers and Daniel M. Cress, 3–25. London/New York: Elsevier.

———. 2004b. "Framing Processes, Ideology, and Discursive Fields." In *The Blackwell Companion to Social Movements,* ed. David A. Snow, Sarah A. Soule, Hanspeter Kriesi, 380–412. Oxford, UK: Blackwell.

———. 2008. "Elaborating the Discursive Contexts of Framing: Discursive Fields and Spaces." *Studies in Symbolic Interaction* 30: 3–28.

Snow, David A., and Leon Anderson. 1993. *Down on Their Luck: A Study of Homeless Street People.* Berkeley: University of California Press.

Snow, David A., and Robert D. Benford. 1988. "Ideology, Frame Resonance, and Participant Mobilization." *International Social Movement Research* 1: 197–217.

————. 1992. "Master Frames and Cycles of Protest." In *Frontiers in Social Movement Theory*, ed. Aldon D. Morris and Carol McClurg Mueller, 133–155. New Haven: Yale University Press.

————. 1999. "Alternative Types of Cross-National Diffusion in the Social Movement Arena." In *Social Movements in a Globalizing World*, ed. Donatella della Porta, Hanspeter Kriesi, and Dieter Rucht. New York: St. Martin's Press.

Snow, David A., and Catherine Corrigall-Brown. "Falling on Deaf Ears: Confronting the Prospect of Non-Resonant Frames." In *Rhyming Hope and History: Activism and Social Movement Scholarship*, ed. David Croteau, Charlotte Ryan, and William Hoynes, 222–238. Minneapolis: University of Minnesota Press.

Snow, David A., and Richard Machalek. 1984. "The Sociology of Conversion." *Annual Review of Sociology* 10: 167–190.

Snow, David A., and Susan Marshall. 1984. "Cultural Imperialism, Social Movements, and the Islamic Revival." In *Research in Social Movements, Conflicts, and Change*, vol. 7, ed. L. Kriesberg, 131–152. Greenwich, CT: JAI.

Snow, David A., and Doug McAdam. 2000. "Identity Work Processes in the Context of Social Movements: Clarifying the Identity/Movement Nexus." In *Self, Identity, and Social Movements*, ed. Sheldon Stryker, Timothy Owens, and Robert White, 41–67. Minneapolis: University of Minnesota Press.

Snow, David A., and Cynthia Phillips. 1980. "The Lofland-Stark Conversion Model: A Critical Reassessment." *Social Problems* 27: 430–447.

Snow, David A., Daniel Cress, Liam Downey, and Andrew Jones. 1998. "Disrupting the Quotidian: Reconceptualizing the Relationship between Breakdown and the Emergence of Collective Action." *Mobilization: An International Journal* 3: 1–22.

Snow, David A., Burke Rochford Jr., Steven K. Worden, and Robert D. Benford. 1986. "Frame Alignment Processes, Micromobilization, and Movement Participation." *American Sociological Review* 51: 464–481.

Snow, David A., Sarah A. Soule, and Daniel Cress. 2005. "Identifying the Precipitants of Homeless Protest Across 17 U.S. Cities, 1980–1990." *Social Forces* 83: 227– 254.

Snow, David A., Rens Vliegenhart, and Catherine Corrigall-Brown. 2007. "Framing the French 'Riots': A Comparative Study of Frame Variation." *Social Forces* 86: 385–415.

Snow, David A., Louis A. Zurcher, and Sheldon Ekland-Olson. 1980. "Social Networks and Social Movements: A Microstructural Approach to Differential Recruitment." *American Sociological Review* 45: 787–801.

Solo, Pam. 1988. *From Protest to Policy: Beyond the Freeze to Common Security*. Cambridge, MA: Ballinger.

Soule, Sarah A. 1997. "The Student Divestment Movement in the United States and Tactical Diffusion: The Shantytown Protest." *Social Forces* 75: 855–883.

————. 2004. "Going to the Chapel? Same-Sex Marriage Bans in the United States, 1973–2000." *Social Problems* 51(4): 453–477.

———. 2004. "Diffusion Processes Within and Across Social Movements." In *The Blackwell Companion to Social Movements*, ed. David A. Snow, Sarah A. Soule, Hanspeter Kriesi, 294–310. Oxford, UK: Blackwell.

———. Forthcoming. *Contention and Corporate Social Responsibility*. New York: Cambridge University Press.

Soule, Sarah A., and Brayden G. King. 2006. "The Stages of the Policy Process and the Equal Rights Amendment, 1972–1982." *American Journal of Sociology* 111(6): 1871–1909.

Soule, Sarah A., and Brayden G. King. 2008. "Competition and Resource Partitioning in Three Social Movement Industries." *American Journal of Sociology* 113(6): 1568–1610.

Soule, Sarah A., and Susan Olzak. 2004. "When Do Movements Matter? The Politics of Contingency and the Equal Rights Amendment." *American Sociological Review* 69: 473–497.

Soule, Sarah A., Doug McAdam, John McCarthy, and Yang Su. 1999. "Protest Events: Cause or Consequence of State Action? The U.S. Women's Movement and Federal Congressional Activities, 1956–1979." *Mobilization* 4:239–250.

Spilerman, Seymour. 1970. "The Causes of Racial Disturbances: A Comparison of Alternate Explanations." *American Sociological Review* 35: 627–649.

———. 1971. "The Causes of Racial Disturbances: A Test of Alternate Explanations." *American Sociological Review* 36: 427–442.

———. 1976. "Structural Characteristics of Cities and the Severity of Racial Disorders." *American Sociological Review* 41: 771–793.

Stillerman, Joel. 2003. "Space, Strategies, and Alliances in Mobilization: The 1960 Metalworkers' and Coal Miners' Strikes in Chile." *Mobilization* 8: 65–85.

Staggenborg, Suzanne. 1988. "The Consequences of Professionalization and Formalization in the American Labor Movement." *American Sociological Review* 53: 585–605.

Stark, Rodney, and William S. Bainbridge. 1980. "Networks of Faith: Interpersonal Networks and Recruitment to Cults and Sects." *American Journal of Sociology* 85: 1376–1395.

Steinberg, Marc W. 1999. "The Talk and Back Talk of Collective Action: A Dialogic Analysis of Repertoires of Discourse among Nineteenth-Century English Cotton-Spinners." *American Journal of Sociology* 105: 736–780.

Straus, R. 1976. "Changing Oneself: Seekers and the Creative Transformation of Life Experience." In *Doing Social Life*, ed. John Lofland, 252–272. New York: John Wiley.

Takahashi, Lois M. 1998. *Homelessness, AIDS, and Stigmatization: The NIMBY Syndrome in the Unites States at the End of the Twentieth Century*. New York: Oxford University Press.

Tarrow, Sidney. 1994. *Power in Movement: Social Movements, Collective Action and Politics*. New York: Cambridge University Press.

———. 1998. *Power in Movement: Social Movements, Collective Action and Politics*. 2nd ed. New York: Cambridge University Press.

———. 2005. *The New Transnational Activism*. New York: Cambridge University Press.

Taylor, Verta. 1989. "Social Movement Continuity: The Women's Movement in Abeyance. *American Sociological Review* 54: 761–775.

Taylor, Verta, and Nella Van Dyke. 2004. "'Getup, Stand Up': Tactical Repertoires of Social Movements." In *The Blackwell Companion to Social Movements*, ed. David A. Snow, Sarah A. Soule, and Hanspeter Kriesi, 262–293. Malden, MA: Blackwell.

Taylor, Verta, and Nicole C. Raeburn. 1995. "Identity Politics as High-Risk Activism: Career Consequences for Lesbian, Gay, and Bisexual Sociologists." *Social Problems* 42: 252–273.

Taylor, Verta, and Nancy Whittier. 1992. "Collective Identity in Social Movement Communities: Lesbian Feminist Mobilization." In *Frontiers in Social Movement Theory*, ed. Aldon D. Morris and Carol McClurg Mueller, 104–129. New Haven: Yale University Press.

———. 1995. "Analytical Approaches to Social Movement Culture: The Culture of the Women's Movement." In *Social Movements and Culture*, ed. Hank Johnston and Bert Klandermans, 163–187. Minneapolis: University of Minnesota Press.

Thomas, Janet. 2000. *The Battle in Seattle: The Story Behind and Beyond the WTO Demonstrations*. Golden, CO: Fulcrum Publishing.

Thornton, Thomas Perry. 1964. "Terror as a Weapon of Political Agitation." In *Internal War: Problems and Approaches*, ed. Harry Eckstein, 71–99. New York: Free Press of Glencoe.

Tilly, Charles. 1978. *From Mobilization to Revolution*. Reading, MA: Addison-Wesley.

———. 1995. *Popular Contention in Great Britain, 1758–1834*. Cambridge, MA: Harvard University Press.

———. 2000. "Spaces of Contention." *Mobilization* 5: 135–159.

Tilly, Charles, Louise Tilly, and Richard Tilly. 1975. *The Rebellious Century, 1830–1930*. Cambridge, MA: Harvard University Press.

Trotsky, Leon. 1959 (1932). *The History of the Russian Revolution*, ed. F. W. Dupre. New York: Doubleday.

Turner, Ralph H. 1969. "The Theme of Contemporary Social Movements." *British Journal of Sociology* 20: 390–405.

———. 1970. "Determinants of Social Movement Strategies." In *Human Nature and Collective Behavior: Papers in Honor of Herbert Blumer*," ed. T. Shibutani, 145–164. New Brunswick, NJ: Transaction.

———. 1983. "Figure and Ground in the Analysis of Social Movements." *Symbolic Interaction* 6: 175–181.

Turner, Ralph H., and Lewis Killian. 1987. *Collective Behavior*. 3rd ed. Englewood Cliffs, NJ: Prentice-Hall.

Useem, Bert. 1998. "Breakdown Theories of Collective Action." *Annual Review of Sociology* 24: 215–238.

Useem, Bert, and Peter Kimball. 1989. *States of Siege: U.S. Prison Riots 1971–1986.* New York: Oxford University Press.

Vallochi, Steve. 1990. "The Unemployed Workers Movement of the 1930s: A Reexamination of the Piven and Cloward Thesis." *Social Problems* 37: 191–205.

Van Biema, David. 2002. "Rebels in the Pews." *Time,* June 17: 54–58.

Van Dyke, Nella. 1998. "Hotbeds of Activism: Locations of Student Protest." *Social Problems* 45: 205–219.

Van Dyke, Nella, Sarah A. Soule, and Verta A. Taylor. 2004. "The Targets of Social Movements: Movements Beyond a Focus on the State." In *Authority in Contention: Research in Social Movements, Conflict, and Change,* vol. 25, ed. Daniel J. Meyers and Daniel M. Cress, 27–51. London/New York: Elsevier.

Varon, Jeremy. 2004. *Bringing the War Home: The Weather Underground, the Red Army Faction and Revolutionary Violence in the Sixties and Seventies.* Berkeley: University of California Press.

Verba, Sidney, Kay Lehman Schlozman, and Henry E. Brady. 1995. *Voice and Equality: Civic Voluntarism in American Politics.* Cambridge, MA: Harvard University Press.

Walker, Daniel. 1969. *Rights in Conflict* (Report to the National Commission on the Causes and Prevention of Violence). New York: Bantam Books.

Wallis, Roy. 1984. *The Elementary Forms of the New Religious Life.* London: Routledge & Kegan Paul.

Walsh, Edward J. 1981. "Resource Mobilization and Citizen Protest in Communities around Three-Mile-Island." *Social Problems* 29: 1–21.

Watanabe, Thomas, and Hector Becerra. 2006. "500,000 Cram Streets to Protest Immigration Bills." *Los Angeles Times,* March 26: A1, A20.

Weiss, Robert F. 1963. "Defection from Social Movements and Subsequent Recruitment to New Movements." *Sociometry* 26: 1–20.

Weist, Dawn, Jackie Smith, and Ivana Eterovic. 2002, unpublished paper. "Uneven Globalization? Underlying Variable Participation in Transnational Social Movement Organizations."

Werum, Regina, and Bill Winders. 2001. "Who's 'In' and Who's 'Out': State Fragmentation and the Struggle over Gay Rights, 1974–1999." *Social Problems* 48: 386–410.

Westby, David L., and Richard G. Braungart. 1966. "Class and Politics in the Family Backgrounds of Student Political Activists." *American Sociological Review* 31: 690–692.

Whalen, Jack, and Richard Flacks. 1989. *Beyond the Barricades: The Sixties Generation Grows Up.* Philadelphia: Temple University Press.

Whittier, Nancy. 2004. "The Consequences of Social Movements for Each Other." In *The Blackwell Companion to Social Movements,* ed. David A. Snow, Sarah A. Soule, and Hanspeter Kriesi, 531–551. London: Blackwell.

Wilkinson, Tracy. 2002. "In Growing Numbers, Palestinian Boys Are Choosing the Brief Life of a 'Martyr'." *Los Angeles Times,* June 10: A1, A11.

Williams, Rhys H. 2004. "The Cultural Contexts of Collective Action: Constraints, Opportunities, and the Symbolic Life of Social Movements." In *The Blackwell Companion to Social Movements*, ed. David A. Snow, Sarah A. Soule, and Hanspeter Kriesi, 91–115. London: Blackwell.

Williams, Rhys H. 1995. "Constructing the Public Good: Social Movements and Cultural Resources." *Social Problems* 42(1): 124–143.

Wilson, John. 1973. *Introduction to Social Movements*. New York: Basic Books.

Wilson, Bryan, and Karel Dobbelaere. 1994. *A Time to Chant: The Soka Gakkai Buddhists in Britain*. Oxford: Oxford University Press.

Wiltfang, Gregory, and Doug McAdam. 1991. "Distinguishing Cost and Risk in Sanctuary Activism." *Social Forces* 69: 987–1010.

Woodward, C. Vann. 2001 (1955). *The Strange Career of Jim Crow*. Afterword by William C. McFeely. New York: Oxford University Press.

Young, Michael P. 2002. "Confessional Protest: The Religious Birth of U.S. National Social Movements." *American Sociological Review* 67: 660–688.

Zablocki, Benjamin. 1971. *The Joyful Community: An Account of the Bruderhof, a Communal Movement Now in Its Third Generation*. Chicago: University of Chicago Press.

———. 1980. *Alienation and Charisma*. New York: Free Press.

Zald, Mayer N., and John D. McCarthy. 1987. *Social Movements in an Organizational Society*. New Brunswick, NJ: Transaction.

Zawadski, Bohan, and Paul E. Lazarsfeld. 1935. "The Psychological Consequences of Unemployment." *Journal of Social Psychology* 6: 224–251.

Zhao, Dingxin. 2001. *The Power of Tiananmen: State-Society Relations and the 1989 Beijing Student Movement*. Chicago: University of Chicago Press.

———. 2008. "Organization and Place in the Anti-U.S. Protests after the 1999 Belgrade Embassy Bombing." *Mobilization*: 2008:14:107–129.

Zuo, Jiping, and Robert D. Benford. 1195. "Mobilization Processes and the 1989 Chinese Democracy Movement." *Sociological Quarterly* 36: 131–156.

Zurcher, Louis, and David A. Snow. 1981. "Collective Behavior: Social Movements." In *Social Psychology: Sociological Perspectives*, ed. R. Rosenberg and R. Turner, 447–482. New York: Basic Books.

INDEX

abolitionist movement, vii, 142
abortion discourse, in United States vs. Germany,
  83
absolute deprivation or immiseration thesis,
  34–36
acceptance, as movement outcome, 213
access influence model, 221
accommodation (diffusion process), 197, 198–99
accommodative subcultures, 105
  in Estonia, 105–6
action mobilization, 111, 140
  dilemma of, 133
  See also mobilization
action-reaction model, 221
adaptation (diffusion process), 197, 198
affinity groups, 157–58
Afghanistan, madrasas in, 103–4
African Americans
  in children's books, 217, 226
  protests of
    and African American congressional
      representation, 75
    and divided government, 73
    and media as diffusion channel, 196
    student sit-ins (1960), 95, 102–3, 194, 196
    by students for African American studies,
      215
    and right to vote, 203, 251n.1
    and women's suffrage argument, 203
Albany, Georgia, King's civil rights marches
  in, 167
allies, influential, 74–75, 223–24
Almeida, Paul, 79–81
Al Qaeda terrorist movement, 104, 168, 172
Amenta, Edwin, 74, 210
Andrews, Kennneth, 194, 195, 196
animal rights movements
  affinity groups in, 158
  See also PETA
Anthony, Susan B., 203
anti-abortion/pro-life movement, 120, 212
  Operation Rescue, 82
anti-cult countermovement, 186
anti-government movement, "constitutional
  confrontations" carried out by, 179

anti–Iraq War movement
  affinity groups in, 158
  and media coverage, 180
  and risks of petition against, 115
  Win Without War coalition, 160
antinuclear movement, *See* nuclear disarmament
  or freeze movement
antiwar movements, *See* peace movement
Aquino, Benigno, Jr., viii
Argentina
  protest as response to oppression in, 79
  women's protests in, 38, 177
attribution of blame or responsibility, 54–55
Augustine, Saint, 46
Austin, Texas
  NIMBY mobilization in (vs. Salvation Army),
    4, 54–56
  Nuclear Disarmament Movement in, 152, 176
authority(ies), 11
  commitment to, 11
  and movement consequences, 212–17
  repressive capacity of, 75–84
  social movements as challengers or defenders
    of, 7–12, 202

Baby Milk Action, 156
Beijing student-led democracy movement
  (1989), 1–2, 76–78
  authority as target of, 11–12
  and contextual conditions, 65
  ecological factors in, 99, 137
  framing problem of, 59–60
  as one of worldwide appropriations of public
    space, 177
  as organized, 18
  participants' lives affected by, 218
  and political opportunity, 71
  repression of, 2, 82, 86
  as unintended consequence, 206
  Western themes adapted for, 198
Benford, Robert, 59, 137–38, 152, 176, 197
Berlin Wall, fall of, 2
Beyerlein, Kraig, 131
Biggs, Michael, 194, 195, 196
bin Laden, Osama, 172